Garden in the Grasslands

Garden in the Grasslands

Boomer Literature of the
Central Great Plains

BY

DAVID M. EMMONS

UNIVERSITY OF NEBRASKA PRESS · LINCOLN

Publishers on the Plains
UNP

Copyright © 1971 by the University of Nebraska Press
All Rights Reserved
International Standard Book Number 0–8032–0753–0
Library of Congress Catalog Card Number 70–125100

Manufactured in the United States of America

To my family

Contents

A section of illustrations follows page 114.

Preface

The central Great Plains region was, at mid-nineteenth century, one of America's least attractive frontiers. Condemned by many as a Great Desert, it presented a particularly stubborn obstacle to America's continental expansion because of its climate and vegetation. Americans were used to something better, and it was with considerable disappointment and apprehension that they confronted the Plains frontier. Many of their values depended upon the maintenance of an open area of Edenic character to which the dispossessed of older and hence less favored regions could retreat. But this haven involved more than just an escape; the so-called safety valve had to emit people into a better and freer world. Only then could it relieve the older sections from an unsettling and perhaps mutinous overpopulation. Should the Plains prove a desert, they could only frustrate retreat to a nearer west as one of the principal features of the American condition. Thus the railroads that traversed the Plains and the people who inhabited them had a vested interest in encouraging others to join them. By stimulating immigration and settlement they not only furthered their own interests but contributed as well to the notion that the United States had not exhausted its supply of gardenlike frontiers.

To the promoters fell the job of breaking down the notions of desert sterility and proving to an anxious world that the central Great Plains region was a true and worthy frontier capable of working the same miracles as its predecessors. They accepted their assignment willingly, distributing thousands of pieces of promotional literature designed not only to entice immigrants but also to reeducate those who continued to embrace the desert theory.

A part of the promotional barrage was for town sites, but urban growth in the central Plains, though important in their development, was not a part of the Edenic image. The Garden was agricultural; it did not promise the substitution of western cities for eastern. Other promoters might sell their town lots, but those who would transfer the Garden to the grassland recruited new immigrants on the basis of the agricultural potential of the central Plains.

The western promoters promised the prospective immigrant almost every conceivable comfort. Not only were the Plains not a desert, they were the most complete expression of America as a garden. They were made to appear the perfect home for the yeoman, a place where the poor and dispirited could find immediate relief. The climate was pure and healthful, the soil was of the highest fertility, the population was refined, and, most important, the rainfall was abundant and constantly increasing.

This last promise was the key to the promotional campaigns. The alleged aridity of the Plains was the most tenacious element of the desert theory. In a burst of inspired promotionalism the boomers discovered a counter theory which could put to rest all of the remaining fears of desert sterility on the Plains. That theory dealt with the increased rainfall attendant upon settlement. It was believed, or at least fervently hoped, that Americans would bring their rain with them, that by plowing the soil they would so upset meteorological conditions that bountiful rainfall would result. Here was the perfect promotional device. It catered to the American sense of superiority over nature and it assured all prospective immigrants that the Plains were an ideal home.

These promises were a part of the promotional effort throughout the Great Plains province. From Montana and the Dakotas to West Texas and Oklahoma, the land boomers used the same battery of arguments. But the promotional flurry began in the central Plains. Kansas and Nebraska were the first Plains states to be settled, hence the first to be systematically promoted. The methods employed there, and in Colorado and Wyoming, though owing much to earlier campaigns, served as a model for the later promotional effort in the northern and southern Plains.

This, then, is a study in the literature of land promotion. But it is also a study of the potency of an idea, for the land boomers were doing more than just attracting newcomers; they were sustaining, or attempting to sustain, the notion of America as a garden. They had to keep alive the traditional belief that America had "homes for the homeless," not an enviable assignment on the central plains, and one which resulted in a good deal of misrepresentation and geographical legerdemain.

This study began as a dissertation under the direction of Professor Robert Athearn of the University of Colorado. The completed product owes much to his patient guidance. Any errors which remain are, of course, mine alone. The final preparation was aided by a small grant from the University of Montana and several larger ones from my father, Joseph F. Emmons. I thank them both. Thanks are also due Mrs. Mary Wilson and Mrs. Mary Schwarz, who handled the typing in expert fashion. Finally, I make public acknowledgment of the contribution of my wife, Suzanne. She read and helped proof the manuscript, all the time keeping the family reasonably solvent and the children reasonably civil during the lean and busy years of preparation.

DAVID M. EMMONS

Garden in the Grasslands

CHAPTER ONE

Introduction

———————————————————

The American people had always expected much of their frontiers. These outlying regions, whether located in the Connecticut River valley or in the blue grass hills of Kentucky, served as a constant pull upon the American imagination. Their challenges and promises supplied a part of the generative energy that propelled the settlers westward. It was little wonder that a grateful people invested their frontiers with hazy images of the garden regained, describing them in language reserved for Edenic landscapes only. The people who lived within them were thought to enjoy the favors only an Eden could supply.

The vast material wealth the frontier offered, the fertile soil and benign and productive climate, afforded predictable and conventional rewards: there a man could make a decent living. Similarly, as the number of settlers increased, new resources and markets would be made available to the more developed regions farther east. A nation constantly growing, it was thought, was a nation constantly prospering; and this growth, this westering, was central to the thinking of those who envisioned a powerful and self-sufficient nation. But economic prosperity was not the only benefit Americans could expect to receive from their frontiers. There were political and spiritual rewards as well. A frontier, by definition, would be settled by agriculturalists, and most Americans shared Jefferson's belief that these were the chosen of God's people. The American agriculturist, the yeoman, had been selected as the standard-bearer of American culture. Simple in his tastes, frugal in habits, he was the ideal republican, and upon him rested much of this nation's cultural and political identity. A constant supply of frontiers must be provided for his occupation.[1]

1. The literature of the garden and the yeoman is vast and extensive. The seminal work is Henry Nash Smith, *Virgin Land: The American West as Symbol and Myth* (New York: Vintage Books, 1962), but see also Leo Marx, *The Machine in the Garden* (New York: Oxford University Press, 1964); Charles Sanford, *The Quest*

1

Of equal importance was the frontier's well-sung role as a safety valve for urban discontent. Simply by virtue of its being away and apart from the more industrialized East, the frontier was thought a haven for those ill-suited to meet the demands of the older regions. Emigration to the west offered a new start, a chance to regroup in an economic and social environment more open and fluid. But those who emigrated were not to be the only beneficiaries of their removal. The threat of social upheaval was thought to decrease in direct proportion to the number of discontent who defected from the East to the West. Similarly, the wages and working conditions of those who remained in the older regions improved in direct proportion to the emigration of those who had once competed with them for the same jobs. Emigration, then, or so the theory would have it, removed from the East and from Europe those whose presence constituted a social hazard, depositing those undesirables in areas which needed them for its own development and which could offer them the kind of opportunities lacking in the older, more advanced regions. Given these theories, it is not surprising that when Americans sought evidence of providential favor—and they often did— they regularly referred to their western regions, their frontiers. Likewise, when Europeans sought similar evidence, they too noted the existence of a frontier, a region to which Americans could escape, an area capable of absorbing the excess and sometimes destructive energies of the American people.[2]

---

for Paradise: Europe and the American Moral Imagination (Urbana: University of Illinois Press, 1961); and R. W. B. Lewis, *The American Adam* (Chicago: University of Chicago Press, 1955). This list could be extended almost indefinitely, but these four may be taken as representative.

2. Among those Europeans and Americans who commented on the safety valve, the following are of particular importance: Hector de Crèvecoeur, *Letters from an American Farmer* (New York: New American Library, 1963), p. 74; Benjamin Franklin, "Observations Concerning the Increase of Mankind," *The Papers of Benjamin Franklin*, ed. by Leonard Labaree, 12 vols. (New Haven: Yale University Press, 1961), 4: 227–28. Thomas Jefferson made repeated reference to the safety valve. For one of the clearest expressions of his interest, see Jefferson to James Madison, December 20, 1787, in *The Writings of Thomas Jefferson*, ed. by Paul Leicester Ford, 10 vols. (New York: G. P. Putnam's Sons, 1892–99), 4: 479–80. For European comment on the safety valve, see Adam Smith, *An Inquiry into the Nature and Causes of the Wealth of Nations* (New York: Modern Library, 1957), p. 533; Thomas Malthus, *An Essay on Population*, 2 vols. (London: J. M. Dent & Sons, 1958), 2: 30–37; Karl Marx, *Capital*, trans. by Eden and Cedar Paul, 2 vols. (London: J. M. Dent & Co., 1930), 2: 856–58; Lord Macaulay to H. S. S. Randall, May 23, 1857, in *The Life and Letters of Lord Macaulay*, ed. by George O. Trevelyan, 2 vols. (New York: Harper & Bros., 1877), 2: 408.

In 1844 the labor journal *Working Man's Advocate*, reflecting the workers' obvious interest in this frontier theory, memorialized the Congress, pleading the case for free land. Unless the land was thrown open, according to the *Advocate*, the frontier would not function according to theory, and Americans generally, not just labor, would be the losers. As the memorial made clear, there was much to lose. Reference was made, first of all, to the republicanizing tendency of residence in the West. By increasing the number of freeholders the Congress would decrease antirepublicanism proportionally. In addition, city populations would diminish, with a concomitant gain in political virtue. There would be no need for a standing army—the yeomen could serve its function and serve it more efficiently than professional soldiers. National prosperity and the prosperity of the masses would be coincident. Capitalism could never become repressive or exploitative of human resources. There would be no office beggars, less bureaucracy, and, of equal importance, few laws and fewer lawyers. And finally, the safety valve for American and European labor would remain open to work its wondrous magic upon hours and wages.[3]

This, then, was the dazzling prospect held out by the American West. So long as the garden remained to offer its resources, both material and spiritual, the morality play which was the American experiment had every chance of continued success. The gift of this one resource, encompassing so many other benefits, was ample evidence of heavenly favor, and until the mid-nineteenth century there seemed to be no diminution of God's beneficence. From the Atlantic Ocean to the Missouri River, from the Great Lakes to the Gulf of Mexico, North America presented a continuing spectacle of incredibly fertile land, land capable of effecting the promises made in its name. There were, of course, reversals and disappointments as Americans moved out across this region, but generally they were well treated by the land and the frontier theory contained just enough credibility to ensure its continued acceptance.

There was, however, an obvious, though all too often overlooked corollary to this theory. For a western region to successfully meet the demands made upon it, it had to be fertile. The yeoman could not farm hard scrabble; the safety valve was of little use if it substituted one set of intolerable conditions for another; America's cultural mission

3. *Working Man's Advocate*, November 30, 1844, quoted in John R. Commons et al. eds., *A Documentary History of American Industrial Society*, 13 vols. (Cleveland: Arthur H. Clark Co., 1910), 7: 318–20.

did not include bitter and prolonged struggles against an intractable environment. An American frontier, by definition, had to be productive. Anything less was thought an aberration, a denial of faith. Some people, however, suspected that the supply of fertile frontiers was limited.

There was another part of America where the gardenlike images which surrounded earlier frontiers was singularly out of place. This was the region west of the Missouri River and east of the Rockies known as the central Great Plains, considered, for our purposes, to include what is now Kansas and Nebraska and the eastern one-third of Colorado and Wyoming. Here Americans found no Eden, but its opposite, an area of seemingly infinite barrenness and sterility. The only truly comprehensible features of these plains are their vastness and their semi-aridity. In addition, they are perversely unpredictable in their rainfall patterns. There is nothing idyllic about the Plains; their climate is cruel, their dimensions lonely and frightening. They are, in brief, not the stuff from which gardens are made. As a consequence, the American people in the nineteenth century said a number of different things about the Plains, not all of them kind; they did a number of different things to the Plains, not all of them wise. But what they said and what they did profoundly affected not only their history but the history of a region.

Among the first things they said was that these Plains were a desert, a notoriously imprecise term generally, but in this instance one which elicited a fairly predictable response. Some Americans used "desert" to describe any unoccupied land, and the word became a synonym for "wilderness," regardless of the fertility of the soil.[4] But these "deserts" contained at least the promise of productive good. The Plains, though they shared, even surpassed, the harshness of these earlier Wests, seemed to some to offer no redeeming economic or social utility. They were not only frightening and ugly, they seemed totally without value. Here, truly was a desert, total and absolute.

How firmly and extensively the desert theory was held is open to debate. This is true, in part, because many refused to accept, in their entirety, the reports of the desert theorists. These reports were simply too incompatible with accepted American values. Adding to the confusion is the problem of locating, with any degree of precision, the limits of the desert, assuming one was found and reported. Most important, however, is the fact that the reports, whatever their judg-

4. See Marx, *Machine in the Garden*, p. 43, and Roderick Nash, *Wilderness and the American Mind* (New Haven: Yale University Press, 1967), pp. 1–7.

ments on the utility of the Plains, were read by only a select and educated few. It seems certain, then, that whatever the reason, there was no unanimity of feeling regarding the potential of the central Plains—the desert theory had to compete for public attention with both counter theories and uninterestedness.[5]

But in spite of this fact, the desert theory still had an enormous influence. Witness if nothing else the lengths to which the western promoters went to refute it. Whether the general public was aware of Pike's report, or Long's, Parkman's, or Gregg's is here irrelevant.[6] Those who had a vested interest in promoting the settlement of the Plains were aware of them and beginning in the 1850s felt obligated to disprove them. Desert notions conjured up alien images. The Plains were "a novelty," according to John C. Frémont, that "excited Asiatic, not American ideas." Max Greene, one of the first to promote the settlement of the Plains, was even more specific. "To the dweller by the Atlantic," he wrote in 1856, "it is difficult to picture aright those scenes of Asian wildness within our natural borders. From childhood, we have so linked descriptions of piles of scorial and treeless, grassless slopes with dimmest legends of the olden time that we cannot well persuade ourselves that such things are American realities."[7]

Obviously such notions could not go unchallenged. Americans needed those "treeless, grassless slopes" as homes for future yeomen, as a safety valve for future laborers. "These inarable lands must at no distant day be the subject of important consideration," wrote Commissioner Joseph Wilson of the General Land Office in 1868, "and their reclamation will become a matter of necessity." Thus far the fertile Mississippi

5. See Martyn J. Bowden, "The Perception of the Western Interior of the United States, 1800–1870: A Problem in Historical Geosophy," *Proceedings of the Association of American Geographers* 1 (1969): 16–21.

6. These four were among the more prominent desert theorists. See Elliott Coues, ed., *The Expedition of Zebulon Montgomery Pike*, 3 vols. (New York: Francis P. Harper, 1895), 2: 525. Long's desert theory is best summarized in Edwin James, "Account of an Expedition from Pittsburgh to the Rocky Mountains, 1819–1820," in *Early Western Travels*, ed. by Reuben G. Thwaites, 39 vols. (Cleveland: Arthur H. Clark Co., 1904–1907), 15: 232, 251. For Parkman, see Francis Parkman, *The Oregon Trail* (New York: Modern Library, 1949), pp. 31, 59, 161. For Gregg, see Josiah Gregg, *Commerce of the Prairies*, ed. by Max L. Moorhead (Norman: University of Oklahoma Press, 1958), pp. 50, 355.

7. John C. Frémont, *Report of the Exploring Expedition to the Rocky Mountains in the Year 1842* (Washington: Gales & Seaton, 1845), p. 48; Max Greene, *The Kanzas Region, Forest, Prairie, Desert, Mountain, Vale and River* (New York: Fowler & Wells, 1856), pp. 47–48.

Valley had proved capable of supporting the land-hungry pioneer. But that day, Wilson predicted, would soon end and then "the question will be earnestly asked, what can be done to remove this impediment, this obstacle to the progress of the nation ... to relieve this belt from natural inarability and make it fit for the habitation of man?"[8]

Fortunately for the desert conscious, counter theories had been proposed long before Wilson issued his urgent warning. In fact, one of the strange ironies of American history is that while the Great American Desert theory was being most actively publicized, Americans were beginning to proclaim their Manifest Destiny over the same condemned regions. Theirs was a divine mission to people the wilderness, extending the blessings of liberty from sea to sea; that man "must know little of the American people, who supposes that they can be stopped by any thing in the shape of mountains, deserts, seas, or rivers."[9] The Americans prided themselves on their ability to convert the raw wilderness into areas fit for civilized habitation, and the natural order was totally impotent before this generative impulse. If Nature was impudent enough to place obstacles in the way of America's advance, they were removed. "Nothing can resist us," wrote Thomas Carlyle of the Anglo-Saxons; "We war with rude Nature; and, by our resistless engines, come off always victorious, and loaded with spoils." A purely American statement of the same confidence was presented by the early industrialist Timothy Walker. Mechanization, the introduction of the machine not to destroy but to build the garden, was Walker's tool of conquest. "Where [Nature] denied us rivers," he announced, "Mechanism has supplied them. Where she left our planet uncomfortably rough, Mechanism has applied the roller. Where her mountains have been found in the way, Mechanism has boldly levelled or cut through them." Nature became man's servant, to "fetch and carry at his command," and the reverence once reserved for God and Nature had become instead a self-congratulatory tribute to man and his tools of conquest.[10] This youthful optimism inspired the belief that the American republic could transform any type of country through sheer

8. Joseph Wilson, "Report of the Commissioner of the General Land Office, 1868," in *Report of the Secretary of the Interior, 1868* (Washington, D.C.: Government Printing Office, 1869), pp. 137–38. Hereafter the Government Printing Office will be cited as GPO.

9. [Joshua Pilcher], U.S., Congress, House, *Exec. Doc. 39*, 21st Cong., 2d sess., 1831, p. 19.

10. The Carlyle and Walker comments are cited by Marx, *Machine in the Garden*, pp. 171, 182–83.

force of will, and the Great Plains, like the forests and prairies before them, must eventually succumb. It was manifestly destined.

This apotheosis of the American will was but one indication of a general romantic vision of the New World. Of equal significance in the history of the Plains region were the observations of those early nineteenth-century scientists who attempted in their methodology to discover in the natural world what they knew must be the overarching unity of God's plan. Alexander von Humboldt and Arnold Guyot were of this cosmological school as was, in a less scientific way, Walt Whitman. Von Humboldt and Guyot insisted that an American desert was geographically impossible, that the basic unity of the great concave interior basin between the Allegheny-Appalachian range and the Rockies ensured a similarity of form between prairies and plains.[11] Whitman offered a poetic expression of this same theory. All lands, he wrote, were welcome to the American, "mountains, flats, sands, forests, prairies." All were part of a general "Kosmos" which bound man and his institutions to the earth. As for the Plains specifically, Whitman called them "a newer garden of creation . . . the crown and teeming paradise, so far, of time's accumulations."[12]

The Plains were thus being reevaluated through the dim light of romanticism. The errors of omission and commission of the desert theorists were being partially corrected and the Plains were beginning to assume their place as part of the Garden. This land was different, to be sure, but for all its strangeness, it was still part of God's plan, still part of the essential unity and pattern of the American environment. Thus, the much cherished assumption that the purposes of Nature, God, and humanity were one remained credible.

The political spokesman of this new confidence was Missouri's Senator Thomas Hart Benton. Benton's initial interest in the Plains was limited to the region's possible utility as a route to the Far East. The rivers of the Plains were destined to "become lines of communication with Eastern Asia," but, unfortunately, according to Benton, settlement of the lands along their banks would be frustrated by the natural

11. Alexander von Humboldt, *Views of Nature; or, Contemplations on the Sublime Phenomena of Creation*, trans. by E. C. Otte and H. G. Bohn (London: George Bell & Sons, 1896), p. 32; Arnold Guyot, *The Earth and Man* (New York: Charles Scribner's Sons, 1897), pp. 207–26, 284.

12. Whitman, "Song of the Broad-axe," "Kosmos," and "The Prairie States," in *Complete Poetry and Selected Prose*, ed. by James Miller (Boston: Houghton Mifflin Co., 1959), pp. 135, 276–77, 282.

sterility of the area.[13] With the addition of California and Oregon to the American union, however, Benton began to revise his original estimate of the productive capacity of the Plains, and his expansionism became concerned less with passages to the East and more with the development of an introspective empire.

The construction of a transcontinental railroad was vital to this object. "The western wilderness," he prophesied in 1849, "from the Pacific to the Mississippi, will start into life under [the railroad's] touch."[14] Then came the reversal of his original judgment on the Plains: They had already been adequately prepared for settlement, he insisted, and they lacked nothing to make them the most desirable region in North America. Like Humboldt, Benton admitted that

> there may be persons to impugn it and cry down the country. That is an old business—as old as Moses and the twelve messengers. . . . This is what happened to the promised land and it is not to be expected that the distant and unknown countries of the Great West are to fare better. . . . But truth is powerful and must prevail.[15]

It was Benton's self-appointed task to correct this error. The truth he possessed was not just powerful, it was astounding. After years of Great American Desert stories, the American people witnessed a United States senator speaking of Kansas as "rich like Egypt and tempting as Egypt would be if raised above the slimy flood, waved into gentle undulations, variegated with groves and meadows, sprinkled with springs, coursed by streams." Nor were his idyllic descriptions limited to the prairie regions of eastern Kansas. The Huerfano River valley in present-day eastern Colorado was described as "carpeted with soft grass—a sylvan paradise. . . . The humidity of the Sierra mountains had given great fertility to this region." Let there be no mistake, "this is the bucolic region of our America."[16]

Benton's remarks were supplemented and given added credence by the explorations and reports of his son-in-law, John Frémont. In 1842 Frémont had commented on the harsh and alien landscape of the Plains region, but in the early fifties, under the influence of Benton, he

13. Cited in Smith, *Virgin Land*, pp. 26–27.

14. U.S., Congress, Senate, *Congressional Globe*, 30th Cong., 2d sess., 1849, 20, pt. 1: 473.

15. Thomas H. Benton, *Discourse of Mr. Benton of Missouri before the Boston Mercantile Library Association . . . Delivered in Tremont Temple at Boston, December 20, 1854* (Washington: J. T. & L. Towers, 1854), pp. 16, 18.

16. Ibid., pp. 4, 5, 6–7.

became increasingly enthusiastic about the possibilities of the region. As Frémont himself stated, "I saw visions." [17] Among them was his idealized picture of the Kansas River valley, which he described as "a beautiful and wooded country of great fertility of soil, well adapted to settlement and cultivation." It was joined in this condition by the country of the upper Arkansas River valley, which was "continuously well adapted to settlements . . . well watered and fertile." As an added bonus, Frémont reminded his listeners that the central region of the Plains which he was discussing ran very near the 39th parallel, that miraculous line where "the valetudinarian might travel . . . in his own vehicle . . . for the mere restoration of health and recovery of spirits." [18]

Together, Benton and Frémont tried to reverse many of the legends which had so long surrounded the Plains. Quite as much as Whitman and cosmologists like Humboldt and Guyot, they were able to introduce a new and cheerful note into discussions on the future of the Plains. If nothing else they gave political expression to the buoyant optimism of the romantic movement.

Neither Benton nor Frémont, however, developed a systematic logic to explain the precise role of the Plains in future American development. This was left to William Gilpin, companion of Frémont on the Pathfinder's 1843 expedition to Oregon, student of Humboldt, lawyer, geographer, soldier, philosopher, and, from 1836 to 1890, prophet of the new wisdom of the Plains. Most of Gilpin's writing was done after the Civil War, after the desert theory had been all but erased, but in style and mood Gilpin was of an earlier era. His ideas were formed during Benton's generation. He felt more at home with the theories of Humboldt than with those of the post–Civil War land promoters. Gilpin managed to codify and bring into order many of the random notes on conditions in the West. His method, though it owed much to Humboldt and Darwin, was peculiarly his own in its regional limitations. His science, according to Bernard De Voto, was typically nineteenth-century, "which is to say that much of it was *a priori*, deduced, generalized, falsely systematized, and therefore wrong." [19]

17. John C. Frémont, *Memoirs of My Life* (Chicago: Belford, Clarke & Co., 1886), p. 65.

18. See *Discourse of Mr. Benton before the Boston Mercantile Library Association*, p. 6; and letter from Col. Frémont to the Railroad Convention, St. Louis, April, 1850, in *Central National Highway from the Mississippi River to the Pacific* (Louisville: Lost Cause Press, Microcard, 1960), pp. 6, 8.

19. Bernard De Voto, "Geopolitics with Dew on It," *Harper's Magazine* 188 (March 1944): 314.

The mission Gilpin set for himself was immense. He would correct the misconceptions regarding the central United States, and make known to the people the "divine light issuing from the obscurity of the past, shining upon our country and our people, illuminating alike the recesses of nature and the intellect of man."[20] Gilpin saw in the sweep of the North American continent a structural unity which, if recognized in time, could ensure the success of America's mission. All he witnessed was good. God and Nature had not betrayed the American people in presenting them with the Great Plains. On the contrary, science, once perceptive of the laws governing this region, would at once acknowledge the balance and harmony of God's divine plan. Gilpin's obvious debt to Humboldt did not go unacknowledged. Humboldt alone had "spoken worthily of America to her own people." He alone had recognized the essential unity of the American continent, "its symmetry and . . . grand simplicity of configuration." Now it was time for an American to speak worthily and apply the general universal laws of Humboldt's cosmos to a fuller understanding of American conditions.[21]

The essential fact about North America was its concave structure. Gilpin called the continent "a vast amphitheatre," opening "towards heaven . . . to receive and fuse harmoniously whatever enters within its rim." From the Alleghenies to the Rockies the heartland of America presented the appearance of a giant bowl, down whose sides tumbled a people who were one in language, customs, and institutions. Nor would those outside this bowl be lost to civilization; there were connecting links, the great rivers which flowed from the mountain flanks into the basin of the Mississippi. So perfect was this design that the great basin formed by the Mississippi River could alone contain 1,310,000,000 people. As for the Great Plains, Gilpin described them as the best and most favored part of this Basin.[22] Only the most misguided or benighted

20. Hubert H. Bancroft, *History of the Life of William Gilpin: A Character Study* (San Francisco: History Company, 1889), pp. 58–60.

21. Message of the Governor of Colorado Territory, September 9, 1861, *House Journal of the Legislative Assembly, Territory of Colorado* (Denver: Thomas Gibson, Colorado Herald Office, 1861), p. 11. See also William Gilpin, *Mission of the North American People: Geographical, Social, and Political*, 2d ed. (Philadelphia: J. B. Lippincott & Co., 1874), pp. 50, 61–62, 123; and William Gilpin, *The Cosmopolitan Railway, Compacting and Fusing Together All the World's Continents* (San Francisco: History Co., 1890), p. iv. See also Bancroft, *Life of Gilpin*, p. 6, for another tribute to Humboldt.

22. *Cosmopolitan Railway*, p. 210; William Gilpin, *The Central Gold Regions: The Grain, Pastoral, and Gold Regions of North America* (Philadelphia: Sower,

could ever have considered them a desert. "No desert," Gilpin thundered, "does or can exist within this Basin." There had been a radical misapprehension of the true character of the Plains, a misapprehension as "complete as that which pervaded Europe respecting the Atlantic Ocean during the whole historical period prior to COLUMBUS." "The PLAINS are not *deserts*," he was fairly screaming now, "but the OPPOSITE, and the cardinal basis of the future empire . . . now erecting itself upon the North American Continent."[23] Thus did Gilpin conclude his analysis of the Plains. By his own accounting he had performed prodigious labors in the counterattack on the desert theorists. And thanks in part to those heroic efforts, the image of the Plains was being refurbished. Gilpin and the others like him had set aside a portion of the Garden and reserved it for the Plains.

By the 1840s a faint Edenic image had begun to emerge, and although it was not yet dominant over the desert concept, it was infinitely more compatible with American values—so much so that by the 1870s it would totally overshadow images of the desert and efforts to impart even a semblance of balance to descriptions of the Plains would be greeted with charges of heresy and consigned to the dusty stockpile of outworn theories. Visionaires like Gilpin had done much to begin this reversal of judgment on the utility of the Plains. By the 1850s what was needed by the antidesert forces was a national issue of sufficient moment to compel the settlement of the area. If the Plains should become vital to national security or to the sectional balance, the American people might be persuaded to believe almost anything about the suitability of the region for occupation. The passage of the Kansas-Nebraska Act in 1854 provided that issue.

In allowing the actual settlers of Kansas and Nebraska to choose their future status, slave or free, the authors of the Kansas-Nebraska Act inspired a round of sectional violence. Free soilers realized that if a majority of free-state northerners could be enticed to Kansas, the western extension of slavery could be arrested. To many Americans of the mid-1850s, no issue was of greater importance. The character and institutions of the people who were to occupy Kansas, according to one free stater, "cannot but decide the destinies of the continent and the

---

Barnes & Co., 1860), p. 20, speech on the Pacific Railway in *Mission*, pp. 67, 147–48; introduction to William Gilpin's *Guide to the Kansas Gold Mines* (Cincinnati: E. Mendenhall, 1859), p. 24.

23. Gilpin, *Mission*, p. 66.

last great experiment of humanity."[24] Many northerners felt that if
slavery were allowed to enter the Plains, the paradisiacal image of the
West would be despoiled and the missionary zeal with which Americans
went about the settlement of earlier wests would be subverted. Earlier
mistakes, such as the introduction of slavery into the South, could be
corrected only with much difficulty. In 1854, however, the Plains were
still free of this taint, and any attempt "to exclude from a vast unoccupied region emigrants from the old world, and free laborers from our
own states" must be denounced as "a gross violation of a sacred
pledge, . . . an atrocious plot" to destroy the ground of the free yeoman.[25] The extension of slavery would be destructive of the very ends
for which America was settled, at least in the minds of its foes; and
their opposition, in turn, prompted William Seward's ringing challenge
to the South: "Come on, then, Gentlemen of the slave States. . . . We
will engage in competition for the virgin soil of Kansas."[26]

Unfortunately for the cause of abolition, the competitive vigor
of the North was matched only by its aversion to settling a desolate
and allegedly sterile waste. Free soil was of negligible personal value
if it was also desert soil, and the advocates of a free Kansas had first
to combat this notion of sterility. The principal agent in that effort
was the New England Emigrant Aid Company, a group whose purpose
was to organize a systematic emigration to the Plains and ensure its
settlement by free staters. This object was particularly essential now,
"in the critical position of the western territories."[27]

In addition to its humanitarian purpose of preventing the extension
of slavery, the Emigrant Aid Company also entertained some not
unreasonable notions that the enterprise of settling Kansas might
"realize . . . a return to the stockholders on the money they have
invested."[28] Generally, however, the primary function of the company

24. The Rev. Chas. W. Upham, *North American Review* 58 (January 1855): 96.
25. Charles Sumner and Salmon Chase, "Appeal of the Independent Democrats,"
in E. E. Hale, *Kanzas and Nebraska . . . an Account of the Emigrant Aid Co.'s
Directions to Emigrants* (Boston: Phillips, Sampson & Co., 1854), p. 189.
26. Cited in William A. Williams, *Contours of American History* (Cleveland:
World Publishing Co., 1961), p. 284.
27. Samuel Johnson, *The Battle Cry of Freedom: The New England Emigrant Aid
Company in the Kansas Crusade* (Lawrence: University of Kansas Press, 1954),
p. 19, and "Report of the Emigrant Aid Company," in Hale, *Kanzas and Nebraska*,
p. 222.
28. Johnson, *The Battle Cry of Freedom*, pp. 33–34. For a complete discussion of
the financial aspects of the company, see Paul W. Gates, *Fifty Million Acres: Con-*

was to secure Kansas as a free state, and any money which might accrue was strictly an incidental benefit. For this central purpose, the company and other like-minded groups commissioned writers to describe the myriad beauties and advantages of Kansas and Nebraska. The books which resulted constitute the first expressions of systematic and purposeful promoting of the central Great Plains.

Typical of this genre was the work of E. E. Hale entitled *Kanzas and Nebraska*, published in 1855. Hale undertook his account "from a wish to assist in the great enterprise of settling Kanzas at once." He was not quite as undiscriminating as that statement would suggest, however. As a director of the Worcester County, Kansas, League, Hale joined in the great object of the New England Emigrant Aid Company, "the colonization of Kanzas with freemen," and he eagerly sought information which would aid him in his mission. Frémont supplied some needed ammunition when he told Hale that the region between the Arkansas and Platte rivers was truly "excellent, admirably adapted to agricultural purposes, and would support a large agricultural and pastoral population." Another informant warned that different agricultural methods would have to be used—"Nature demands that it should be so"—but it was possible that this would prove but a temporary inconvenience. After all, Hale wrote, "it is not too much to hope ... that ... the passage of the desert [will] become shorter, in the western growth of the civilization of these valleys and the eastward progress of California and Oregon." Hale thus suggested the possibility of an amelioration of the desert conditions, at least to the degree that the free northern yeoman could expect a decent competence.[29]

It was the opinion of Charles Boynton and T. B. Mason that there had never been a desert to combat. These two men had been commissioned by the American Reform Tract and Book Society and the Kansas League of Cincinnati to report on the climate, soil, and promise of Kansas. Their findings were universally favorable. "The value of

---

flicts over Kansas Land Policy, 1854–1890 (Ithaca: Cornell University Press, 1954), pp. 1–3 and chapter 3, "Public Land Sales"; William Carruth, "The New England Emigrant Aid Company as an Investment Society," *Kansas Historical Society Collections* 6 (1903): 90–96; Samuel Johnson, "The Emigrant Aid Company in the Kansas Conflict," *Kansas Historical Quarterly* 7 (February 1937): 21–33; idem, "The Emigrant Aid Company in Kansas," ibid. 1 (November, 1932): 429–41; Russell Hickman, "Speculative Activities of the Emigrant Aid Company," ibid. 5 (August 1935): 235–67.

29. Hale, *Kanzas and Nebraska*, pp. vi, 102, 245, 250, 255.

this immense Territory," they wrote, "has not, as yet been duly appreciated." Indeed, they were "quite prepared to expect, that the skill and enterprise of American farmers will find the means of obtaining comfort and wealth in these regions." Certainly, farmers should not be discouraged by reports of a desert; some people had even found New England disappointing. If the prospective emigrant refused to be satisfied with their bland assurances, Boynton and Mason reminded him again of his Christian obligation to prevent the extension of slavery.[30]

Fortunately, this object did not involve any personal sacrifice. God did not expect these free staters to martyr themselves to the desert. In fact, Boynton and Mason insisted, in a close paraphrase of Gilpin, He had more than adequately prepared Kansas for their settlement. Kansas was not deficient in rain, there was plenty of wood for fencing, and if the supply did fail, the osage hedge would serve as an admirable replacement. Coal deposits were everywhere as a substitute for wood fuel. Besides, once the prairie fires of the Indians ceased, the indigenous forest growth would reappear. And the scenery! The majesty and sublimity of the Kansas landscape were unequaled. "There are many scenes . . . that can scarcely be *remembered* even, without tears. The soul melts in the presence of the wonderful workmanship of God." For some these esthetic considerations were of secondary importance, so Kansas supplied them with a soil capable of producing fifty to one hundred bushels of corn and thirty to one hundred bushels of wheat to the acre. Experience had shown Boynton and Mason that Kansas was "capable of producing in perfection, all the grains, vegetables, and fruits which can be grown in the middle states."

There were other accounts of a similar nature published during the 1850s, all designed to encourage the settlement of Kansas by free laborers. Some of them were directly commissioned by eastern abolitionist societies; all of them aided in the counterattack against the desert theorists.[31]

It was important that there be no desert in Kansas. The free yeoman

30. Charles Boynton and T. B. Mason, *A Journey Through Kansas with Sketches of Nebraska* (Cincinnati: Moore, Wilstach, Keyes & Co., 1855). The quotations from this and the following paragraph are taken from pp. v, 46–73 *passim*, 139–41, 187, 199, 202.

31. See, for example, James Redpath and Richard Hinton, *Handbook to Kansas Territory and the Rocky Mountain Gold Regions* (New York: J. H. Colton, 1859); letter from Platte City, Mo., to Georgia, in An Old Settler [C. W. Dana], *The Garden of the World; or, the Great West* (Boston: Wentworth & Co., 1856); and Greene, *The Kanzas Region.*

had to live there if slavery was to be contained, and the yeoman could live only in a productive region. Logic and destiny demanded that Kansas be fertile: fertile she became. This was not the last time that sophistries were resorted to in the settlement of the Plains. Nor did the Emigrant Aid Company and its partners entirely escape criticism on that score in the 1850s. "It has often been alleged against the Company," Company defenders wrote, that it has "portrayed in glowing and deceptive colors the beauty and fertility of Kansas Territory, and thereby allured people to migrate thither who, had the truth been fitly spoken, would never have wandered from their homes." This was patently untrue. "The Company has not endeavored [by artificial devices] to entice people to go to Kansas."[32] By implication, those who went did so on the basis of the undoubted advantages which Kansas had to offer, advantages which were apparent to any right-thinking person. The promoters assumed an air of self-righteous innocence. They were simply stating facts and in the process performing a rare public service, in this case, preventing the extension of slavery. Whatever the promoters' object—and it was probably a humanitarian one—the borders of the alleged desert began to recede as the boomers directed their energies toward reversing the verdict on the utility of the Plains.

But the Kansas question was only one expression of a continuing dispute over the question of slavery in the territories. Eventually, of course, that dispute was to contribute to the coming of the Civil War. But to those who would attack the desert, these preliminaries to war, indeed the war itself, were of incalculable benefit. Attention was drawn to the Plains; their settlement was first made a tactic in a sectional dispute, then a part of the spoils of a sectional war. In both roles the settlement of the region was made an important part of governmental policy.

Northern opponents of the extension of slavery recognized that the simplest and most effective way of realizing their ambitions was to fill the West with one yeoman to every 160 acres. Congenitally opposed to slavery, the yeoman would effectively block the ambitions of the South and close to that section the great bounty of the western lands. Walled up within its own section and cut off from the regenerative powers of expansion, slavery would soon wither and die of attrition.[33] Various

32. "Information to Kansas Emigrants," in [Dana], *The Garden of the World*, pp. 203, 215.

33. See, for example, the remarks of George Julian of Indiana, U.S., Congress, Senate, *Congressional Globe*, 31st Cong., 2d sess., 1851, Appendix, p. 136; and the

plans were considered for settling the western regions with free institutions as quickly as possible in order to build the barrier against the
southern economic system. The most effective seemed to be the most
direct: a free homestead, 160 acres of virgin soil, as a gift of the federal
government.

To southerners, such generosity was not only fiscally irresponsible,
it could permanently deny them entrance to the western regions.
Slavery and the plantation system demanded large acreages, perhaps
minimums of 960 to 1,280 acres. Anything less than that was useless to
them. Thus did the South consciously place herself in opposition to
the gospel of progress so eagerly endorsed by the West and the North,
a gospel which rested largely upon industrial expansion into the lands
beyond the frontier. And thus, too, did the South declare her enmity
to the new Republican party, the political organ of that progress.

It was accepted by the Republicans, almost without question, that
the future growth of the United States depended in great part upon the
exploitation and development of the trans-Mississippi West. The
homestead principle with its Edenic blueprint for peopling this region
with free men and free institutions became a part of the official Republican doctrine. Many arguments were raised in its defense. Passage of
a homestead bill would eliminate the South from further participation
in the American continental empire. In this sense, at least, it was part
of an imperial struggle, a blow for northern domination of the remaining
portions of America's contiguous empire. In addition, a homestead
law would give official sanction to the well-defined belief that a home
for the yeoman was still the best assurance that American institutions
would continue viable.

It was the best assurance, as well, that the economic development
and prosperity of the North would continue, and that the safety valve
as a means and an end of that development would remain operative.
This belief, too, was a part of the Republican creed. The Republican
party, as Horace Greeley reminded his readers, was "the only national
party committed to the policy of making the public lands free in
quarter-sections. . . . Every worker will be enabled to hew out for his
family a home from the virgin soil of the Great West." A quarter
section, "land enough for any man" and available to all for the asking,
could perform a multitude of wonders, Greeley insisted. It "would

---

New York Weekly Tribune, June 12, 1852, in Roy Robbins, *Our Landed Heritage:
The Public Domain, 1776–1936* (Lincoln: University of Nebraska Press, 1962), p. 111.

snatch the landless multitudes from crime and starvation," wrote George Julian, another principal Republican spokesman, "and place them in a situation . . . conducive to virtue."[34]

The Republican party's commitment to growth, development, and free soil required, then, the opening of the western lands. But it also required people to settle those lands. As early as 1854 Representative Benjamin Wade of Ohio, in answering the charge that a homestead bill would encourage the immigration of European paupers, asked, "Why . . . should we not encourage *immigration?*" It seemed reasonable to Wade that the nation would gain immensely by encouraging poor Europeans to take advantage of the regenerative powers of the American garden.[35] The point was not lost on the Republicans. In 1863 Abraham Lincoln, in his third annual message, recommended to the Congress the establishment of "a system for the encouragement of immigration." "Our vast extent, our broad national homestead," not only permits it but demands it.[36]

The following year a special Senate committee reported that of the three factors most conducive to rapid growth—productive soil, Anglo-Saxon vigor, and foreign immigration—only the last was not being adequately dealt with and protected. It was the consensus of the committee that this condition could not be allowed to remain. "Authentic information on the inducements of immigration" should be distributed to Europeans that they might know of the boundless opportunities of American settlement. Senator John Sherman of Ohio was convinced that the appointment of a commissioner of immigration and the distribution of material on "the soil, climate, mineral resources and agricultural products . . . in the different portions of the United States" would increase America's yearly supply of immigrants by 100,000. On July 4, 1864, the National Bureau of Immigration was

34. *New York Tribune*, November 7, 1859, quoted in Smith, *Virgin Land*, p. 238; Horace Greeley, *An Overland Journey from New York to San Francisco in the Summer of 1859*, ed. by A. C. Duncan (New York: Alfred Knopf and Co., 1964), p. 54; speech in the House, January 29, 1851, in George Julian, *Speeches on Political Questions* (New York: Hurn and Houghton, 1872), p. 54. See also U.S., Congress, Senate, *Congressional Globe*, 31st Cong., 2d sess., 1851, Appendix, p. 137.

35. U.S., Congress, House, *Congressional Globe*, 33d Cong., 1st sess., 1854, pt. 3: 1717.

36. December 8, 1863 in James D. Richardson, ed., *A Compilation of the Messages and Papers of the Presidents*, 11 vols. (Washington, D.C.: Bureau of National Literature and Art, 1910), 5: 3383, and "Second Annual Message," December 1, 1862, in ibid., pp. 3334, 3336.

formed and entrusted with this responsibility. That same summer the Republicans made the encouragement of immigration, "the asylum of the oppressed of all nations," a campaign promise which was kept. Most of the European states manifested a "liberal disposition" toward this national campaign and Lincoln was pleased to announce that the increased influx of immigrants was proving to be "one of the principle replenishing streams . . . appointed by Providence to repair the ravages of internal war."[37]

Internal war ended, however; the South was taken back into the Union, and the American people, led by the Republican party, began to prepare in earnest for a united assault upon the untapped resources of the trans-Mississippi region. For many, this seemed the true legacy of the Civil War. Freed from the divisive sectionalism which had frustrated so many of their earlier ambitions, Americans were eager to make up for time lost. The defeat of the southern economic system similarly freed them; now the American genius for exploitation could proceed uninhibited. Their energies were to be directed first at the Great Plains.

Early in 1867 a senatorial excursion party set out on a mission of reconnaissance to discover the potential of the Plains region. All found it promising. The advancement of American institutions, predicted Richard Yates of Illinois, might proceed uninterrupted "to the Kansas, to the Platte, to the Rio Grande, to the Peaks of the Rocky Mountains." Nor should this occasion any surprise. "There is no portion of the earth," Yates asserted, "where . . . the triumphs of peaceful industry and the advance of improvement and material progress will be more visible and marked, than in this heaven-favored region west of the Mississippi River." His partner in the Senate, Lyman Trumbull, was equally confident. "I had heard of an American desert," he admitted, ". . . but I am satisfied that this is a mistake. . . . These plains [are] . . . of the same character as our Illinois prairies." The excursion party reached the vicinity of Fort Harker, Kansas, near the western end of the Union Pacific Railroad, Eastern Division, and very

37. U.S., Congress, Senate, Committee on Agriculture, *Report on the Enactment of Suitable Laws for the Encouragement and Protection of Foreign Immigrants*, 38th Cong., 1st sess., 1864, S. Rept. 15, pp. 2–3; U.S., Congress, Senate, *Congressional Globe*, 38th Cong., 1st sess., 1864: 865; Kirk Porter and Donald B. Johnson, eds., *National Party Platforms, 1840–1956* (Urbana: University of Illinois Press, 1956), pp. 35–36; Lincoln, Fourth Annual Message, December 6, 1864, in Richardson, ed., *Messages and Papers of the Presidents*, 5: 3447.

near the 100th meridian. Hence, the senators were not describing prairie land. They were in the short-grass Plains, but at least one of their number saw no reason to assume that the dominion and power of the federal government would be less recognized here than in the defeated South. The conquest of a people and the conquest of a land, wrote Senator G. S. Orth of Indiana, were both within the abilities of the revitalized Union. The extension of the garden image to the Plains had become part of the official Republican creed.[38]

For those who doubted this sweeping expression of faith, a number of gazettes appeared after the Civil War presenting the potential immigrant with a staggering assortment of crop statistics, personal testimonials, and lyrical promises. These gazettes form an imposing library of the occult science known only to the promoter, but they reveal as well a new appreciation of the Plains as a home for future generations of Americans and can be considered among the first systematic attempts to promote the settlement of the Plains. Many of their promises, in fact, served as models for the even more high powered promotional campaigns which followed. The Plains emerged from their pages as a golden paradise capable of fulfilling all the expectations of a garden. Some of these guidebooks were limited in their approach and did little more than list the myriad benefits of immigration to the West. But others, the more important of them, were contributions to a national crusade, part of the general effort to deny the existence of a desert and maintain the relevance of the postwar definition of the American dream.

It would be impossible to discuss all of these gazettes. They undoubtedly number in the hundreds. One of the most important and widely known of them was Linus Brockett's *Our Western Empire; or, The New West Beyond the Mississippi*. Brockett was something of a court historian for the Republican party. He had previously written campaign biographies for Ulysses S. Grant and Schuyler Colfax, and his massive gazette was likewise consistent with the expressed policy of the party.[39] It contains all the buoyant optimism, all the expansiveness and exploitative energy which the Republicans bequeathed to the nation after the Civil War.

The Plains, in Brockett's mind, were the ideal location for the exercise of these virtues. Nowhere was there a region so receptive to American

38. Speech of Senator Yates of Illinois, *Speeches Delivered at the Southern Hotel, St. Louis, June 14, 1867* (St. Louis: S. Levison, Printer, 1867), p. 13; speech of Lyman Trumbull, ibid., p. 49; speech of G. S. Orth of Indiana, ibid., p. 49.

39. Smith, *Virgin Land*, p. 215.

energies. This western empire was literally overflowing with the resources of material abundance. Its soil was of such extent and fertility that it could supply the world with bread. Its grasslands could support "flocks and herds beyond the dream of the most opulent of the patriarchs of the East." Prosperity for those fortunate enough to settle there was automatic. The Plains had a future which "all the dreams of the poets, or the rapt vision of the seers [could not] describe in too glowing colors—a future which shall make the ancient Paradise a modern reality." Certainly there was a market for a region with so glorious a future. All through Europe, from England to Italy, men lived out their lives in hopelessness and despair. There was no reason for it, no reason for them to submit to the "evils, discomforts, and oppressions" to which they were subject in Europe. Once they were aware of the opportunities which awaited them on the Plains they would "flock thither, as to a New Eden," swelling the population of the western empire from the 11 million who resided there in 1880 to some unknown figure in excess of 100 million in 1950. After all, Brockett reasoned, the nation's productive capacity had not yet been really tested, its arable lands were not one-twentieth developed. Who could possibly predict conditions "twenty years hence . . . when our resources are taken to their full extent?" The crop statistics from the 1870s were remarkable enough and proof of the region's fertility. With advanced technology, yields would become even more prodigious.[40]

Given these conditions, it was not surprising that the pioneer farmers of the Plains were a contented group. They enjoyed material prosperity, good health, and spiritual bliss; and the future promised to be even brighter. The markets of the world were open to them and all were receiving a fair price for grain. It was at this point that Brockett momentarily broke his reverie. He admitted that present market and price conditions might deteriorate, that the prosperity of the past few years could be temporarily interrupted. But even that need occasion no real alarm, at least among the corn growers of the Plains. As Brockett explained, in one of the cruelest jokes of the season, "when the price is low, and markets not easily accessible, corn is burned instead of coal, being somewhat cheaper and making a hotter fire." This, needless to say, was a feature of Plains life in which only Brockett

40. Linus Brockett, *Our Western Empire* (Philadelphia: Bradley Garretson & Co., 1881). The quotations in this and the following paragraph were taken from pp. 131–40, 179, 192, 207, 213, 235–36, 238.

could have found comfort, and generally even he tended to emphasize more conventional advantages—things like copious rains, rich soil, abundant crops. The plainsman appreciated these blessings. He responded to them gratefully and humbly in the only way he knew. According to Brockett, he was "industrious, enterprising, intelligent, moral, law-abiding, God-fearing, and brave." In a word, he was an American yeoman, worthy of the same respect and support accorded all who followed in that tradition.

Another advertiser of the Plains was Frederick Goddard, whose gazette, *Where to Immigrate and Why*, was of the same type as Brockett's. Both men considered their efforts part of a general errand of mercy rather than a mere recital of soil fertility and crop statistics. The areas open to immigration, according to Goddard, were the hope of the world, a chance for personal redemption and social harmony. Goddard approached melodrama in expressing this belief. His discussion of why people emigrate was almost a burlesque of the romantic style: They leave, he wrote, "when . . . some circumstance brings forcibly home the possible loss of health, or failure in business, or lack of employment; or they are worn and wearied with the bustle and din, and vice of our great cities, and yearn for a more quiet and purer life." When this despondent mood hits, he continues, "who has not felt himself inspired with what we may call the instinct of emigration, akin, perhaps, to that of the birds of passage, and turned his thoughts fondly and longingly toward some ideal spot among the broad fields and green pastures, the murmuring streams and long valleys of the West?" The gloomier the cities, the more rampant the vice, "the more attractive do these Arcadian homes appear to us." [41]

And where were these murmuring streams and Arcadian homes to be found? One such location was the Laramie Plains, west of the Black Hills. Here, in some of the cruelest country of present-day Wyoming, Goddard managed to find soil "as ready to-day [1869] for the plow and the spade as the fertile prairies of Illinois." For those who felt that life in that region might prove too rigorous, Goddard supplied a number of alternatives. Western Nebraska, for example, though "erroneously styled the Great American Desert," was similarly endowed. Goddard admitted that there were "a few patches of drift-sand" in

---

41. Frederick Goddard, *Where to Immigrate and Why* (Philadelphia and Cincinnati: Peoples' Publishing Co., 1869). The quotations in this and the following two paragraphs were taken from pp. 12, 13, 21, 177, 193.

places, an obvious reference to the almost fifteen thousand square miles which comprise Nebraska's Sand Hills district, but this was hardly enough to deter the dedicated.

With these inducements before him, it seemed strange to Goddard that a man would elect to remain in the East. Certainly it could not have been a lack of funds which forced him to stay. The Homestead Act—"one of the most beneficent enactments of any age, or country, and one which has done more than any other to honor the American name, and make it loved throughout the earth"—removed that obstacle. The West was open to him, it offered him "the greatest boon on earth—Manhood and Independence."

Less grandiose in his claims, but no less enthusiastic, was Albert D. Richardson. Richardson published his *Beyond the Mississippi* in 1867. In it he displayed many of the attitudes which marked the Republican party in the years immediately following the Civil War. All that party's optimism, all its commitment to growth and progress are revealed in Richardson's pages. He excoriates the slaveholding South for obstructing the inevitable destiny of the American people, and he speaks in rapturous phrases of the golden age which dawned with the defeat of the Confederacy. The West, needless to say, was to be the scene of this final triumph of free progressive institutions. "Its mines, forests and prairies await the capitalist," he wrote; "its air invites the invalid. . . . Its society welcomes the immigrant, offering . . . generous obliviousness of errors past—a clean page to begin anew the record of his life." From the Mississippi River to the Pacific was one vast expanse perfectly suited to fulfill the promise of American life. In this belief Richardson was in accord with William Gilpin and he acknowledged his debt to that "zealous student of the natural sciences." True, Gilpin had been branded by many an "enthusiast," but just eighteen years after he had preached the new gospel of continental expansion his prophecies were everywhere in the West being confirmed. Civilization was pressing westward; "the Conquest of Nature [was] moving toward the Pacific."[42]

As far as can be determined, the gazetteers were not acting in the capacity of official promoters. They accepted free passes from the railroads and were particularly lavish in their praise of the roads'

42. Albert D. Richardson, *Beyond the Mississippi: From the Great River to the Great Ocean, Life and Adventure on the Prairies, Mountains and Pacific Coast* (Hartford: American Publishing Co., 1867). The quotations were taken from pp. i–ii, 77, 79, 136, 559, 567.

contribution, but they seem to have been motivated by nothing more sinister than ignorance. They seem honestly to have believed that the Plains were ideally suited to a farming culture. All succumbed to the optimism of the post–Civil War years, all were convinced of America's ability to convert the harsh, open grasslands of the Plains into thriving villages and comfortable farms. They were wrong, of course; but so were many others who joined with them in the national crusade to people the Plains. Essentially, then, it was altruism which motivated all of them; none evinced any hint of commercial connections in the publication of his gazette. Like so many in the East, Brockett, Goddard, and Richardson believed in the simplistic notion that because the Plains had to be settled, they would be settled. It was a dangerous belief.[43]

Yet the relief which accompanied these gazettes must have been profound. Never had the American people been so eager to descend upon a frontier as they were after the Civil War. Never were they more confident of their mission, surer that they enjoyed God's unique favor. As they read the accounts of the gazetteers they were further confirmed in their faith. But it was the Great Plains these gazetteers were talking about, that region of dust and sterility known to some since the early part of the century as the Great American Desert. It was the policy of the Republican party, however, to give and preserve power to the people, to enable them to become proprietors and to secure them in their homes.[44] In this the Republicans rightfully claimed descent from Jefferson. Unlike their political sire, however, who watched over half a continent of boundless fertility, they were confronted with the other

43. There are a number of other gazetteers who could have been mentioned in this same category. Among the most interesting of them are: Samuel Bowles, *Our New West* (Hartford: Hartford Publishing Co., 1869); L. D. Burch, *Kansas as It Is: A Complete Review of the Resources, Advantages, and Drawbacks of the Great Central State* (Chicago: C. S. Burch, 1878); L. T. Bodine, *Kansas Illustrated: an Accurate and Reliable Description of This Marvellous State* (Kansas City: Ramsey, Mollett & Hudson, 1879); William Baynham Matthews, *The Settler's Map and Guide Book* (Washington, D.C.: W. B. Matthews, 1889); Edward Hepple Hall, *The Great West: Emigrants', Settlers', and Travellers' Guide and Hand Book* (New York: Tribune Office, 1864); Bayard Taylor, *Colorado: A Summer Trip* (New York: G. P. Putnam & Sons, 1867); F. V. Hayden, *The Great West: Its Attractions and Resources* (Philadelphia: Franklin Publishing Co., 1880); B. C. Keeler, *Where to Go to Become Rich* . . . (Chicago: Belford, Clarke & Co., 1880).

44. "Homesteads, the Republicans and Settlers against Democracy and Monopoly, the Record, 1868," in *Kansas Speeches*, 4, Kansas State Historical Society, Topeka. The Kansas State Historical Society is hereafter referred to as KSHS.

half, a region of apparently boundless sterility. This seemed to some a cruel trick, but the Republicans and, following their lead, most Americans, managed to brush aside what remained of the desert myth. There had to be a continuity of development. The institutions which had allowed the North to emerge dominant from the Civil War must be transferable to the trans-Mississippi West. The new West had to be developed, its resources tapped and converted to civilization's use. Immigrants had to be secured either from Europe or from the more crowded areas of the eastern United States. And these were more than just party policies. They were a national calling, a crusade of vast proportions and divine intent. The commitment to them meant that the boomers' task, the massive promotional effort to people the central Great Plains, could now begin.

CHAPTER TWO

Railroad Promotion

The principal agent for implementing the settlement and development policies of the Republican party, and hence the principal force in the boomers' frontier, was the railroad. The homestead law gave land away, but the railroad was expected to market this land, promote its settlement, and carry its resources to the East. In addition, the railroads were to open up the Far Eastern trade, provide for the defense of the western regions, and generally promote the welfare of the nation. In return for these favors the federal government was prepared to surrender vast quantities of land to the roads, land which might be used to finance the construction and the first developmental years of the various transcontinental lines.

In 1862 the first of these grants was issued. With the secession of the southern states, the old conflict between northern and southern routes was settled by default, and the central route from Omaha west was decided upon as the most feasible for the first transcontinental line. The two railroads chosen for this project, the Union Pacific and the Central Pacific, were the grateful recipients of ten alternate sections of land for each mile of track laid. In addition, the government agreed to supply the companies, on a first mortgage loan basis, with $16,000 for each mile of track in level country, $32,000 for track laid in foothill regions, and $48,000 per mile of mountain construction. Generous as these terms were, they failed to attract enough private capital to allow either road to begin construction. After two years of relative inactivity, Congress agreed to double the land grant and take a second mortgage. With this added impetus, Union Pacific crews began to build.

In issuing these grants the Congress closed to actual settlement much of the region through which the railroads passed. The alternate sections which were not a part of the railroad bounty were reserved for sale at $2.50 per acre, but none of these could be sold until the railroads had received their full grant. This, of course, might involve

years, and in the meantime the settler was limited to the sections held
by the railroads and sold at prices ranging from four to ten dollars
an acre. The prospective homesteader, lured by the promise of free
land, was thus forced to exercise his homestead patent on lands outside
the railroad grant and hence of negligible commercial value.[1]

This basic inconsistency between railroad land grants and free
homesteads was for the moment all but ignored. There seemed to be, in
the 1860s at least, room enough for both, especially since the railroads
alone seemed capable of effecting the twin objects of free land: settlement and development. So vital did this function seem that Henry
V. Poor insisted that the railroads themselves were least favored by the
land grants. Both the federal government, as representative of the
nation, and the individual farmer were more directly benefited by their
issuance.[2] The railroads would develop the area between the settled
regions of the Mississippi Valley and those of the Pacific Coast. This was
a contribution which they could not perform unaided; the cost would be
prohibitive. But the cost to the nation if this development did not
occur would be incalculable. It was cheap at any price, even 181 million
acres, the amount awarded eventually to various western roads.

Closely connected with this same problem was the question of
financial maturity. Prior to this time, railroads had followed settlement,
and hence were able to avoid the purely developmental stage of growth
and move directly to the exploitative. They were, in other words,
mature industries financially at the time of their birth. On the Plains,
however, this order was reversed. The roads were to precede and
promote settlement. They were, then, immature industries.[3] Land
grants, the kind gift of a paternal government, were expected to ease
the burdens of financial adolescence. But before true maturity could
be reached, these lands had to be sold and the region developed to the
point where the roads could realize a profit from the carrying trade of

1. Fred Shannon, *The Farmers' Last Frontier: Agriculture, 1860–1897* (New York:
Harper, 1968), pp. 65–66; Paul W. Gates, "The Homestead Law in an Incongruous
Land System," *American Historical Review* 41 (July 1936): 657–58.

2. Henry V. Poor, *Manual of the Railroads of the United States* (New York: H.
V. & H. W. Poor, 1871–1872), p. 417. See also the comments of C. J. Ernst, a railroad
promoter, "The Railroads as a Creator of Wealth in the Development of a Community or District," *Nebraska History* 7 (January–March 1924): 16–22.

3. See Robert Fogel, *The Union Pacific Railroad: A Case in Premature Enterprise*,
Johns Hopkins University Studies in Historical and Political Science, vol. 78, no. 2
(Baltimore, 1960), pp. 17–25. See also William Bell, *New Tracks in North America*
(London: Chapman & Hall, 1870), p. xxv.

the area. In order to hasten this maturity, the lands had to be promoted. The railroads could not sit idly by and wait for the marching legions of American pioneers to reach them. They had to advertise, to stimulate interest, to misrepresent if necessary, but always to sell their lands. The railroads found, according to the Burlington's C. R. Lowell, "that he who buildeth a Railroad west of the Mississippi must also find a population and build up business."[4] This was especially true on the marginal and semiarid lands of the Plains, lands which, unlike those of the humid regions, would not sell themselves.[5] The result was a promotional and marketing campaign which rivaled the most urgent and persuasive advertisements of the twentieth century.

The purpose of this campaign, however, was not necessarily corporate profits. Development was the railroads' object. The railroads, according to a representative spokesman, needed first to "double the population, double the wealth, double the cultivated lands" of the regions through which they passed. None of these goals could be reached if the lands were sold at prices beyond the reach of prospective settlers.[6]

A neat system of interdependence was thus established. The success of the railroads depended upon the rapid development of the regions they served, but this development was possible only with the aid of the roads. In 1867, the people of Cheyenne, Wyoming, welcomed the arrival of the Union Pacific proclaiming, "Farewell to ye eternal solitudes that have held here your reign from creation's dawn. . . . Farewell to yet roaming herds of bison and antelope; your green pastures are [about to pass] into the hands of tillage and husbandry."[7] The Union Pacific undoubtedly joined them in these sentiments and, together with the other lines, determined to speed the bison and antelope on their way.

4. Cited in Richard Overton, *Burlington West: A Colonization History of the Burlington Railroad* (Cambridge: Harvard University Press, 1941), p. 159. See also the report of M. W. Ensign, January 26, 1888, in George Holdrege Papers, Nebraska State Historical Society, Lincoln. The Nebraska State Historical Society is hereafter referred to as NSHS.

5. See James Blain Hedges, *Building the Canadian West: The Land and Colonization Policies of the Canadian Pacific Railway* (New York: Macmillan Co., 1939), pp. 141–42.

6. A. B. Touzalin, land commissioner of the Burlington, 1878, in Overton, *Burlington West*, pp. 150, 251, 385–86, 433; see also *Weekly Tribune* (Lawrence, Kans.), September 22, 1870; for a conflicting view, consult Robbins, *Our Landed Heritage*, p. 255.

7. *Cheyenne Leader*, November 14, 1867.

The earnestness and efficiency with which the railroads pursued this object was remarkable. The promoters operated on the advice given one of their numbers by C. R. Lowell. Their reports, Lowell suggested, should be as urgent, as compelling as a letter to a "lady love . . . describing the Paradise where [they] hoped to pass . . . a blissful middleage."[8] They seldom fell short of this goal. Prospective immigrants were promised everything from longevity to instant riches. The Plains were made to appear capable of producing in abundance every known grain. The beauties of the region were unsurpassed, the climate was healthful and invigorating, and the people who lived there, pure of mind and noble of spirit. Nothing was overlooked, nothing omitted in the campaign to attract new residents to the Plains. At the same time, the promoters invariably paused long enough to add that "the utmost care has been exercised to admit nothing to their [promotional] columns that cannot be depended upon as correct."[9] Every statement concerning the productive capacity of the Plains could be "fully sustained, upon investigation."[10]

These claims of credibility, like many other promotional devices, were modeled after the example of the Illinois Central. The first of the land grant railroads, it had developed a highly sophisticated and successful technique for inducing immigrants to its lands, and many of the trans-Mississippi lines sent observers to watch the Illinois Central in action.[11] They learned their lessons well, too well to suit the Illinois Central. By the 1870s, pamphlets and other promotional literature were being distributed throughout Illinois by the trans-Mississippi lines. So successful were these efforts to stimulate immigration west, that the Illinois Central, along whose route much of this promotional appeal was directed, began to reconsider the advisability of its earlier assistance.[12]

8. Lowell to Henry Thielsen, October 6, 1859, in Overton, *Burlington West*, p. 143.

9. *Western Trail* (Rock Island), May, 1886. All of the railroads across the Plains published promotional newspapers. They will be identified hereafter, for the first citation only, by the name of the paper and the railroad issuing it.

10. *Kansas Pacific Homestead* (Kansas Pacific), January, 1878.

11. Paul Wallace Gates, *The Illinois Central Railroad and Its Colonization Work* (Cambridge: Harvard University Press, 1934), pp. 169–73, 308–9. One Burlington representative thought the Illinois Central spent too much time and money on long detailed newspaper advertisements, but with some other exceptions, the western roads based their promotional appeals on the tried methods of the Illinois Central. See Overton, *Burlington West*, pp. 200–1.

12. Gates, *The Illinois Central*, pp. 209–10; and Gates, *Fifty Million Acres*, pp. 246–47.

Illinois was not alone in facing the threat of decreased rural population. Every state, and many foreign nations, were targets for the same
type of promotion. The resourcefulness of the railroads in this project
and the methods they used to secure its success seemed unlimited. One
of the favorite promotional devices was to dispatch excursion trains for
a tour of the Plains. Newspaper editors were invited to view firsthand
the miraculous opportunities which there awaited the settler. One
editor from Indiana swore he "never saw a finer country in the world
than that part of Kansas passed over by the Atchison, Topeka and
Santa Fe. . . . Corn waist high, wheat in the shock, oats in fine condition."[13] Needless to say, the Santa Fe was delighted, though not
overly surprised, by this testimonial. The railroad had, of course,
financed the entire trip. The excursion began on the twenty-fourth of
June when the plains were admittedly at their loveliest. The editors
were treated like visiting royalty, but their response was no less grati-
fying for all its predictability. In this instance, the visiting editors were
"compelled to repeat in earnest what [they had] often quoted in
derision . . . 'Go West, young man, go West.'"[14]

Another device often used by the western roads was to retain a
permanent and professional advertising correspondent. The best of
these was probably J. D. Butler of the Burlington. Butler was hired in
1869 as a lecturer, a traveling promoter who spoke to interested groups
about the glories of the West, especially that part traversed by the
Burlington. Anonymity was particularly important, and Butler went to
some lengths to disguise his relationship with the road. He could then
advertise Burlington lands and "the people not know [his] motives,
either in lecture rooms or in the columns of the numerous periodicals
to which [he] gained access."[15] Among these "periodicals" were the
reports of the Nebraska State Board of Agriculture. In 1873 he contributed a short statement, the burden of which was the absolute cer-
tainty of successful agriculture throughout the state.[16] This official

13. Santa Fe, *Kansas in 1875: Strong and Impartial Testimony to the Wonderful
Productiveness of the Cottonwood and Arkansas Valleys; What Over 200 Editors
Think of Their Present and Future* (Topeka, 1875), p. 17. Unless otherwise noted,
promotional pamphlets were published by the company involved.

14. Ibid., p. 24. This comment was made at Granada, Colorado, located approxi-
mately on the 103d meridian. See also *Daily Commonwealth* (Topeka), July 13,
1873, for an account of another excursion train.

15. George Harris to Butler, November 20, 1869, in Overton, *Burlington West*,
p. 299.

16. Nebraska State Board of Agriculture, *Fourth Annual Report, 1873* (Lincoln,
1873), p. 27. Hereafter the Nebraska State Board of Agriculture is cited as NSBA.

sanction, together with his anonymity, gave Butler a decided advantage when dealing with prospective settlers on Burlington land. He could and did pose as a disinterested and concerned humanitarian whose sole interest was in finding a good home for deserving people. It was an effective technique.[17]

The railroads' claims of sincerity were given a severe challenge by the activities of men like Butler, but no more so than by the publication of allegedly unsolicited testimonials from settlers already on railroad lands. The Kansas Pacific obtained considerable promotional value out of the comments of one S. P. Donmeyer, farmer extraordinary from Salina County, Kansas. Donmeyer wrote in the January, 1878, issue of the *Kansas Pacific Homestead* of the remarkable yields he had harvested from sixty-two acres of Kansas sod. His wheat averaged twenty-eight bushels per acre, and with the proceeds from its sale he was able to pay off the entire cost of his land. This in itself was a note-worthy accomplishment, but in addition to liquidating his debt to the Kansas Pacific, Donmeyer had almost five hundred dollars remaining for new machinery and farm improvements. Donmeyer's comments, which the Kansas Pacific insisted were sent out of good will, prompted numerous letters from interested parties in the East. Some of these, at least, must have challenged the accuracy of his statements, for Donmeyer was moved to assure his readers that he had "no interest in inducing any one to come West," though in all honesty he had to admit that "a great many could better themselves in coming." [18]

The value of unofficial testimony of this sort was obvious to all of the western roads and most of them tried to secure someone of unquestionable integrity or detachment to comment on the advantages of their land. The Burlington retained the Reverend Darius Jones to handle some of their promotional material and he garnished it with a predictable amount of selfless piety.[19] Another "correspondent" of the

---

See also *Salina County Post*, April 22, 1871, for an account of some of Butler's activities in Kansas.

17. There were, however, warnings to European immigrants to be suspicious of disinterested agents. See, for example, Edward Money, *The Truth about America* (London: Sampson Low, Marston, Searle & Riverton, 1886), pp. 42–51. Two promi-nent Nebraskans were convinced that Butler, specifically, had been uncovered and his usefulness as a promoter compromised. See J. Sterling Morton to Robt. Furnas, January 23, 1873, Furnas Papers, NSHS.

18. Letter from S. P. Donmeyer to the *Kansas Pacific Homestead*, February, 1877.

19. Overton, *Burlington West*, p. 352.

Burlington was a Nebraskan by the name of Moses Syndenham, who appeared to have found a profitable avocation in writing "unsolicited" letters to various promotional agencies, railroad and state, and to many of the gazettes which were published in the 1870s purporting to describe conditions in the West. Syndenham was the ideal correspondent, literate, enthusiastic, and easily compromised. He was particularly effusive in one open letter to George S. Harris, president of the Burlington. "May success attend the energetic efforts of the Burlington," he wrote, "and many benedictions and blessings arise from thousands of homes made happy by the wise dealings and liberal conduct of the company toward those who are homeless and landless in the world." [20] In Syndenham's mind the Burlington was a philanthropic organization: benefactor of oppressed humanity, savior of the home, and protector of the commonwealth. The implication was clear: anyone who did not take advantage of the opportunities offered by the B & M was missing a unique chance to claim for himself a share of the American dream.

One of the most commonly used promotional techniques was the formation of land companies which were technically independent of the railroads but actually, like the dummy construction companies of earlier years, identical in management and financing. The Burlington was especially adept at this sort of promotion. At various times it was dependent upon the Eastern Land Association, the South Platte Land Company, the Lincoln Land Company, and the Lancaster Land Company to market its holdings. [21] The land companies did so successfully, but only by disassociating themselves from the railroads and hence presenting an appearance of detachment. Less well disguised than the Burlington subsidiaries, but equally effective, was the National Land Company, the promotional arm of the Kansas Pacific and Denver Pacific lines. The National Land Company was organized in Chicago in 1869 and concentrated most of its energies on securing entire colonies of immigrants to settle the lines' holdings in Colorado. It enjoyed

20. *Nebraska Herald* (Plattsmouth), September 15, 1870. The Union Pacific benefited from the unofficial testimony of a "disinterested" observer, Fred Hedde (*Pioneer* [Union Pacific], June 1875). Hedde had earlier worked as an immigration agent for Nebraska in Germany.

21. Overton, *Burlington West*, pp. 286–89; C. J. Ernst Manuscripts, NSHS; Interview by J. T. Kearns with W. D. McGinnis, WPA Project, Colorado State Historical Society, Denver. The Colorado State Historical Society is hereafter cited as CSHS.

singular success, especially in the Greeley and Chicago colonies.[22]
Eventually the company set up sixteen such colonies in Kansas and
Colorado, and by 1870 was reported to have sold, in a space of twenty
days, 10,597 acres in Colorado alone. There was much truth in the
statement of the *Rocky Mountain News* that "this company has done
more than any other organization in existence to settle up the Kansas
prairies, and will now send thousands of emigrants to settle up our
beautiful Colorado lands."[23]

If population figures for Kansas and Nebraska are any indication,
this estimate was overly conservative. In 1870 the population of
Kansas was 364,234. A scant four years later it had increased almost 50
percent to 530,367. This in itself represents a remarkable growth, but
the increase in the thirteen counties served by the Santa Fe railroad
was 64 percent. By 1887 the state as a whole contained more than a
million and a half souls, or almost five times as many as resided there
thirteen years earlier.[24] The growth of Nebraska was equally spectac-
ular. In 1875, 246,200 people made their home there. In 1880 the
figure was 452,542, and between 1880 and 1890 another 600,000 joined
them.[25]

The surveyor general of Nebraska attributed much of this growth to
the promotional activities of the Union Pacific and the Burlington, and
to the low rates and easy terms at which they offered their land.[26] He
recognized, as the railroads had much earlier, that low down payments
and easy credit would greatly facilitate the disposal of their land
bounties. All of the lines offered generous terms—in the case of the
Union Pacific, 10 percent down and eleven years credit at 7 percent
per annum.[27]

22. J. F. Willard, "Editor's Introduction," in *Experiments in Colorado Colonization* (Boulder: University of Colorado Press, 1932), pp. xxiv, 238–43.

23. *Rocky Mountain News* (Denver), May 2, 1870; see also, ibid., October 15,
1870, and the *Colorado Tribune* (Denver), May 20, 1870, for further accounts of the
activities of the National Land Company.

24. Lawrence L. Waters, *Steel Trails to Santa Fe* (Lawrence: University of
Kansas Press, 1950), p. 224; Everett Dick, *The Sod House Frontier* (New York: D.
Appleton Century Co., 1937), p. 185.

25. "Report of the Surveyor General of Nebraska," in *Report of the Secretary
of the Interior, 1880* (Washington, D.C.: GPO, 1881), pp. 1004–5.

26. Ibid., p. 1005.

27. Dick, *Sod House Frontier*, p. 188. See also Brockett, *Our Western Empire*,
pp. 351–53, for the rates offered by the Santa Fe. Overton, in *Burlington West*,
discusses those of the Burlington, pp. 337–38.

By the late 1870s the various promotional techniques and methods of the railroads had been tried, proven, and perfected, and few new methods were introduced in the years following. The most sophisticated techniques would have availed them little, however, if the railroads had not also discovered a battery of persuasive arguments to plead their case and stimulate interest in their lands. As might be expected, some of these contained promises impossible to fulfill. The Plains were made to appear a land singularly blessed, no easy task and one which involved a not overly sensitive conscience.

Richard C. Overton and James B. Hedges, two particularly prominent railroad historians, insist that, of all the promotional agencies operating after the Civil War, the railroads were the least irresponsible in their advertising. Both men emphasize the railroads' oft-repeated warning that only those of hard-working disposition and unwavering perseverance should consider immigration to the Plains. The promotional literature of the railroads, writes Hedges, "contained . . . many frank statements of the difficulties ahead," statements which, according to Overton, appeared "even when times were hard and [land] sales falling." [28] There can be no doubting the accuracy of these contentions. But is this reason enough to assign to the railroads the mantle of responsible advertising? Listen, for example, to a statement made in 1876 by the Santa Fe:

> If hard work doesn't agree with you, or you can't get on without luxuries, stay where you are. If you don't have enough capital to equip or stock a farm, if you are susceptible to homesickness, if you do not have pluck and perseverance, stay where you are. . . . Wealth here is won only by work.[29]

This was not a warning, it was a challenge, and a challenge of a particularly seductive sort. John Miller, an agent for the Kansas Pacific, expressed similar sentiments in 1871. Miller's responsibility was to attract settlers, and he told one prospect "plainly that America is not the place for young men who have *not made up thier* [sic] *minds to work*. . . . America and Kansas in particular, is the place for all who will persevere. . . . *God forbid that I should tell you lies*." Was this a negative condition, a harsh fact which, in truth, must be mentioned? Or was it rather a positive feature which Kansas to her glory shared

28. James B. Hedges, "Promotion of Immigration to the Pacific Northwest by the Railroads," *Mississippi Valley Historical Review* 15 (September 1928): 201; Overton, *Burlington West*, pp. 447–48.

29. Santa Fe, *How and Where to Get a Living* (Boston, 1876), pp. 45–46.

with the rest of the nation? Miller obviously thought the latter.[30]
The railroads realized that few would admit that they lacked the
requirements for material success. Hard work, perseverance, the
simple life, all were a part of the American tradition. It represented
no break from this tradition for the promoters to warn prospective
immigrants that they would have to work to succeed on the Plains.
"America is the land of labor," Benjamin Franklin had written in 1782,
and it remained such a century later. The Edenic image, the image of
America as a cultivated garden, demanded that this be the case. Productive labor was glorified. It was an absolute if America was to fulfill
her manifest destiny. To require it on the Plains was not to repel
potential immigrants, but rather to confirm that the area was, in fact, a
true and worthy frontier.

The wilderness of the Plains was to be converted by hard work and
the railroads based their promotion on this belief. But there was a
necessary consequence of this appeal. Those who performed this vital
function were to be honored as pioneers. Such had always been the case,
and the railroads were quick to make the connection. The Union
Pacific, for example, compared those who bought and settled their
lands to Abraham, Columbus, and the Pilgrims. They were "the advance
column of civilization," a proud breed of men worthy of the highest
laurels of a grateful nation. For all their sturdiness, however, they were
"a peaceable, even tempered race, who hate war, love peace, . . . honor
their wives, raise honest children, live within their income, and grow
rich out of Kansas soil." [31] In other words, they were yeomen, followers
in a grand tradition. The fact that they also grew rich seems almost an
afterthought.

More important to the image than riches was the fact that here
"every man can become his own landlord." "Free citizenship and
equality of civil rights" were offered to all who emigrated. Here were
independence and freedom, a "poor man's paradise," where a comfortable subsistence was all but guaranteed.[32] This was the basic promise

30. John Miller to Bertie Cator, January 18, 1871, in Angie Debo, ed., "An
English View of the Wild West," *Panhandle Plains Historical Review* 6 (1933): 27.
31. *Pioneer*, July, 1874.
32. *Kansas Pacific Homestead*, January, 1878; Union Pacific, *Guide to the Union
Pacific Railroad Lands, 12,000,000 Acres* . . . (Omaha, 1871); Union Pacific, *The
Emigrant Guide and Handbook of the Central Branch, Union Pacific R.R., &c.: Homes
for the Homeless and Superior Locations for Capitalists and Other Business Men*
(Omaha: Advertising Co., 1878).

of the Plains, and if one became rich in the process, it was a welcome fringe benefit.

Nonetheless, it was a benefit which the railroads chose not to ignore. Visions of yeomen pioneers were of negligible value if they involved poverty and sacrifice. The Plains, to be successfully promoted, had to appear a potential garden, capable of supplying those who worked them with sufficient rewards, and it was at this point that the railroad promoters confronted directly the theory of the Great American Desert. Much of their energy was devoted to dispelling it. The Plains were to receive a new image, a promotional face-lifting. They were to become an organic part of the Edenic landscape. Unfortunately, if they were unrecognizable as a desert, they were absurd as a garden.

In spite of the labors of men like Benton, Frémont, and Gilpin, and in spite of the commitment of the Republican party, enough Americans remained stubbornly desert-minded to warrant railroad attention. As late as 1871, a Kansas Pacific representative was lamenting that the East was still "profoundly ignorant of the facts" about Kansas.[33] It was the railroads' objective to correct this ignorance, to "rediscover" the Plains and display to the world their unsuspected treasure. In the words of J. D. Butler, the true discoverer of the region "was not Major Long, nor yet any of those wayfarers who beheld only its barrenness. Its true Columbus was he who ... first detected its latent capabilities." In the process, this second Columbus, "with one sweeping blow, [would throw] down the barriers which hid the un-exampled progress which was going on in spite of the ignorance of the East."[34] Once these obstacles were lifted, the immense fertility of the Plains would become manifest, and Kansas and Nebraska would then become as celebrated as Kentucky and those other obsolete gardens.

What remained of the desert barrier was thus subjected to a massive counterattack. Kansas was identified as "undeniably ... a paradise."[35] For those who were unconvinced and continued to ask why they should emigrate there, the Rock Island had a ready answer: "Because it is the garden spot of the world. ... Because it will grow anything that any other country will grow and with less work. Because it rains

33. W. Weston, ed., *Weston's Guide to the Kansas Pacific Railway* (Kansas City: Missouri Bulletin Steam Printing and Engraving House, 1871), p. 195.

34. *Nebraska, Its Characteristics and Prospects* (Omaha: Privately printed, 1873), p. 10.

35. A. B. Linquist, "The Swedish Immigrant in Kansas," *Kansas Historical Quarterly* 29 (Spring 1963): 5, commenting on a Kansas Pacific pamphlet.

here more than in any other place, and just at the right time."[36] This was no desert, but an arcadia. Rainfall was abundant; the soil was of the highest fertility. There were "no stones, no stumps, no stubborn clays" to harass the farmer. The plow glided through the deep black mold as easily as in the well cultivated fields of Pennsylvania, "tickling the Plains and producing in return the laughter of bountiful harvests."[37]

The desert makers, however, had implied more than just sterility when they spoke of the barrenness of the Plains. The scenery was portrayed as singularly unattractive. The climate, apart from its significance for agriculture, was extreme and unhealthy. It was to these secondary problems that the railroads next directed their promotional zeal. A Union Pacific promotional pamphlet of 1868 insisted that "the scenery [was] one vast ever changing panorama."[38] The climate of this inspiring land was equally magnificent. That of Kansas, wrote a Union Pacific promoter in 1871, was "genial and healthful." The entire state basked under almost perpetual sunshine. The air was dry and pure and effectively free of the miasmic influences of more humid regions. Good health was one of the natural consequences of residing in Kansas, and after all, the Union Pacific reasoned, "what doth it profit a man to buy a farm . . . if he and his family lose their health?"[39]

It is interesting to note that eleven years later, after most of its lands in the eastern part of the state had been sold, the Union Pacific began to warn prospective buyers that eastern Kansas was notoriously unhealthy and that they should "get to the higher elevations of the central part of the state." There, the reader was not surprised to learn, the Union Pacific still held five million acres.[40]

36. *Western Trail*, January, 1887.

37. *Kansas Pacific Homestead*, January, 1878; Kansas Land and Emigration Co., *Emigration to Kansas, the Glory of the West* (London: Privately printed, 1871), p. 12; this company was the agent of the National Land Company in England, Ireland, and Wales. The comment on "tickling the Plains" comes from the *Western Trail*, May, 1886. This was a favorite slogan of the promoters of the 1880s.

38. Union Pacific, *Omaha to the Mountains on the Union Pacific Railroad* (Chicago, 1868), p. 11.

39. Union Pacific, *Guide to the Union Pacific Railroad Lands, 12,000,000 Acres* . . . (Omaha, 1871); Union Pacific, *Five Million Acres, the Union Pacific Guide, Farms and Homes in Kansas and Colorado at Low Prices and Eleven Years' Credit* (Kansas City, 1882), p. 14. The Santa Fe and the Kansas Pacific made similar claims as to the salubrity of the Kansas climate. See, for example, *Star of Empire* (Santa Fe), July, 1869, and *Kansas Pacific Homestead*, July, 1878.

40. Union Pacific, *Five Million Acres*, p. 10.

For those who might still doubt that the central Great Plains were the most healthful region on the globe, the railroads used the theory of isothermal lines. In terms reminiscent of William Gilpin, the Santa Fe wrote of its route along the Arkansas River and near the 39th parallel as "the parallel of grain and flowers, and orchards and vineyards." This was no doubt comforting news, but the 39th parallel was more, it was "the parallel of physical power" and the route of empire.[41] The climatic advantages within this zone were well known and indisputable. There were no extremes of temperature. The rays of the sun struck at precisely the right angles and with an almost supernatural effect. Bodily vigor and mental alertness were inevitable consequences of residence in this most favored land.[42]

Only the most greedy could have asked more from a region than was offered by the central Great Plains. Wealth, independence, good health, good neighbors, and the chance to perform a vital national service were among the opportunities granted to those fortunate enough to live there. This conviction led the railroads to some rather lofty predictions regarding the future growth and population of the area. None of these could match the heady figure of 1.3 billion people projected by Gilpin, but Carl Schmidt of the Santa Fe was convinced that Kansas could support 33 million in comfort and wealth. A somewhat less sanguine Union Pacific promoter revised that figure downward to 19 million but this total was to be achieved by 1920. After that date, the number was likely to multiply so prolifically that even a railroad promoter hesitated to offer a prediction.[43] These were figures to make a railroader's heart sing. The heroic effort to depict the Plains as a verdant paradise had been rewarded. People were coming, and as J. J. Hill once stated, "You might put a railroad in the Garden of Eden and if there was nobody there but Adam and Eve, it would be a failure."[44] Fortunately for the railroads, the existence of such a garden ensured rapid population

41. Santa Fe, *A New Sectional Map of Seven Counties in the Arkansas Valley of Kansas* (Topeka, 1883).

42. The Union Pacific also promoted on this basis. See *Pioneer*, July, 1874. See also Goddard, *Where to Immigrate and Why*, p. 548, and Weston, ed., *Weston's Guide to the Kansas Pacific*, pp. 163–64.

43. Carl B. Schmidt, *Official Facts about Kansas* (Topeka: AT & SF, 1884), p. 1. Union Pacific, *The Great Northwest, the Most Successful Farming Region of Kansas! Well Watered, Cheapest Lands* (Omaha, n.d.), p. 4.

44. "Development of the West," *Proceedings of the Fourth Dry Farming Congress*, Billings, Montana, October 26–28, 1909 (Billings, 1910), p. 35.

growth and the Plains were indisputably a garden. Adam and Eve were well advised to prepare for neighbors.

There existed only one possible deterrent to continued and permanent success on the Plains. A Union Pacific pamphlet made explicit reference to it in 1876. Conventional farming in western Kansas, the Union Pacific told its readers, was an impossibility. "The small farmer can never succeed here on his 160 acre homestead."[45] To admit that even a portion of the Plains was not suitable for cultivation was tantamount to heresy and quite out of character for a railroad promoter. A corrective, however, had been supplied by the Union Pacific some years earlier. From Fort Kearny to the Rocky Mountains, the company had written in 1868, irrigation was necessary to secure abundant crops.[46] This was one of the first instances in which a railroad promoter mentioned irrigation. It was an alien method to the Americans, especially in the 1860s, but the Union Pacific hastened to assure prospective settlers that it was simple, inexpensive, and foolproof.[47]

In spite of the bland assurance offered by the Union Pacific, many of the railroads were concerned about the sale of their lands west of the 100th meridian. They were resigned to the melancholy fact that irrigation was necessary west of this line, but they never ceased to search for an alternative method more in keeping with American experience. Until such an alternative was found they were forced to admit that the semiarid, short grass Plains presented an entirely new set of problems and that certain adjustments in their price schedules were required. Burlington lands, for example, ranged in price from eight to twenty dollars per acre in central Nebraska to two to six dollars in the western part of the state,[48] an obvious attempt to stimulate interest in lands which had either to be irrigated or devoted exclusively to stock raising.

This did not mean, of course, that the railroads had abandoned interest in the western half of the Plains, but simply that new methods would

45. Union Pacific, *Kansas, The Golden Belt Lands along the Line of the Kansas Division of the U.P. R'W* (Kansas City, Mo., 1876).

46. Union Pacific, *Progress of the Union Pacific Railroad West from Omaha . . . across the Continent . . .* (New York, 1868), pp. 18–19; they had said essentially the same thing in 1867 in *Union Pacific Railroad across the Continent West from Omaha, Nebraska* (New York, 1867), p. 11.

47. *Progress of the Union Pacific*, p. 20. Irrigation had been practiced for years by the trappers at old Bent's Fort and they had enjoyed considerable success. See Thomas Farnham, "Travels on the Great Western Prairies," in *Early Western Travels*, ed. by Reuben G. Thwaites, 27:173.

48. Overton, *Burlington West*, p. 335. This was from 1871 to 1872.

have to be used in order to realize the promise of the region. That the promise was there became an article of faith with the railroads. The Kansas Pacific in 1870 invited all who doubted the productive capacity of western Kansas to "have their incredulity dispelled by calling at [our] office."[49] There they would be shown examples of the grains grown under irrigation in the Arkansas River valley of southwestern Kansas. Those who chose to visit the Sante Fe's office in Topeka could discover just how simple an effective irrigation system was to construct, while all of the roads gave prominent attention to the pastoral advantages of the short grass country and the ease with which cattle could be fattened and marketed, especially if irrigation were used as an adjunct to stock raising.[50]

Irrigation and stock raising, however, were little more than temporary expedients, and satisfactory ones only so long as the railroads had land east of the 100th meridian. While this was the case there was no very compelling reason to promote the western half of the Plains on any other basis. Once these marginal lands were all that remained, the railroads would display more resourcefulness in their promotion, and the earlier argument that the land west of the 100th meridian was suited only for irrigation and stock raising would be refuted by the same lines which once so enthusiastically endorsed it.

Originally most of the people of the central Great Plains seem to have been pleased with the promotional efforts of the railroads. They recognized their mutual dependence on the roads in this vital matter and considered themselves "supremely fortunate" in having their nongovernment lands transferred to corporations whose interest in promotion so closely paralleled their own. The *Nebraska Farmer*, for example, was convinced that the railroads' chief aim was not to realize a profit from the sale of their lands but to secure "occupancy and development of the country." To this end, "they have advertised the advantages and resources of the State in every quarter of the globe, with unremitting zeal."[51] In Kansas, the *Lawrence Weekly Tribune* of September 22, 1870, expressed its appreciation of the "admirable

---

49. *Daily Colorado Tribune* (Denver), citing the *Kansas City* (Mo.) *Bulletin*, October 12, 1870.

50. Santa Fe, *Guide to the Arkansas Valley Lands of the Atchison, Topeka, and Santa Fe Railroad Company in Southwestern Kansas* (Topeka, 1879); *Omaha Daily Herald*, June 5, 1870, contains a statement by a Union Pacific official on the stock-raising possibilities of western Nebraska; see also *Western Trail*, May, 1886.

51. *Nebraska Farmer* (Lincoln), January, 1877.

provisions" made by the National Land Company "for the transportation and settlement of emigrants on the rich lands of Kansas and
Colorado." Two years later, an Omaha newspaper announced its
"entire satisfaction with the course [the Burlington] has pursued, and
is now pursuing, toward the State of Nebraska in the advertisement and
sale of its immense land subsidy."[52] A more official expression of these
same sentiments came from Governor William James, who publicly
acknowledged the obligation he felt the state owed the Burlington and
Union Pacific for their efforts in advancing Nebraska's interest.[53]

In spite of this approbation, there were always a few in every state
who doubted the effectiveness of the railroads' promotional campaigns.
Most of these critics complained that the roads were not doing enough
in the way of advertising or that what advertising they did perform was
discriminatory against certain sections or towns. The Pueblo, Colorado,
Chamber of Commerce, for example, was highly critical of the National
Land Company for its alleged discrimination against the Arkansas
Valley in its promotional literature. The fact that the Kansas Pacific,
for whom the company was promoting, did not travel the Arkansas
River route was conveniently ignored.[54] The Wichita, Kansas, Chamber
of Commerce was similarly distressed at the action of the Santa Fe in
reducing its rates for passage to Hutchinson, Kansas. It had not
reduced its fares to Newton on the spur line through Wichita, and the
chamber interpreted this to mean "that the intention of the road is to
force emigration as far west as Hutchinson, so that by no possibility
could Sedgwick [of which Wichita was the county seat], Sumner,
Butler, and Cowley counties receive their fair share of the emigration."[55]
At about this time the charge was heard in Nebraska that the Burlington
exhibit at the Centennial Exposition in Philadelphia was not large
enough and did not represent the varied capacity of the state. This was
quite in contrast to the magnificent display the Burlington provided for
Iowa, and seemed to indicate that the road was either insensitive to

52. *Omaha Daily Tribune and Republican*, September 14, 1872. See also *Nebraska
Herald* (Plattsmouth), December 16, 1869. Newspapers throughout the Plains
contained stories on the progress of the railroads in disposing of their grants. See,
for example, *Topeka Capital*, May 11, 1888; *Omaha Herald*, July 16, 1873, and
February 21, 1880; *Omaha Republican*, July 23, 1876.
53. Outgoing message of Acting Governor William James, January 10, 1873, in
Messages and Proclamations of Nebraska Governors, 3 vols. (Lincoln: NSHS, 1942),
1: 360.
54. *Colorado Chieftain* (Pueblo), May 12, 1870.
55. *Wichita Weekly Beacon*, April 5, 1876.

the needs of Nebraska or ignorant of the state's enormous potential. A. E. Touzalin answered for the Burlington and tried to assuage some of the hurt feelings by assuring Governor Garber of the railroad's continuing devotion to Nebraska's welfare.[56] State paranoia was not easily corrected, however. In 1887 the *Atchinson Champion* declared simply and somewhat petulantly that "the Kansas Pacific . . . never did very much to advertise our state or even its own lands,"[57] while three years later the *Kansas City* (Missouri) *Star* of January 27, 1890, protested because the Santa Fe passenger trains traveled through western Kansas only at night. "Are the people of any section of Kansas," they asked, "not entitled to a daylight train that travelers may see the country?"

A far more important consideration was whether, having seen the country, the traveler would be able to buy a part of it—whether, in other words, the railroads had secured final patent on their grants and were offering the land for sale. By the mid-1870s this problem was becoming an increasingly pressing one. At issue was the alleged inconsistency between the land grants and the need for more land open to homestead entry. The Homestead Act was expected to encourage immigration and development; the land grants were intended to do likewise, but increasingly in the 1870s it seemed they were operating at cross purposes to this object. Land given to the railroads was withdrawn from the public domain and hence could not be homesteaded. While the roads were being constructed, this land was held in a kind of escrow account awaiting the completion of the project, a policy which left thousands of acres of Plains soil out of the reach of the prospective settler. Prior to the mid-seventies this inconsistency was thought to exist in theory only. In practice, it was widely believed, conflict could arise only if the railroads did not proceed with reasonable dispatch in marketing their lands. This possibility was considered unlikely since no railroad was expected to hold its lands off the market longer than was necessary. Unfortunately for the cause of state-railroad relations, the roads found a number of different reasons for doing precisely what people thought they would never do—delay the sale of their lands or offer them for sale at prices which would postpone development.

Though the policy of delay was most often practiced in the seventies and eighties, the railroads gave ample evidence before then that a rapid marketing of their lands might be impossible or undesirable.

56. A. E. Touzalin to Garber, June 25, 1876, Garber Papers, NSHS.
57. May 8, 1887.

As P. B. Maxson, commissioner of the Union Pacific, Eastern Division, wrote to Governor Samuel Crawford of Kansas, "The U. P. is as anxious for the country to be opened to settlement as any one but I want our RRds built and the lands will do it much quicker than the money being received for them, viz. $1.25–$2.00/acre." In less obscure language, he wanted to postpone the sale of Union Pacific land until the railroad was completed and the value of its lands had proportionately increased. To that end he asked Crawford to curtail the activities of G. W. Veale, Kansas agent for the sale of railroad lands. Maxson urged, "Please see that our lands are kept from the market for a while yet."[58]

Policies of this sort led many in the Plains states to doubt the wisdom of the entire land grant program, and to insist that the grants, far from hastening development, locked up the resources of the new regions and prevented their exploitation by land-hungry settlers. This was certainly the attitude behind Nebraska's protest of the 1866 ruling by the secretary of the interior which withdrew from private entry ten alternate sections on each side of the projected Burlington route. J. Sterling Morton, a leading citizen of the territory, complained bitterly that the withdrawal order would injure Nebraska by excluding homesteaders from an unnecessarily large portion of the public domain. The Burlington's answer was simple and direct. The injury complaint was "bosh—with the even sections open to Homesteads, no settler need be turned away for forty years to come." Nobody, they reminded their listeners, was more interested in the early settlement of the state than the Burlington.[59]

In spite of such disclaimers, state disenchantment with the railroads increased in the 1870s and '80s. Again, only a very few criticized the extent of railroad promotional activities as the roads put down a heavy barrage. The problem arose over the timing of this campaign and the location of the lands being promoted. In the less settled regions of the Plains the railroads not only did little promoting, they did not file for patents on the land. Because of this, critics of railroad land policy made numerous attempts to secure the forfeiture of grants already made and to prevent the issuance of new grants. Their motives varied. Some objected to the fact that until the railroads had taken out final patent

58. P. B. Maxson to Samuel Crawford, July 24, 1868, Crawford Papers, KSHS. Crawford, a year earlier, had told Maxson that railroads should be able to sell or not sell their lands at their pleasure (Crawford to Maxson, May 25, 1867, Governor's Letter Press Books, Crawford, KSHS).

59. Overton, *Burlington West*, pp. 269, 281.

the lands were still part of the public domain and hence untaxable. Others insisted that the grants were incompatible with the homestead principle.[60] Advocates of reform secured a partial victory in 1871 when their constant agitation forced Congress to discontinue the land grant policy. A more important issue, however, was the forfeiture of existing, unearned grants. The land reformers were hindered in their efforts in this direction by the 1874 Supreme Court decision in *Schulenberg* v. *Harriman*. The Court held that forfeiture must be initiated by the grantor of the lands, that is, the United States Congress. If the Congress refused to take action, the railroads' title remained unimpaired, regardless of the fact that many of the roads had not technically earned their grants.

In spite of this temporary setback the critics of land grants continued to press for forfeiture. Congress could, after all, be persuaded to reverse its earlier generosity and revoke the subsidies. In 1890 an act was passed forfeiting the grants opposite uncompleted roads. This was obviously an unsatisfactory solution since it did not apply to lands already patented to completed lines. Demand for a general forfeiture law continued, but it was effectively checked in the Senate.[61] After all as one congressman reminded his listeners, "we gave [the railroads] an empire composed of an arid desert . . . a vast region of country . . . unfit for the habitation of man." In return, he continued, the railroads, through their promotional campaigns, have given the nation "an empire of hardy and industrious citizens."[62]

It was precisely this point, however, that many critics of the land grant program could not accept. They were emphatic in their belief that the railroads were not using their grants to promote settlement; that, in fact, settlement was being delayed by the roads' refusal, for whatever reasons, to patent and market their lands. In 1874 there was more controversy regarding the Burlington grant in Nebraska, a controversy in which Senator Phineas Hitchcock of Nebraska insisted that there existed "a serious question whether the Company is entitled to this

60. David M. Ellis, "The Forfeiture of Railroad Land Grants, 1867–1894," *Mississippi Valley Historical Review* 33 (June 1946): 38.

61. Ibid., pp. 30–31, 54, 55–60.

62. Rep. Charles E. Hooker of Mississippi, U.S., Congress, House, *Congressional Record*, 51st Cong., 1st sess., 1890, 21, pt. 8: 1889–90. For more detailed treatment of the forfeiture issue, see, in addition to Ellis's article, Leslie Decker, *Railroads, Lands, and Politics: The Taxation of the Railroad Land Grants, 1864–1897* (Providence: Brown University Press, 1964), pp. 30–56, 69–73; Gates, *Fifty Million Acres*, pp. 249–94; Robbins, *Our Landed Heritage*, pp. 278–85.

vast body of land—a question which retards the prosperity and hinders the settlement and development of our State." [63] Others quickly joined in the chorus of dissent. In 1876 Grover Cleveland stated unequivocally that railroad land grants were "a check to our national development." [64] Three years later a traveler in Kansas remarked on the large number of absentee-owned farms and attributed this perversion of the democratic principle to the sale of railroad land to speculators and corporations. [65] That same year Senator George Julian of Indiana, one of the early backers of a homestead bill and a devoted champion of the pioneer farmer, lent his potent influence to the cause for land grant forfeiture. Land grants and land speculation, Julian stated, left huge amounts of fertile land in unproductive hands. The government, in issuing these grants, deprived the settler of his legacy, cheated the producing classes, and effectively blocked the operation of the Homestead Act. [66] In 1883 Julian returned to this theme. He excoriated the railroads for monopolizing the land of the Plains and preventing its sale and distribution among the needy yeomen of the nation. He deplored the continuing subversion of American institutions which was the inevitable consequence of this blind and selfish policy of aggrandizement. But Julian's attack this time was composed of more than just vaguely defined generalizations of corporate greed. One railroad in particular, the Santa Fe, was singled out for criticism. The Santa Fe was the possessor of an illegal claim running from Fort Riley to the Kansas-Colorado border, an empire of land closed to those who most needed it and were best prepared to make productive use of it. This, in Julian's mind, was an unconscionable abuse of corporate rights, but unfortunately it was symptomatic of the entire land grant program. [67]

Julian based his argument against the Santa Fe on charges introduced in Kansas by former governor Samuel Crawford. Crawford, one of the most energetic promoters in the state, had become by the early 1880s a bitter critic of railroad land subsidies, especially those given the Santa Fe. The Santa Fe claimed as part of its grant over a million acres in the Arkansas River valley. Crawford was convinced that the line had no legal hold on this land and that their pretensions of legality

63. Quoted in Overton, *Burlington West*, p. 405.

64. Quoted in Robbins, *Our Landed Heritage*, p. 278.

65. "Kansas Farmers and Illinois Dairymen," *Atlantic Monthly* 46 (December 1879): 722.

66. George Julian, "Our Land Policy," ibid. 43 (March 1879): 328.

67. George Julian, "Railway Influence in the Land Office," *North American Review* 136 (March 1883): 237–56, esp. 248.

were depriving prospective settlers of their God-given right to the soil.[68] He asked that no more land be granted to the Santa Fe and that the lands already granted revert to the Department of the Interior. Only then could the legal rights of the people be secured.[69] Crawford, moreover, had earlier offered incontestable evidence that they were not being secured under the present system. Aaron Bobb, a settler in Rice County, near the Great Bend of the Arkansas, had been removed from his preemption claim on the basis of prior appropriation by the Santa Fe. The removal order initiated by the road was not only a flagrant abuse of power, it was inconsistent with the expressed policy of promoting immigration and development.[70]

Crawford's real concern, however, was not with the alleged infringement of settlers' rights, but rather with the real infringement of the rights of the state to promote settlement. Here the Santa Fe was not necessarily the only guilty party; the entire system of land grants must be indicted. The Kansas Pacific, another land grant road, was charged with arresting development simply because it had not taken final patent on its lands. Until this final patent was secured the lands could be neither sold nor given away—an intolerable situation in a new and undeveloped state.[71]

Crawford was partially successful in his suit against the Santa Fe. The railroad forfeited a part of its grant to the Department of the Interior, and the land was then restored to the public domain.[72] Potential immigrants to Kansas were now able to secure patent to these lands, a triumph which prompted the *Kansas City* (Kansas) *Times* of October 12, 1883, to predict another "OKLAHOMA EXCITEMENT upon the soil of Kansas."

Kansans could not forget, however, that for years the Santa Fe had held this land illegally; nor could they dismiss the fact that the line was

---

68. Crawford to Gov. S. W. Glick, September 26, 1883, Glick Papers, KSHS.

69. S. J. Crawford, "Brief . . . in the Matter Relating to the Excess of Lands Certified to the Atchison, Topeka and Santa Fe Railroad Company" (Washington: GPO, 1883), p. 17, in *Kansas Claims Pamphlets*, 2, KSHS. See also *Daily Commonwealth* (Topeka), August 25, 1883, and *Kansas City* (Kans.) *Times*, October 12, 1883.

70. "Definite Location of the Atchison, Topeka and Santa Fe Railroad through Rice County, Preemption Rights of Aaron Bobb and Other Settlers, Opinion of S. J. Crawford, 1883," in S. J. Crawford, *Briefs in Private Cases, 1882–1904*, KSHS.

71. Samuel Crawford, *In the Matter of the Kansas Pacific Railroad Grant and Withdrawal of Lands, Rights of the State and Citizens of Kansas, Petition and Argument for the State* (Topeka, 1883), passim; *Daily Commonwealth* (Topeka), October 3, 1883.

72. *Kansas City* (Kans.) *Times*, October 12, 1883.

still in possession of land in excess of its lawful claim. One Kansas
newspaper estimated this excess at ninety thousand acres. "At ninety
acres per family," the story continues, "this one theft has cost the
state ten thousand families, or fifty thousand people."[73] With this
in mind, the Kansas House of Representatives passed a resolution
protesting the fact that lands had been withdrawn and were then
withheld from market, and that the citizens of the United States had
been deprived of their lawful right to such lands under the homestead
and preemption laws.[74]

The attitude of the states toward railroad promotion had gone, in the
space of twenty years, from one of almost unbounded enthusiasm to
one of suspicion and resentment. This change was not necessarily
owing to any unwillingness by the railroads to promote; they continued
to flood the eastern and European immigrant market with pamphlets
and brochures describing the myriad benefits of life on the Plains. The
reason for state discontent stems rather from the selective distribution
of railroad lands. For reasons little understood at the time, the roads
carefully selected the lands they wished to promote in hopes of securing
to themselves the most favorable financial arrangement. Unfortunately,
by the mid-1870s it had become abundantly clear that the prosperity of
the railroads and that of the states was not as mutually dependent as it
was once thought. The real fault for this development must be affixed
not on the railroads entirely, but on a land policy which gave tacit
approval to what the roads were doing.[75] And there was little doubting
just what that was. The railroads, in their conscienceless pursuit of
gain, were accused of corroding the very fabric of American culture.
They were perverting almost beyond recognition the myth of the
garden, and in the process, upsetting America's mission to humanity.
The irony and tragedy of this centered in the fact that Americans,
through an exercise in geographical sleight of hand, had converted a
desert into a paradise. Now, just when that paradise was most in
demand, the railroads, with the aid of the federal land system, were
pursuing policies antithetical to that demand.

73. *Junction City Tribune*, January 27, 1887.
74. House Concurrent Resolution 12, *Session Laws of Kansas, 1887* (Topeka, 1887), pp. 347–48.
75. See Gates, "The Homestead Law in an Incongruous Land System," pp. 658–65; Gates himself has offered a partial corrective to the views expressed in this article. See his "The Homestead Act: Free Land Policy in Operation, 1862–1935," in *Land Use Policy and Problems in the United States*, ed. by Howard Ottoson (Lincoln: University of Nebraska Press, 1963), pp. 28–46.

CHAPTER THREE

State and Local Promotion

In spite of the arguments over the timing and targets of railroad promotion, there was a close bond between the railroads and the Plains states they served. Each was interested in the success of the other but, more important, the success of both was dependent upon their ability to attract new residents to the Plains. The states, moreover, were at least as assiduous in the pursuit of this object as the railroads. As territories at first, each of the Plains states appointed public bureaus to compose and distribute their promotional material, and more often than not, these official state publications exceeded even those of the railroads in the wealth of promises held out to the prospective immigrant. The states were competing for a valuable prize, a share of the rich supply of human resources which every year entered the United States and dispersed itself among the sections of the new land. It was a prize worth capturing, an investment in the future prosperity of the states, and it warranted whatever time and money were expended to attract it.

Various estimates were made in the 1870s and '80s of the per capita cash value of an immigrant, and though no precise figure was ever agreed upon, these estimates must have supplied pleasant topics of speculation among the state promotional agencies. Friedrich Kapp, commissioner of immigration for the state of New York, computed the value of a healthy male immigrant at $1,500. The female was discounted by one-half, making the average value of an immigrant $1,125. Kapp hastened to add, however, that the capital value differed considerably according to the immigrant's station in life and the civilization of the nation from which he came. "The German," for example, "must be measured by another standard than the Mexican or South American." Charles L. Brace (an amateur in the field, according to Kapp) took some exception to Kapp's figures. Without denying the immense value of "this golden tide" of immigrants, Brace insisted upon adding another element to the computation: the demand for the immigrant's services.

After all, he reminded Kapp, "a cow or a horse is worth not alone what it costs to produce it, but what the demand will bring." With this in mind, Brace corrected Kapp's figures to $1,000 to $1,100 a head for each male, and a proportionate amount less for a female depending upon her state of health and whether or not she was pregnant.[1] Edward Young, chief of the Bureau of Statistics for the Department of the Interior and commissioner of immigration for the United States, revised the figure downward even further. Although he admitted that $1,000 was usually considered the average value of each permanent addition to the population, he noted that these estimates did not take fully into consideration the consumptive capacity of the immigrants. Their productive capacity was latent only, and until it was fully activated, the immigrant was simply a consumer. Young felt, then, that $800 a head was a more realistic appraisal of an immigrant's cash value, a sum endorsed as well by the Treasury Department.[2]

A number of amateur mathematicians also attempted to determine the value of America's newest arrivals. Some, figuring the immigrant to be worth twice as much as an antebellum slave of similar talents, hit upon the figure of $1,000 for a farmer or unskilled laborer.[3] Andrew Carnegie, on the other hand, perhaps remembering his own immigrant background and contrasting that with the immense fortune he then controlled, inflated the value per capita to $1,500.[4]

Whatever sum a state chose to accept, there could be no question that, in the words of a Nebraska promoter, "*it pays* and *pays well* to draw to [our] borders, the men and women, the muscle and brain, the cash and chattels of older and richer lands." The experience of Nebraska itself offered incontestable proof of this. Figured on the basis of $1,000 apiece, the 1,000 immigrants attracted to the state in 1874 were worth $100,000, while the cost to the state in attracting them was only $10,000 "or the small sum of $10 per man."[5] A return of 100 times on

1. Friedrich Kapp, "Immigration and the Commissioners of Emigration of the State of New York, 1870," in *Historical Aspects of the Immigration Problem*, ed. by Edith Abbott (Chicago: University of Chicago Press, 1926), pp. 373–75.

2. Edward Young, *Special Report of Immigration Accompanying Information for Immigrants* (Washington, D.C.: GPO, 1872), pp. vii–ix.

3. John Higham, *Strangers in the Land: Patterns of American Nativism, 1860–1925* (New Brunswick, N.J.: Rutgers University Press, 1955), p. 17.

4. Andrew Carnegie, *Triumphant Democracy; or, Fifty Years' March of the Republic* (New York: Scribner's, 1886), p. 34.

5. H. D. Noteware, *Report of the Superintendent of Immigration for Nebraska, 1874* (Lincoln, 1875), pp. 242–44.

money expended was an investment of incalculable benefit, a bargain which no state sincerely interested in its progress could ignore. Lewis Weise, an immigration agent for Kansas in Hamburg, Germany, made this same point in 1866. It cost the state $2,800 annually to retain his services, or $2.80 for every one of the 1,000 immigrants he had attracted to her borders. Omitting all reference to per capita cash value, Weise gently reminded his employer that taxes on 160 acres amounted to $20 a year. One thousand immigrants, he continued, represented approximately 400 families. If only half their number took up a quarter section, the tax increment to the state alone would be $4,000—all this for an initial expenditure of $2,800.[6]

The immigrant was thus considered a part of a complicated system of commercial exchange. His value to the state which attracted him was one of its principal sources of revenue and growth, especially if he arrived, as did the Mennonites in Nebraska, with "well-filled wallets."[7] But even if he arrived with an empty wallet he was a treasure to be prized and admired. He provided relief from the heavy tax burdens necessary in all new commonwealths. His coming meant better schools and roads, more and improved state services, expanding markets and more complete development of natural resources.[8] The Colorado Territorial Board of Immigration even attributed to his arrival the territory's escape from most of the hazards of the financial crisis of 1873.[9]

This cash register approach was not the only one taken, however. The agricultural immigrant added a certain tone to a community. He imparted a semblance of order and permanence, virtues conspicuously lacking in frontier areas, especially those like Colorado and Wyoming, where mining and stock raising served as the economic bases. Colorado, claimed one promotional pamphlet, need not apologize for those who extracted her mineral wealth. Mining was a profitable and socially acceptable enterprise. But agriculture must one day become its dominant interest; it was the "conservative element. . . . It alone steadies, preserves, purifies, and elevates" a commonwealth.[10] The same thing

6. Lewis F. Weise to Samuel Crawford, May 25, 1866, Crawford Papers, KSHS.

7. The *Daily State Journal* (Lincoln), July 29, 1874.

8. See, for example, the message of Gov. George T. Anthony of Kansas, January 10, 1877, in *Messages of Kansas Governors*, 4 vols. (Topeka: State Printer, 1937), 1, 1861–81: 33. See also the *Greeley* (Colo.) *Tribune*, December 20, 1871.

9. Colorado Territorial Board of Immigration, *Report . . . 1874* (Denver, 1874), p. 7.

10. Chicago-Colorado Colony Constitution and By-laws, Longmont, Colorado

was true, however, of those areas where agriculture was already the "dominant interest." Kansas, for example, could never have too many small farmers. The more their number multiplied, "the surer, the stabler, the more thriving and progressive will be every power."[11] The immigrant was a potent force for good, and "no crop to be harvested by the farmers of Kansas next summer," wrote the state's Bureau of Immigration, "will be equal in value [to] the harvest of people that may be gathered."[12]

This "human harvest" had to be carefully cultivated. The East must, of course, be further disabused of the notion that the Plains were subject to drought and grasshoppers, but of equal importance, the competition from other state promotional agencies had to be met. By 1865, a number of states from all parts of the Union employed immigration bureaus. Of the Plains states, Kansas was the first to take action to meet this competition.[13] As early as 1863, S. D. Houston, a land office employee in Junction City, wrote to Governor Thomas Carney and offered his enthusiastic support for a bureau of immigration. The drought of 1860, the Civil War, and the possibility that Kansas might soon become a battlefield of that war—all were conspiring to repel potential immigrants. Perhaps, Houston suggested, a state agency similar to those then being formed in Minnesota and other states of the upper Mississippi Valley could be used to counter some of the unfavorable notices which Kansas was receiving. The entire state, excepting a thin strip on its western border, was eminently suited to agriculture; indeed, Houston was convinced that even western Kansas would "grow more wheat and, take a series of years, more corn, than Iowa or Illinois." If people could but be made aware of this, they would pour into Kansas in grateful hordes, and the prosperity of the state would be assured.[14]

Houston and others like him proved to be persuasive spokesmen, and in January of 1864 Carney included in his annual message reference

---

Territory, July 1, 1871, in *Experiments in Colorado Colonization*, ed. by J. F. Willard, p. 141.

11. Inaugural Address of Gov. Thomas Carney, January 14, 1863, in *Messages of Kansas Governors*, 1: 11.

12. Kansas Bureau of Immigration, *Report . . . 1868* (Topeka, 1869), p. 9.

13. Ibid. See also John P. Swenson to Gov. Crawford, February 2, 1865, Crawford Papers, KSHS.

14. S. D. Houston to Gov. Thomas Carney, August 5, 1863, Carney Papers, KSHS.

to the need of actively promoting immigration.[15] Carney's successor, Samuel J. Crawford, fully agreed with these views, and asked of the state legislature an appropriation to cover the expenses of employing an immigration agent in the older states.[16] The legislators proved balky, however, and Crawford was forced to issue a promotional pamphlet on his own authority and at his own expense. It was evidently well received, both by the Kansas press and by those to whom it was sent, but as Crawford well knew, this type of publication was no substitute for official state activity and he continued his agitation for the appointment of a public bureau to handle immigration promotion.[17] In March, 1867, the legislature finally acceded to his request and approved an appropriation for the creation of a bureau of immigration.[18] The object of the new bureau was announced by its directors in their first report to the legislature. "It was our desire," they wrote, "to fill, upon the map of Kansas, the blank space heretofore allotted to the 'Great American Desert'—that myth of the old Geographers." [19]

They went about it with unmatched zeal. The climate of the state was "without exception, the most desirable in the United States. . . . Since the year 1860 [Kansas] has been blessed with an abundance of rain." Earlier the Bureau of Immigration had described Kansas summers as lasting until December, while "at the close of February we are reminded by a soft gentle breeze from the South, that winter is gone." In the interim from February to December Kansans produced crops which would have shamed the best farmers of Illinois. And why should they not? "Kansas has, undoubtedly, a vastly greater proportion of rich soil to the bad, good land to the poor, or waste than any State in the Union." [20]

15. January 13, 1864, in *Messages of Kansas Governors*, 1: 13. *Kansas Farmer* also suggested a bureau of immigration, January 1, 1864.

16. S. J. Crawford, Message to the Legislature, January 10, 1866, in *Kansas Senate Journal* (Topeka, 1866), p. 32.

17. Annual Message, January 9, 1867, in *Messages of Kansas Governors*, 1: 24–25; unidentified newspaper clippings in the *Crawford Scrapbook, 1865–1910*, KSHS. One Kansan, the Reverend I. S. Kalloch, did criticize Crawford for including false information in the pamphlet. Kalloch was quickly rebuked by the Kansas press. See, for example, *Daily Journal* (Leavenworth), December 30, 1866, in the *Crawford Scrapbook, 1865–1910*, KSHS.

18. *Laws of Kansas, 1867*, chap. 65, sec. 1, March 7, 1867 (Topeka, 1867).

19. Kansas Bureau of Immigration, *Report . . . 1868*, p. 6.

20. Kansas Bureau of Immigration, *Kansas as She Is:—Free Homesteads in the Garden of the World*, 2d ed. (Lawrence, 1870), p. 8; Kansas Bureau of Immigration, *The State of Kansas: A Home for Immigrants . . . Great Inducements Offered to*

Unfortunately, the state had no statistical service, and hence the bureau had to rely on unsubstantiated evidence for much of its information. The members of the bureau were forced to adopt the "cheap expedient" of printing vaguely phrased circulars and distributing them to "every name, postoffice, newspaper, and county office . . . East, South, and North."[21] They did secure from the legislature an appropriation of $2,500 for the publication of C. C. Hutchinson's promotional gazette, *Resources of Kansas.* Although it presented a vivid picture of the prodigious yields of the Kansas farmer, the gazette was also forced to rely on hazy estimates of just what these yields were.[22]

Events in Nebraska were remarkably similar. In 1861, Territorial Governor Alvin Saunders recommended the employment of a "traveling agent of emigration" to reside in New York and steer new arrivals toward the territory. The agent's job would be an easy one by virtue of Nebraska's undoubted potential and the federal homestead law of 1862. When this irresistible combination was made known to them, thousands of new settlers were expected to be drawn to her borders.[23] Like Kansas, however, Nebraska was slow in appropriating the necessary funds for either an agent or a bureau of immigration. In 1865 the quasi-public Nebraska Bureau of Immigration was formed, and the following year it published a short pamphlet in both English and German on the resources of the territory.[24] There was no question, in this pamphlet, that Nebraska was singularly blessed, but the commissioner of the project admitted that a more permanent and more official promotional agency was needed if the territory was to gain its share of immigrants.[25] Governor Algernon S. Paddock agreed that more needed to be done, and even suggested the appointment of four foreign agents to help complete Nebraska's recruitment campaign. The legislature proved not only unresponsive to Paddock's enthusiasm,

Persons Desiring Homes in a New Country (Topeka, 1867), p. 4; *Kansas as She Is,* pp. 8, 45.

21. Kansas Bureau of Immigration, *Report . . . 1868,* p. 6.

22. C. C. Hutchinson, *Resources of Kansas* (Topeka, 1868), p. vi.

23. Opening Message to the 8th Session of the Territorial Legislative Assembly, December 2, 1861, in *Messages and Proclamations,* 1: 165. See also Opening Message to the Legislative Assembly, 9th Session, January 8, 1864, ibid., 1: 169; and Opening Message to the Legislative Assembly, 11th Session, January 9, 1866, ibid., 1: 197.

24. *Nebraska: Containing a Brief Account of the Soil, Productions, Agricultural and Mineral Resources . . .* (Lincoln, 1866).

25. Ibid., p. 1., and *Council Journal, Nebraska,* January 16, 1867 (Omaha, 1867), p. 56.

but they voted eighteen to seventeen not to renew the token appropriation granted the semiofficial Bureau of Immigration.[26]

To Governor David Butler, first chief executive of the new state of Nebraska, this was a clear case of legislative dereliction, and he began a three-year campaign to convince the legislators of their folly.[27] In March of 1870 his earnest appeals were gratified by the creation of the Nebraska Board of Immigration, with a commissioner in New York. The board was charged with directing as much of the immigration to Nebraska as its finances and staff would allow.[28] This included, in the short space of two years, the publication and distribution of "110,000 pamphlets . . . containing 1,440,000 pages, 20,000 homestead circulars, and 21,000 maps" in addition to "not less than 100,000 copies of the newspapers of the State."[29] Among the means not at its disposal, however, was a statistical bureau; Nebraska, like Kansas, was unable to present to the prospective immigrant any detailed or precise information on just how prodigious a corn or wheat yield he could expect.[30]

This proved to be minor inconvenience to the Nebraska bureau. Who needed statistics to confirm the obvious? Nebraska, after all, was the place "where moneyless men may become landowners by a mere residence, and men of small means, property-holders at once." Of equal importance, civilization was ready-made in Nebraska. Railroads, wagon roads, churches, and school houses "have here preceded civilization, instead of following it, after the usual course."[31] This was in striking contrast with areas farther west. In Colorado, for example, the immigrant would find himself among people "who wandered thither as *adventurers*," and as everyone knew, such men constituted an unsettled element in any society. Even more destructive of civilized ways was "the liberal intersprinkling of Indians and Spaniards" which

26. Opening Message, 12th Session of the Legislative Assembly, January 11, 1867, in *Messages and Proclamations*, 1: 239, and *House Journal of the State Legislature of Nebraska . . . 1867* (Omaha, 1867), pp. 156, 185.

27. David Butler, Extra Session Message, May 17, 1867, in *Messages and Proclamations*, 1: 271; Second Inaugural, January 8, 1869, ibid., p. 283; Extra Session Message, February 17, 1870, ibid., p. 298.

28. *Session Laws of the State of Nebraska*, March 4, 1870 (Lincoln, 1870), pp. 21–23; Governor Butler expressed his appreciation in his Third Inaugural, January 6, 1871, *Messages and Proclamations*, 1: 307.

29. Report of the Superintendent of Immigration, J. H. Noteware, *Nebraska Senate Journal, 1875* (Lincoln, 1875), p. 239.

30. *Omaha Republican*, February 4, 1873.

31. George Brown [state secretary of immigration], *The State of Nebraska as a Home for Emigrants* (Lincoln, 1875), p. 5.

frustrated Colorado's progress. By now the reader was almost surely disabused of any notions of going to Colorado, and the amenities of Nebraska must have seemed even more appealing to him. By going to Nebraska he could surround himself with "sober, hardy but enterprising folk, each of whom brought his wife and his little household, seeking out a quiet spot, where the beneficence of our noble government . . . should achieve for him and his that comfortable competence which the older and more crowded communities do not afford the poor man."[32] Here was heaven indeed, a place of comfort and sustenance. Nature willed it, for in addition to ready-made civilization, Nebraska was also blessed by her location "within that isothermal belt which by natural laws not only has always produced the highest type of muscular and mental development, but also the grandest achievements of human invention, skill and enterprise."[33] This should have been enough to convince even the most skeptical, but the bureau insisted upon including in one of its pamphlets mention of the "hardships and trials of a pioneer life." Only the stalwart and hard working should attempt to confront these hardships. The weak and those who "work upon the delusive principal [sic] that 'there is some easier way of getting a dollar than fairly and squarely earning it'" should stay home.[34]

But for those who were adequately equipped, the state offered untold advantages. "The present fertile State of Nebraska," wrote the State Board of Agriculture, "was known only a few score years ago as . . . the 'Great American Desert.'" A decade and a half had changed all that and the 'American Desert' had "vanished into the air." Indeed, so extraordinary was this change that nurserymen in the East were now advised to import some Nebraska soil for use with their more delicate plants. Nor need they be particularly discriminating as to what type of soil they chose. They had only to "send their order to any postmaster or railroad agent, and tell him to dig the first dirt he comes to and send it along."[35]

As was the case in Nebraska, Colorado did not wait for statehood

32. Ibid., pp. 6–7.

33. J. H. Noteware, *The State of Nebraska* (Lincoln, 1873), p. 5.

34. George S. Alexander [commisioner of immigration], *Nebraska: Its Resources, Prospects, and Advantages of Immigration . . . Together with Suggestions to Immigrants* (Lincoln, 1870), p. 16. See also Brown, *The State of Nebraska*, p. 6, and Nebraska State Board of Immigration, *Nebraska: A Sketch of Its History, Resources, and Advantages It Offers to Settlers* (Nebraska City, 1870), pp. 10–12.

35. Noteware, *The State of Nebraska*, p. 19.

to commission an immigration bureau. The need to promote had been recognized as early as 1862 when a Denver newspaper mentioned, ironically, that Territorial Governor William Gilpin's unauthorized mobilization of the Colorado Volunteers had created the impression that Colorado was in a state of anarchy, and had dealt "a death blow almost to her prospects."[36] The territory survived Gilpin, however, and in 1870 Governor Edward McCook recommended strongly the formation of an agency which would collect and distribute promotional material.[37] The initial response of the territorial legislature was to amend the statutes to encourage private promotional associations. These associations could buy, sell, or otherwise dispose of property as part of their stated function.[38] But this use of private corporations for promotion proved only partially successful, and in 1871 the legislature approved the appropriation for a territorial board of immigration.[39]

Like similar agencies in other states, the Colorado board relied heavily on official information from the United States General Land Office. It realized that, fertile and salubrious as Colorado might be, it was the Homestead Act which captured the imagination and allegiance of easterners and Europeans.[40] With this in mind, George T. Clark of the Board of Immigration requested, from Commissioner of the General Land Office Willis Drummond, one hundred copies of the land office's "Brief Description of Public Lands."[41] The information contained in the "Description" was then incorporated into the board's *Official Information of the Resources of Colorado.* This pamphlet, which was reprinted many times, was the board's principal promotional weapon. It was mailed to all parts of the United States and Europe and elicited a gratifyingly large number of responses for more information. Typically, however, the board considered its good work to be

36. *Rocky Mountain News* (Denver), February 22, 1862.

37. *Daily Colorado Tribune* (Denver), January 5, 1870.

38. "An Act, Amendatory to Chapter 18 . . . Concerning Corporations, General Laws, Joint Resolutions, Memorials and Private Acts," *Eighth Session of the Legislative Assembly of the Territory of Colorado . . . 1870* (Denver, 1870), p. 13.

39. Colorado Territorial Board of Immigration, *Report . . . for the Two Years Ending December 31, 1873* (Denver: Wm. Byers Public Printer, 1874), p. 2.

40. See, for example, George T. Clark, commissioner of the Colorado Territorial Board of Immigration, to J. B. Chaffee, February 23, 1872, Letter Press Book of the Colorado Territorial Board of Immigration, Colorado State Historical Society, Denver (hereafter cited as CTBI, CSHS).

41. Clark to Drummond, March 8, 1872, CTBI, CSHS.

handicapped by the unavailability of statistical information, and they pressed for the formation of a statistical division within their agency.[42]

In Wyoming, two factors—the dominant role of the farmer-hating cattlemen and the territory's late start in securing political organization —conspired to prevent any promotional effort similar to that of her neighboring states. Governor John A. Campbell in 1873 had suggested to the territorial legislature the creation of a bureau of immigration so that Wyoming might keep pace with the population growth of the other western states, and the stock interests, surprisingly, endorsed the plan. They soon recovered from this indiscretion, however, and in 1875 the already meager appropriations for the infant bureau were allowed to lapse.[43] The agricultural interests of the state were forced to wait until the late 1880s before the grip of the cattlemen was relaxed and promotional activities could begin again.

Though the enthusiasm of its advocates never waned, state-sponsored promotion suffered in its early years from a lack of funds. The costs of compiling, printing, and distributing information for immigrants were far greater than many had expected, and thrifty state legislatures were often loath to appropriate more than seemed absolutely necessary. Few doubted the importance of securing immigrants, but fewer still were willing to bankrupt the treasury to attract them. This cautious policy drew Kansas Governor Samuel Crawford's criticism as early as 1867, when he appealed to the legislature's sense of duty in requesting more funds.[44] The legislators were unmoved. In 1868 they refused to vote any promotional funds at all, which prompted George A. Crawford, commissioner of immigration for the state, to appeal over their heads to the people. Crawford reminded his readers that Minnesota distributed 60,000 pamphlets in 1867, and that Kansas must at least match that figure if her tax burden was to be more equitably divided.

---

42. Colorado Territorial Board of Immigration, *Official Information of the Resources of Colorado, 1872* (Denver, 1872). It was reprinted under title of *Resources and Advantages of Colorado* (Denver, 1873). For the response it evoked, see *Report . . . for the Two Years Ending December 31, 1873*, pp. 5–6, 9.

43. *Message of Governor Campbell to the Third Legislative Assembly of Wyoming Territory . . . 1873* (Laramie, 1873), p. 7. For the repeal of the bureau, see *Message of Governor J. W. Hoyt to the Sixth Legislative Assembly of Wyoming Territory . . . 1879* (Cheyenne, 1879), p. 38. Typescript copies of both are in the Wyoming State Historical Society, Cheyenne, hereafter referred to as WSHS.

44. Annual Message of Gov. Samuel Crawford, January 9, 1867, in *Messages of Kansas Governors*, 1: 24–25.

Millions of dollars and hundreds of thousands of people were the prizes to be gained. "It would not be characteristic," he added with prophetic accuracy, "for Kansas to hide under a bushel."[45] But hidden it remained for the moment, and in 1869 Governor James Harvey was forced to reiterate Samuel Crawford's appeal for more money—with similar result. The legislature, for the second time, refused to vote any appropriation for Crawford's bureau.[46] In 1871 the state legislature did manage to find $2,500 for publication of C. C. Hutchinson's *Resources of Kansas,* but this financial support was not repeated until later in the decade.

The promotion of immigration in Nebraska and Colorado suffered from similar neglect. The *Omaha Republican,* for example, maintained in 1877 that the state's reluctance to advertise had cost her 5,000 men in the last year alone, or, to use a more popular method of computation, $500,000.[47] The *Nebraska Farmer,* principal agricultural journal of the state, echoed these sentiments. It was a "penny wise and pound foolish policy" to refuse adequate appropriations for the encouragement of immigration. "The state . . . [was] full to overflowing of all the resources that a native or foreign immigrant could wish for," and it was almost criminal to leave prospective immigrants ignorant of this.[48]

In Colorado, reported the *Rocky Mountain News* of December 18, 1872, the Board of Immigration was doing all that its limited means would allow. With an appropriation of only $3,000 per year, this was certainly not much—not enough, for example, to send agents outside the territory, not enough even to finance the publication and distribution of its promotional literature. One pamphlet had been printed in Chicago at a cost which absorbed all the remaining funds appropriated to the board by the territorial legislature. Since they had no way of paying for the pamphlet's transit from Chicago to Denver, the board appealed to the Kansas Pacific Railroad in getting the work "dead headed from Chicago," adding that it was meant "to bring people to

---

45. *An Appeal from the Kansas Bureau of Immigration to the People of Kansas, March 7, 1868, George A. Crawford, Commissioner.* Copy in KSHS library.

46. Annual Message of Gov. James Harvey, January 7, 1869, in *Messages of Kansas Governors,* 1: 38. Crawford took this occasion to resign. See George A. Crawford to Governor Harvey, January 29, 1869, Harvey Papers, KSHS.

47. September 15, 1877; see also the edition of February 4, 1873, in which Fred Hedde, Nebraska's agent in Germany, complained of lack of funds.

48. *Nebraska Farmer,* February, 1877.

Colorado and the roads leading from Chicago to Kansas City are as much interested in this as we."[49]

They were, indeed. Short of the premature patenting of their lands, the railroads tried to cooperate in whatever way they could with the various state and territorial immigration bureaus, one reason the states were able to reduce their own promotional efforts. The roads issued free passes to immigration agents going out of the states and reduced their rates for prospective immigrants coming in.[50] They shared the expenses of maintaining overseas agents, exchanged promotional material and statistics, and displayed throughout the world prize winning examples of a state's agricultural products.[51]

In none of these activities, of course, were the railroads motivated by altruism, in spite of a Burlington official's insistence that his road had aided Nebraska "from pure good will."[52] They tended to benefit equally from this collaboration with the states. Nor was the cooperation all one-sided. Nebraska, for example, lent to the Burlington a copy of a promotional tract written for the state by Professor Samuel Aughey. The Burlington then submitted the material to the *New York Tribune* for inclusion in the paper's emigration column.[53] In Colorado, membership in the Territorial Board of Immigration was given to William N. Byers, an officer and publicist of the National Land Company, the promotional subsidiary of the Kansas Pacific Railroad. Byers was the editor of the *Rocky Mountain News*, one of the founders of the Colorado State Agricultural Society, and an inveterate promoter. He brought to the board an infectious enthusiasm for the agricultural

49. George T. Clark, secretary of the board, to B. R. Keim, ticket agent for the D.P., January 31, 1873, CTBI, CSHS.

50. George T. Clark to E. R. Drunnel, October 17, 1872, ibid.; A. E. Touzalin, Burlington RR, to D. H. Wheeler, secretary of the Nebraska State Board of Agriculture, September 14, 1872, Letter Press Book of the NSBA, NSHS; Colorado Territorial Board of Immigration, *Official Information, Colorado, 1872* (Denver, 1872), p. 32.

51. For the exchange of agents, see *West Point Republican*, May 12, 1871, WPA Writers' Project, NSHS; *Omaha Republican*, February 4, 1873; for the exchange of information, see George T. Clark to B. R. Keim, November 14, 1872, CTBI, CSHS; NSBA, *Fourth Annual Report, 1873* (Lincoln, 1873), pp. 5–28; for the railroads' use of state products, see Gov. Silas Garber to O. C. Davis, October 10, 1876, and Garber to A. E. Touzalin, October 10, 1876, Garber Letter Press Books, NSHS; T. H. Leavitt to H. D. Wheeler, September 12, 1872, NSBA Letter Press Books, NSHS.

52. A. E. Touzalin to Silas Garber, June 25, 1876, Garber Papers, NSHS.

53. Touzalin to Garber, March 30, 1878, ibid.

potential of the territory, especially that part traversed by the Kansas Pacific. He wrote much of the copy for the pamphlet *Colorado and Its Resources*, agreed to print the board's annual reports for a minimal fee, and was instrumental in securing free passes for territorial immigration agents.[54]

All of the states benefited from the railroads' heavy involvement in promotion, and there seemed little reason for the states not to cooperate with the lines. This was especially true when the unstable condition of western finances was taken into account. The railroads had to promote anyway. Why, then, should the states not cut back on their own promotional budgets? Colorado was particularly eager to solicit railroad help. The newest of three commonwealths under discussion, she was the least able to finance a vigorous promotional campaign without some form of outside assistance. The railroads provided that assistance. Cooperation appeared to be to the advantage of both parties.

By the mid-1870s, however, this cooperation seemed unnecessary if not unwise. Some legislators were even more disposed than before to cut appropriations to state agencies as an economy measure. There were some who questioned the wisdom of this position, but the reason for it seemed clear enough. "Is it not," asked the *Nebraska Farmer* in February of 1877, "because the Union Pacific and the Burlington and Missouri Companies are so liberal in their efforts to advertise us?" In part it was, as the editors fully realized. Just a month before their rhetorical question appeared, they had congratulated Nebraska on her supreme good fortune in having her nongovernment lands transferred to railroad companies, whose only desire was to develop these lands for the good of the state. Seven years earlier the *Nebraska Herald* had commented similarly on the promotional efforts of the Burlington's George Harris. Harris was a source of great pride and comfort to the state. He was doing "more to advertise Nebraska ... than all the immigration societies the Legislature can charter in the next five years. We believe in Immigration Societies," the paper continued, "but we believe in Harris more."[55]

54. See Deryl V. Gease, "William M. Byers and the Colorado Agricultural Society," *Colorado Magazine* 43 (Fall 1966): 327–38. For his appointment to the board, see George T. Clark to D. C. Collier, March 29, 1873, CTBI, CSHS, and Colorado Territorial Board of Immigration, *Report ... for the Two Years Ending December 31, 1873*, p. 4.

55. *Nebraska Herald* (Plattsmouth), March 17, 1870; see also the issue of December 16, 1869.

But there were others in the Plains states who did not believe in Harris at all. It was not that these skeptics doubted the determination of Harris and the other railroad promoters, only their credibility. Their suspicions led them to conclusions entirely different from those who would cut promotional appropriations, and introduced into the boomers' frontier a new and highly effective promotional tactic, the use of state agricultural agencies to promote.

The chief sin of the railroad promoters, according to these critics, was their overly beatific descriptions of life on the Plains. A Nebraska newspaper as early as 1866 accused the Burlington of "unbounded misrepresentation" in its promotional appeals. The results were not only unethical but, more important, destructive of the purposes of promotion—the attraction of affluent and genuine settlers capable of making the hard adjustment to Plains life.[56]

In 1873 a similar charge was brought against the Santa Fe in Kansas but in this instance the newspapers of the state moved quickly to the railroad's defense. The *Topeka Daily Commonwealth* of July 13, 1873, was convinced the charges were totally without foundation. The Santa Fe, it claimed, "would not tell a falsehood to make the sale of a whole county." This bland assurance probably surprised even the Santa Fe's officials. Certainly it left one critic unappeased. In a letter to Governor George T. Anthony, J. F. Everhart accused the Kansas railroads of blatant misrepresentation. "It is familiar knowledge," he wrote, "that the extravagant statements of advantage for settling in Kansas, made by nearly every Railway company in the State has attained such a morbid character *that but little interest attaches to their efforts.*" People had become inured to the impossible claims made by the various lines and as a result the railroads' "usefullness as promotional agents has greatly depreciated."[57] A Nebraskan felt that their usefulness had not just depreciated but had become self-defeating. E. W. Arnold insisted that the land in the Grand Island district was selling so fast on its own merits that any attempt to advertise it, regardless of how responsibly phrased, would repel rather than attract immigrants. So suspicious had potential settlers become regarding railroad promotion

56. *Nebraska Statesman* (Nebraska City), June 9, 1866, WPA Writers' Project, NSHS.

57. J. F. Everhart to Gov. George T. Anthony, April 5, 1877, Anthony Papers, KSHS (emphasis mine); see also the *Champion* (Atchison), September 9, 1880, for further comment from Kansas on the charges of misrepresentation.

that the roads would better serve themselves if they limited their activities to delivering the people and letting the land sell itself.[58]

Two other Nebraskans were even more concerned, but in this instance concern led to a solution and a new promotional tactic. J. Sterling Morton and Robert Furnas were among the more prominent citizens of the state, and one of their abiding interests in the early 1870s was promotion, the attraction of new money and new muscle to Nebraska. They recognized the interest of the railroads in this campaign, but both, by 1873, had come to doubt the roads' effectiveness. Railroad promotion, in fact, had reached a point of diminishing if not disappearing returns. Morton explained:

> Railroad and Emigration pamphlets are regarded with suspicion by the public and charged with mendacity generally. An agent to secure Emigration or to sell railroad lands, if known as such, meets with about the same cheerful and cordial reception which generally greets a solicitor of Life Insurance.[59]

Even J. D. Butler, the Burlington's undercover promoter, was suffering from this crisis of credibility. His latest effort, according to Morton, was "able, pleasant, and truthful. But he is known as a writer for the B & M and so his work does not do so much good as it ought to."[60] Making the situation doubly unfortunate for the cause of promotion was the fact that state immigration agents were similarly hindered. Like their railroad colleagues, they were too readily identifiable, their mission was too obvious.

What was clearly needed was a suitable cover for the publication of state promotional material. Morton thought he had found one. "To succeed," he wrote Furnas, "we must not appear as seeking Emigration by Agents, who bear that obnoxious name. We must deodorize the state in that regard. The Board of Agriculture is the only organization which can do any good." The reason, as Morton explained later, was "that [the reports of the Board of Agriculture] are singularly a record of the facts and experiences published for our own use and not, *ostensibly*, for the purpose of inducing emigration or alluring land buyers and speculators."[61] Now if only Harris could be convinced to republish

58. E. W. Arnold to Gov. Silas Garber, May 28, 1878, Garber Papers, NSHS.
59. Morton to Furnas, January 24, 1873, Furnas Papers, NSHS.
60. Ibid., January 23, 1873.
61. Ibid., and Morton to Furnas, February 13, 1873 (emphasis mine).

Butler's latest article, "leaving Butler's name off, and giving the imprint of the State Board of Agriculture," much good could be accomplished.[62]

Events in Kansas followed a fairly similar course, though never were Kansans as ready to trust their promotional interests entirely to the railroads. They were, however, taken by the promotional possibilities of the State Board of Agriculture. As early as 1872, very soon after the organization of the state board, men began to consider its usefulness as a bureau of immigration. Governor George T. Anthony, in his annual message of 1877, reminded his constituents that they lived in a heavenly region and that once this fact became more common knowledge, others would flock to join them. What better agency for the dissemination of such information than the Board of Agriculture? It was well established, adequately financed, and (although this went unmentioned) did not include promotional matters among its objects. The last item was, of course, an especially attractive feature. The reports of the board could only be interpreted as a contribution to scientific understanding, not an attempt to induce unsuspecting immigrants to join the Kansas legions. Statistical and promotional material could be presented with clinical detachment and, as a result, with greater effect.[63]

In 1885 the board summarized its promotional efforts, and explained why it had been chosen to lead the state's campaign. In 1877, the report stated, "it became apparent . . . that to meet the widespread and constantly increasing demand for more general and complete information relating to Kansas," either a new agency would have to be formed or the scope of an existing agency would have to be extended. Kansas chose the latter course and the Board of Agriculture was authorized to involve itself in affairs "much beyond the limit which would seem to be indicated by the name given to the organization at its inception."[64] No longer was it a mere fact-finding agency; indeed, it was destined to become, especially under the leadership of Foster Dwight Coburn, the best known and most vigorous promotional bureau in the Plains.

Coburn did not assume command until 1895 but even before then the board had given ample evidence of its new nature. A case in point was the comment in the 1883 biennial report that Kansas, due to its "fertility of soil . . . and mildness of climate," possessed "abundant facilities

62. Ibid., January 23, 1873.

63. Annual Message of Gov. George T. Anthony, January 10, 1877, in *Messages of Kansas Governors*, 1: 262.

64. KSBA, *Fifth Biennial Report . . . 1885–1886* (Topeka, 1887), p. 7.

for the maintenance of ten millions of people." [65] On another occasion the board published a booklet on the resources and capabilities of the state which left the reader with the unmistakable impression that yields of sixty bushels of wheat per acre were the norm everywhere in Kansas. Curiously, eastern Colorado, even that part immediately bordering on Kansas, required irrigation to produce harvests only half as great. [66]

Kansas and Nebraska were back in the promotion trade, this time through their agricultural bureaus rather than their boards of immigration. It was an effective technique and apparently won the allegiance even of those who preferred to leave such matters to the railroads.

Neither Colorado nor Wyoming displayed quite the same fervor in considering the issue of immigration. In both states, the sentiment remained strong that the railroads and other private agencies were better equipped to deal with promotional affairs. In 1885 a group of Denver real estate operators petitioned Governor Benjamin Eaton for a new bureau of immigration, but to no effect. [67] Two years later one of the leading agricultural papers in the state repeated this suggestion, mentioning in this regard the activities of promotional bureaus in Kansas and Nebraska. [68] Again the response was less than overwhelming. The legislature did form the Bureau of Immigration and Statistics in 1889, and a seventy-five page pamphlet was published under the auspices of the new agency. [69] It was the only publication to come from the bureau, and the only effective piece of official propaganda to be issued by the state until the early 1900s. [70] Wyoming promoters fared little better. Governor Francis Warren noted in 1890 that the territory was "in quest of immigration and [that] the highest results are attained by legitimate and enlightened advertising." He managed to secure an appropriation of $2,500 for the publication of 12,000 copies of

65. KSBA, *Third Biennial Report . . . 1881–1882* (Topeka, 1883), p. 5.

66. KSBA, *Kansas: Its Resources and Capabilities, Its Position, Dimensions, and Topography* (Topeka, 1883), pp. 22–24. This booklet was also published in German and Swedish and distributed widely in both nations.

67. Denver Real Estate Exchange, Petition to Gov. Benjamin Eaton, ca. 1885, Eaton Papers, Colorado Archives.

68. *Field and Farm* (Denver), February 5, 1887.

69. Colorado State Bureau of Immigration and Statistics, *Natural Resources and Industrial Development and Conditions of Colorado* (Denver, 1889).

70. For criticism of this neglect, see Colorado State Board of Agriculture, *Agricultural Statistics of the State of Colorado, 1892 . . .* (Denver, 1894), p. 4, and ibid., *1893*, p. 5.

Resources of Wyoming, but the fund was quickly exhausted and never replenished.[71]

Whatever the degree of official involvement in promotion, however, all the states of the Central Plains encouraged as much activity by private agencies as possible. This was true regardless of their attitudes toward railroad promotion or the extent of their own efforts. There were a number of these agencies to which they could turn. One source of private promotion, indeed the most representative example of the mood of western boosterism, was the local newspapers. No one ever doubted the press's commitment to growth or its eagerness to engage in promotional hyperbole. And fortunately, the local paper considered itself all but immune from charges of vested interest. Printed railroad circulars, one newspaperman mentioned in 1876, "may exaggerate, people are everywhere suspicious of farming handbills." But the newspapers were free from this suspicion, they were "something more, ... a living sample of the enterprise, and the vitality of the region in which [they were] published." For this reason among others, Nebraska instituted a policy of sending abroad twenty-five copies of each newspaper in the state in an attempt to interest potential immigrants.[72] The following October the *Nebraska Farmer*, after granting the fact that everyone in Kansas and Nebraska was interested in inducing immigration, suggested that the best way to accomplish this end was to add another subscription to the local paper; "and mail a copy to this friend, and next week mail another copy to that friend, and so on." It would be impossible to determine how many Kansans or Nebraskans heeded this advice, but for every one who did there were a number of eastern "friends" who were subjected to some of the most outrageous promotional literature to come out of the West.

The *Caldwell* (Kansas) *Commercial* of May 6, 1880, succumbed to pure fantasy as it described its location:

> Dimly in the north beyond the rising and falling billows of the flower-spangled prairie, may be seen a dark line of timber skirting the sandy shores of the Chicaskia, with here and there a white speck upon its rich bottoms, showing that the husbandman has found a land which, if not now flowing with milk and honey, is destined at no distant day to become richer and fairer than Canaan.

71. *Biennial Message of Francis E. Warren ... to the Eleventh General Assembly, 1890* (Cheyenne, 1890), pp. 18–19.
72. *Lincoln Journal*, August 10, 1876.

For other newspapers, prose, regardless of how full-blown, was inadequate to the task. The *Kirwin* (Kansas) *Chief* of February 26, 1876, reprinted Lucy Larcom's poem "A Call to Kansas" as a means of attracting newcomers. The poem was imploring:

> Yeoman strong; hither throng!
> Nature's honest men,
> We will make the wilderness
> Bud and bloom again.

In the same issue the editors explained how this was to be done. "Energy, thrift and enterprise characteristic of our western pioneers, will fast transform the 'Great American Desert' into fields of corn and wheat."

At the same time, there was the implication that the "desert" would offer no real challenge. Fuel and water were abundant, the soil was a rich black loam, the corn yield in 1875 was eighty bushels to the acre, and the climate was healthy and salubrious.[73] But for those who insisted upon a desert, the Millbrook, Kansas, paper, entitled the *American Desert*, was willing to supply one, at least poetically. Yes, the paper admitted on May 1, 1887, there had once been a desert in western Kansas:

> But Time's unceasing pulses throbbed,
> And waves of population rolled
> In slow aggressive lines
> That dared the desperate desert's hold.

Dared it successfully, needless to add, and then watched as:

> Lo! like many a tale of old,
> That spring and grow, by Fancy kissed,
> The terror of the desert shrank,
> And faded like the morning mist.

The desert faded to reveal, in the Kirwin district anyway, fields of corn which yielded one hundred bushels to the acre, wheat averaging fifty bushels, potatoes that weighed four pounds, turnips of fourteen pounds each, radishes of twenty-eight pounds, and most remarkable of all, a 220-pound pumpkin.[74] The *Lusk* (Wyoming) *Herald* of May 27, 1886, was less specific in its claims, but no less extravagant. Eastern

73. *Kirwin* (Kans.) *Chief*, February 26, 1876.
74. Ibid.

Wyoming, contrary to some published reports, "contains a large area of fine agricultural lands where small grains . . . grow so immensely that it is almost incredible to state the facts." In Colorado, the "facts" were equally incredible, so much so that the *Springfield Herald* despaired of ever being able to describe this land of promise to its eastern readers.[75] Only the "imaginative genius of a Milton" would be adequate to this task; an epic struggle had been joined, and only an epic poet was prepared to chronicle it.[76]

In analyzing these claims it is important to note that, with few exceptions, the appeal was not to the prospective settler's acquisitive instincts, but rather to his yearning for personal independence. Large yields could be expected to provide a good living, of course, but seemingly more important was the fact that a man could "hither come and upward grow."[77] The Plains offered "HOMES! HOMES!! For the Needy and Worthy"; they offered "an advanced civilization already provided."[78] The climate was healthful, the air was pure and sweet, churches were either under construction or already well established, schools were the first priority, society was refined and virtuous.

The plainsman was doing more than simply promoting in making these claims. He was refuting the desert and the desert makers. In the process he was confounding those who believed that the Plains would frustrate America's continental expansion, that they would prove, in the words of yet another bit of newspaper poetry, "the barrier of the race."[79] This barrier was being lifted by the "Saxon bands with gun and share" who marched upon the desert and converted it to productive use. Here, then, was the place for the yeoman. Here, on the same Plains that Pike had likened to the Sahara, was a paradise literally regained.

Occasionally, it must be admitted, a more mercenary approach to the blessing of immigration crept into the promotional accounts. The references to large yields infer as much. So too does the mention of a rapid rise in land values. Many prospective immigrants undoubtedly read suggestions similar to one in the San Francisco *Argonaut* urging

75. In *Cheyenne Wells* (Colo.) *Gazette*, February 11, 1888.

76. *Burlington Blade*, in ibid., February 1, 1888.

77. *Kinsley* (Kans.) *Mercury*, April 30, 1887.

78. *Atwood* (Kans.) *Pioneer*, October 23, 1879; see also *Kirwin* (Kans.) *Chief*, February 26, 1876.

79. *American Desert* (Millbrook, Kans.), May 1, 1887.

them to invest in Kansas lands and watch their investments double within five years.[80]

A far more common economic argument, however, was that presented by the *Coffeyville* (Kansas) *Journal* of April 22, 1883. Prodigious crops and ready markets made the Coffeyville area a prosperous one, so prosperous that many of the farmers "paid for their farms out of last year's crops, and seem to be glad they came to Kansas." In other words, one year's time was enough to produce a self-sufficient farmer, a participant in the fee-simple empire which the United States was so generously providing. An appeal of this sort was more likely to attract a man with limited means and limited ambitions. But it was for such a man, after all, that the American garden had been created. Regardless of the basis of their appeals, the newspapers were obviously an important part of any promotional campaign, and the states, whether they were doing any official promoting or not, counted heavily on the press to attract new immigrants.

Nor were newspapers the only form of private recruitment to which the states could turn. Promotion was considered a civic duty and all who deserved well of the commonwealth were expected to participate in it. Every individual, it was assumed, realized that the prosperity and progress of his "State, his county, and his neighborhood depended upon his personal efforts to 'push things'" and he acted accordingly.[81] This involved, most particularly, sending letters to friends and relatives in the East and Europe describing for them the happy life to be found on the Plains. The Kansas Bureau of Immigration had recognized as early as 1868 that such letters constituted one of the most effective forms of advertising available to the state, and recommended strongly that citizens of Kansas cooperate in this enterprise.[82] In order to ensure that these were favorable notices it was important that the immigrants to a region be received as cordially as possible. As the Kansas agent in Hamburg wrote to Governor Crawford, "We will have to confront all these men sooner or later. . . . Their minds . . . is [sic] a blank sheet. . . . May we not mould these minds as long as they are elastic enough to have impressions?"[83] It was widely believed that the new arrivals,

80. *San Francisco Argonaut* in the *American Desert* (Millbrook, Kans.), May 1, 1887.

81. *Historical and Descriptive Review of Kansas*, vol. 1, *The Northern Section* (Topeka: Jon. Lethem, 1890), p. 8.

82. Kansas Bureau of Immigration, *Report . . . 1868*, p. 5.

83. Lewis F. Weise to Samuel Crawford, May 25, 1866, Crawford Papers, KSHS.

properly molded of course, would serve as living testimony to the beneficence of Kansas, and that their correspondence would reflect general satisfaction. The promotional value in this was considerable, as a letter from the Reverend Olaf Olsson to friends still in Sweden attests:

> We do not dig gold with pocket knives nor do we expect to become bountifully rich in a few days or in a few years, but what we aim at is to own our own home. We are like the Swedish yeoman in our freedom. . . . The advantage which America offers is not to make everyone rich without toil and trouble.[84]

The disclaimer of easy wealth was not designed to deter immigration but rather to confirm the impression of America as a land of free and independent labor. Few Europeans of the nineteenth century could have desired more.

Another alternative to official promotion was the inclusion of descriptive material in the yearly reports of the territorial governors to the Department of the Interior. In 1878 when the Interior Department took over the responsibility of administering the territories, Secretary Carl Schurz issued an invitation to the governors to include in their reports statements on the climate, soil, natural resources, and general inducements for immigration in their territories. The governors were quick to take advantage of this opportunity, especially when the Interior Secretary began to publish these promotional accounts in his yearly report. With the imprimatur of the federal government attached to them, these territorial reports were soon considered the most reliable sources of information for the prospective immigrant, in spite of the fact that, more often than not, the governors simply borrowed material verbatim from territorial immigration pamphlets. Even when they did exercise some originality there was little attempt made to disguise the fact that the report was intended to attract immigrants and not to give a recital of the political development of the area.[85] A perfect case in point is the 1887 report from Governor Thomas Moonlight of Wyoming Territory.

As mentioned before, Wyoming was seriously limited in her promotional efforts by the large cattle interests who dominated the terri-

84. Emory Lindquist, ed. and trans., "Letters of the Reverend and Mrs. Olaf Olsson, 1869–1873, Pioneer Founders of Lindsborg," *Kansas Historical Quarterly* 21 (November 1955): 499.

85. Earl Pomeroy, *The Territories and the United States, 1861–1890* (Philadelphia: University of Pennsylvania Press, 1947), p. 22–24.

tory. Moonlight, a firm champion of agricultural interests, was determined to break this hold and introduce Wyoming to the manifold blessings of yeomanry. He was convinced that if the people of Wyoming could only be made aware of the enormous agricultural potential of the area they would quickly abandon stock raising and turn to the plow. Even more important, a recognition of this central fact would induce the "sturdy, hardy settler, poor perhaps, but energetic and determined" to settle the territory. His report to the Secretary of the Interior seemed the ideal forum for this effort at public education. "The first great important demand," he wrote, "is farmers, practical, every-day farmers, who will put their hands to the plow and not look back." Unfortunately, it was thought that Wyoming was fit only for pasturage, "that crops would not grow in response to the tillage." Moonlight's object in the remainder of his report was to refute that charge, to clear the good name of the territory, and to issue a warm welcome to the deserving yeoman. Certainly Wyoming had much to offer, most particularly a soil and climate capable of producing "bountiful harvests of grains, vegetables, and grasses . . . more nutritious in quality and more abundant in quantity than can be produced in the old and well-settled States farther east." The land was open and the bars to agricultural settlement thrown down.

Unfortunately, Moonlight went on, the potential settlers were not always aware of this, and until such time as the Wyoming legislature should awaken to its true responsibility and establish an official promotional bureau, they would remain ignorant of the possibilities of the territory. Moonlight took some comfort in the formation of private immigration companies such as the recently formed Colonization Corporation of Cheyenne, but he was convinced that real progress in this vital area would come only when the territory began to promote on a more systematic basis. Until then he hoped that his own reports to the Interior Department would continue to be used to supplement the information published by newspapers and other private agencies concerned with immigration matters.[86]

There were many such private agencies throughout the Central Plains, many of them associated with railroads, and they, too, relieved the states of some of the promotional burden. Occasionally, as in Colorado,

86. Report of Gov. Thomas Moonlight of Wyoming to the secretary of the interior, September 27, 1887, copy in the files of the WSHS. For another example of state promotion in federal publications, see Nebraska's entry in Young, *Special Report of Immigration*, pp. 101–7.

the state or territory would specifically request that private concerns send agents to the East Coast as quasi-public servants. These agents would, of course, emphasize their own special interests, but territorial officials in Colorado hoped that the interests of all would be secured by investing them with a degree of official authority.[87]

Generally, the cooperation between state and private agencies was not so overt. In Kansas, however, Foster Dwight Coburn managed to share his promotional talents with both the State Board of Agriculture and the Husted Investment Company of Kansas City.[88] It was Coburn who compiled the rainfall statistics which played so conspicuous a role in the promotional campaign of the Husted Company. Coburn quoted statistics purporting to show that the rainfall in Kansas in 1888 had totaled a soggy 44.17 inches; in 1889, said Coburn, 43.99 inches fell over the state as a whole. These figures, needless to say, are open to dispute. There are few stations in Kansas which have ever received the precipitation that Coburn claims for the whole state. By combining the rainfall of stations all over the state, unreasonable as this total is, Coburn managed to avoid making the necessary distinction between eastern and western Kansas—good evidence that he understood fully the unlimited possibilities of his profession.[89]

Few of the many private promoters were more careful or responsible in their claims. Stephen Marcou, one of the most energetic of the Kansas promoters, spoke of the Cottonwood Valley in the central part of the state as "the 'Italy of America.'" The climate of the region was distinctly Mediterranean in its temperance. It was capable of producing in abundance almost any crop native to southern Europe except possibly olives. Marcou was insistent that settlers "COME NOW, [and not] permit a few dollars in the price of . . . property in the east prevent [them] from coming now, for [they] could repurchase here at figures that would warrant [them] in selling out at home for what [they] could get."[90]

87. George T. Clark to the Secretaries of the Union, Saint Louis, Chicago, Fountain, and Tennessee Colonies, February 20, 1872, CTBI, CSHS.

88. *Topeka Capital*, January 12, 1882.

89. Husted Investment Co., *Some Facts About Kansas*, comp. by Foster D. Coburn (Kansas City, 1890), pp. 3–4.

90. Stephen Marcou, *Homes for the Homeless: A Description of Marion County, Kansas, and the Cottonwood Valley! The Garden of the State!* (Marion Centre, Kans.: Marion County Record Book and Job Office, 1874), p. 12; see also Marcou to Gov. James M. Harvey, May 24, 1871, Harvey Papers, KSHS, for an account of Marcou's promotional activities in France.

Marcou and Coburn were only two of many. Samuel Crawford, former governor of the state, was also actively involved in promotion, as was T. C. Henry, one of the largest land holders in central Kansas.[91] There were, in addition, many local and regional agencies involved in promotion. The Cheyenne Wells Town and Investment Company of Colorado and the Northern Kansas Immigration Association are two examples,[92] in addition to the Colonization Corporation of Cheyenne.

With assistance of this sort, it was understandable that some considered any concerted activity on the part of the states to be super-fluous. Railroads, newspapers, private citizens, and investment companies were all committed to population growth. All were prepared to pursue their commitment in whatever way seemed most likely of success. The result was a barrage of pamphlets, brochures, land guides, and announcements holding up for public inspection the alleged bounties of individual regions. Boomer literature followed the prospective immigrant from the time he left Europe or the eastern United States until he had finally settled on a location for his home. And even then he was subjected to continuous inducements to move again, to search for the final West. The mobility of the American farmer had been converted into a big business.

But even this assortment of promotional possibilities does not complete the list. There was one other tactic which the states could use in booming the settlement of their lands—submitting displays to the various fairs and expositions which were so popular in the nineteenth century. This involved a degree of official participation greater than what many legislators would have preferred, but it seemed to produce excellent results in relation to the time and money expended. The states used these expositions as a kind of road show, an opportunity to display to the world the blessings of their region. In theory these expositions were called to commemorate some important past event; in the carnival

91. Crawford had helped form the Kansas Land and Emigration Company (unidentified clipping in *Crawford Scrapbooks*, KSHS). For Henry, see *Henry's Advertiser* (Abilene), a blatantly promotional journal dedicated to the sale of Henry's estate and, for a time, the sale of Union Pacific lands in the area. Complete run in KSHS.

92. *Cheyenne Wells Gazette*, March 28, 1886; Northern Kansas Immigration Association, *Corn is King: The Advantages Northern Kansas Offers to Home Seekers and Land Buyers* (Kansas City, Mo.: Ramsey, Millett & Hudson, 1888). See also the land guide prepared by Daniel Witter, *The Settlers' Guide to the Entry of Public Lands in Colorado* (Denver: News Printing Co., 1882).

atmosphere which resulted all were expected to behave with the harmony and accord of a grateful people celebrating a national anniversary. In fact, however, they became highly charged, competitive sessions in which states and railroads vied with one another for the year's crop of the dissatisfied and discontented elements of European and American society. These ceremonial events were a boomers' paradise, and promoters from all over the West descended upon them, eager to display their wares.

The newspapers did their share as well in making sure that the official notices which accompanied the state displays were distributed to a wider audience than those in actual attendance. The *Saint Louis Democrat*, for example, at the time of the Saint Louis fair, proclaimed Colorado the state "where Nature has done so much for the creature, man. There is no wonder," it concluded, "that the exclamation LET'S ALL GO TO COLORADO! should be heard."[93] The same paper also gave a favorable notice to the displays of the Kansas Pacific Railroad and to the efforts of that road to dispel the heretical notion of a Great American Desert.[94]

By 1876 when the Centennial Exposition opened in Philadelphia, the central Great Plains states were fully aware of the enormous promotional possibilities opened to them by the centennial commission. The western states, wrote one interested observer, "have a special object . . . in exhibiting. . . . They are immigrant states and desire to show to the world what resources, interests and advantages they have to induce immigration."[95] Nebraska certainly was prepared to put its best foot forward. J. Sterling Morton and Samuel Aughey, two of the state's most able promoters, were among its delegation. Both were quite aware that Nebraska's object at the exposition was not necessarily to pay homage to America's 100 years of freedom but to prove to the world that their state was continuing that long tradition—and growing an abundance of corn besides. A number of visitors to their displays must have come away favorably impressed, for Governor Garber was able to report that Nebraska had secured a number of highly promising immigrants through her efforts at the exposition.[96]

93. *St. Louis Democrat*, in *Daily Colorado Tribune* (Denver), October 12, 1870.

94. *St. Louis Democrat*, October 3, 1871, in ibid., October 11, 1871.

95. A. L. Brisbane to Gov. Silas Garber of Nebraska, December 4, 1875, Garber Papers, NSHS.

96. J. Sterling Morton to Samuel Aughey, June 26, 1876, in Garber Papers, NSHS. Second Inaugural Message, Silas Garber, January 5, 1877, in *Messages and Proclamations*, 1: 465.

Two years after the centennial of the United States the French government sponsored the International Industrial Exposition in Paris. Here was another excellent opportunity to promote directly, to influence prospective European immigrants on their own soil and with the tacit approval of their own government. The State Department was particularly eager that the several states and territories "assist in the proper representation of the productions of U.S. industry, and of the natural resources of the country." The United States had agreed to appoint twenty commissioners in addition to those the states were expected to send. The only federal restriction was that no person appointed by the states should have any personal interest in immigration. This was not expected, however, to hinder in any way the "promotional advantages to be derived from this beneficent undertaking."[97] Nor, it may safely be assumed, did it prove a bothersome restriction. By the late 1870s a general boom was in progress throughout the West. The Paris exposition, and others like it, were too valuable a part of that boom for the states to have limited their participation.

By the mid-1880s the rush to secure a piece of the Plains reached proportions which exceeded the expectations of all but the most visionary promoters. A few years of above average rainfall had convinced many that the Plains were not only cultivable but contained the richest land on earth. In 1885, in the midst of this vast migration, New Orleans sponsored the World's Industrial and Cotton Centennial Exposition, and once again the Plains states were given an opportunity to parade their resources. Robert Furnas, Nebraska's representative to the exposition, was determined to sustain the momentum of the past few years. "In presenting *Nebraska* to the world," he wrote, "I am making *the grand effort of my life....* [But] it requires money to do this!"[98] He hardly overstated the case. Nebraska kept on constant display enough promotional material to fill six advertising tables. This included matter, furnished by the railroads and real estate operators of the state, in numbers approaching "the hundreds of thousands." Much of the material, in addition, was put up in prepaid wrappers for visitors to send their friends. The general consensus was that Nebraska had the finest state exhibit at the exposition and Furnas expected many thousands to choose that "land of plenty" as their future home.[99]

97. F. W. Seward, acting secretary of state, to Silas Garber, January 2, 1878, Garber Papers, NSHS.
98. Furnas to Gov. Wm. Dawes, November 29, 1884, Dawes Papers, NSHS.
99. Robert Furnas, *Report of [the] . . . Commissioner for Nebraska at the World's*

Governor James Dawes was delighted with the news. Furnas's efforts, he told the state legislature, had occasioned "wonder and astonishment at the great extent and variety of her resources. This is Nebraska's opportunity, and she must not fail to improve it."[100] With Furnas directing the effort there was little fear of that. As he wrote from New Orleans, "I am anxious to go to London next year, and give Nebraska one more *grand boom*. . . . If the Rail Roads will give $1,000 I can then raise $1,000 more. I want a $2,000 fund so that what I do will be done in a grand scale."[101] Furnas made it to London and it is safe to assume that he promoted on just such a scale.[102]

The Colorado commissioner to New Orleans, H. F. Sickles, was no less certain of the importance of his position. Sickles, in a letter to Governor Benjamin Eaton, expressed his complete confidence that a "material benefit to the state has been awakened by our display." He was equally sure that much more could be done by the continuance of this type of advertising and that if "capital and immigration could be attracted to [Colorado] . . . the people could be made prosperous and happy."[103]

Important as New Orleans was to the efforts of the western states, it could not match for promotional appeal the World's Fair and Columbian Exposition hosted by Chicago in 1893. The fair's directors issued the usual invitation to the states to send representatives and displays. The response from the Plains was predictably favorable. The *Nebraska Farmer* of April 3, 1890, was convinced that it would be "'the biggest show on earth'." Anything less than that, it may be assumed, would have been considered unsatisfactory, for Nebraska had an important message—she was going to prepare a display which would finally "open the eyes of foreigners and effete easterners who think this fairest domain on earth is the Great American Desert." The reference to the

Industrial and Cotton Centennial, New Orleans (Lincoln, 1885), pp. 5, 8–9, 11; Furnas to Dawes, November 29, 1884, Dawes Papers, NSHS.

100. James Dawes, Second Inaugural Address, January 8, 1885, in *Messages and Proclamations*, 1: 589. He then requested an additional $10,000 appropriation to aid Furnas in his efforts.

101. Furnas to Dawes, May 21, 1885, Dawes Papers, NSHS.

102. Burnett Landreth to Dawes, August 11, 1886, ibid.

103. H. F. Sickles to Benjamin Eaton, July 15, 1885, Eaton Papers, Colorado Archives. The Denver Real Estate Exchange was similarly persuaded and they urged Eaton and the legislature to do all they could to finance Sickles's important mission (undated petition from the Denver Real Estate Exchange to Eaton, Eaton Papers, Colorado Archives).

desert at this late date was rather unusual, as was the rather smug dismissal of the easterner as effete. Normally, Nebraska was not that defensive. A more positive approach to the state's role at Chicago was presented by Governor John M. Thayer who, in asking the legislators for a special appropriation, assured them that the exposition would be the best advertisement the state ever had. It was a splendid opportunity to dispel old myths and create new ones, to perform the necessary acrobatics and transform a desert into a garden.[104]

Kansas was so excited about this prospect that she began active preparation for the exposition in 1891 with the State Board of Agriculture sending out information sheets to determine crop yield statistics. The results would then be used to dazzle the visitors to Chicago and insure for Kansas an appreciable increase in population.[105] Enthusiasm ran at least as high in Colorado. One of the leading agricultural newspapers in the state suggested as early as 1891 that the legislative penuriousness so common in the state should cease just long enough to finance a worthy exhibit. The world's fair was Colorado's great chance to attract settlers who had gone to Kansas and Nebraska. The state needs people, the paper concluded, and the exposition seemed the place to get them.[106] The state legislators obviously agreed. They voted $20,000 in 1891 and an additional $30,000 in 1892 in order to finance the state's exhibit. Even this sum proved insufficient, however, and Governor John Routt appealed to certain well-placed and "public spirited gentlemen" for yet another $30,000. They proved receptive, and Routt hoped that with $80,000 Colorado would be able to make a representative showing in Chicago.[107]

Even in Wyoming the promotional fever was evident. Governor Francis Warren, a leading cattleman, admitted that an exhibit "would give to the world some idea of the vast and wonderful resources of Wyoming." The benefits of such a display were obvious. Warren reminded his listeners that those who visited the centennial at

---

104. John M. Thayer, Third Inaugural Address, February 5, 1891, *Messages and Proclamations*, 2: 67.

105. Kansas State Board of Agriculture, *Monthly Report, April, 1891* . . . (Topeka, 1891), p. 11; *Topeka Capital*, March 17, 1891. The Kansas State Board of Agriculture is hereafter cited as KSBA.

106. *Field and Farm* (Denver), January 31, 1891.

107. Message of John Routt to the Ninth General Assembly, January 7, 1893, *Colorado Executive Records*, 8: 34. Davis Waite, Routt's successor, also favored a liberal appropriation for the World's Fair (Inaugural Message, January 10, 1893, in ibid., 8: 65).

Philadelphia in 1876 and witnessed the grand displays made there by many of the western states, "especially Colorado, Nebraska and Kansas," were aware of the immense benefits resulting from an exhibit. These were benefits which Wyoming must also secure if she were to grow and prosper.[108] Unfortunately, she was inadequately prepared for the effort. Displays and exhibits were expensive, especially in a state where agriculture was considered by many an unworthy or at least unprofitable profession. In 1898, at the time of the Trans-Mississippi Exposition, Governor William Richards was forced to admit that Wyoming would not be able to prepare an exhibit of her agricultural products. As Richards explained, "there was not a sufficient amount of them available."[109]

This was a problem which the other states of the central Great Plains did not have to face. Even in Colorado, agriculture, especially under irrigation, was a thriving industry and there was never any difficulty in getting up a proper display. Kansas and Nebraska, of course, were even better situated in this regard. The expositions gave these states adequate opportunity to bring to the attention of the world the progress they had made in conquering the desert. Obviously, nothing of a negative character was allowed to creep into their promotional efforts and as a result the expositions became vast arenas in which the western states could recruit new immigrants.

Kansas and Nebraska were obviously the most active of the central Great Plains states in promoting immigration. By the 1870s both had developed a vast and interconnected system of recruitment. In Colorado and Wyoming, events conspired to limit the promotional effort. A short history and the presence of mining and cattle interests made it difficult for either to undertake as ambitious a program of advertising as their older and more agricultural neighbors to the east. It was not that Colorado and Wyoming were unaware of the importance of attracting new immigrants. They simply realized that with limited funds and limited agricultural acreage, promotion could better be served by private agencies. No such modesty was apparent in Kansas or Nebraska. Here, on the eastern edge of the Plains, was an abundance of fertile soil—or so the promoters liked to believe. Few cattlemen and fewer miners disrupted the idyllic rural landscape. There were no desperadoes

108. Biennial Message of Francis E. Warren to the Eleventh Assembly, 1890 (Cheyenne, 1890), p. 33.

109. Retiring Message of Gov. William A. Richards . . . 1898, in Wyoming, *Messages of the Governors, 1890–1933* (Cheyenne, 1934), p. 27.

left from the pioneer days of the late sixties, only tillers of the soil and merchants to supply them. Colorado and Wyoming could only dream of one day possessing such a degree of harmony; Kansas and Nebraska insisted they already had it, and that the world should share in it. Their promotional campaigns manifested this confidence, the belief that the Plains were being conquered, not by nomadic stock growers or miners, but by the American farmer. It was with missionary zeal that they set about informing the world of this fact. They flooded the East and Europe with their promotional literature. Together with the railroads and other private agencies they openly courted the dispossessed and the dissatisfied, hoping always to convince them that their future was secured once they had set foot on the blessed soil of Kansas or Nebraska.

Their appeal was a convincing one. Thousands accepted it and acted upon it. But equally important, many who had absolutely no intention of leaving the East or Europe accepted it also, agreeing with the notion that the corporate good was best secured by encouraging immigration to the Plains. It was this acceptance by the East of the basic appeal of the western promoters that gave vitality to the boomers' frontier. Had there been no one promoting *emigration*, the call of the Plains might have gone unheeded. As it was, however, the prospective settler was besieged from both sides: the East and Europe urging him to leave, rejecting him, the West inviting him to come, welcoming him. It was a difficult argument to resist.

CHAPTER FOUR

Implementing the Safety Valve: The East

It was not surprising to anyone that the western states promoted immigration. They needed people; their lands were empty and unproductive. In years past other frontier areas, confronted with the same problem, had behaved similarly and advertised their wares to the world. One indirect result of such promotion was the settling of a continent, a process which had been in operation since the seventeenth century, but one which was rapidly nearing an end. It was the realization that the continent was approaching exhaustion that gave such urgency to the settlement of the last part of it. It was this realization as well that accounted for the favorable response in the East to western promotion. Easterners not only sympathized with the West's desire to attract new people and money, they also recognized the importance to their own section of maintaining an open frontier as a safety valve. The settled regions had been the first to acknowledge the awful significance of a Great American Desert; they were, then, the first to applaud the West's efforts to conquer this desert, even though that conquest was more literary than actual. The western boomer told them the desert was gone. The easterners wanted very much to believe him. It was important that the boomer be right; if the safety valve were to remain open he had to be right.

One of the first easterners to recognize this central fact was the philanthropist Peter Cooper. Though a self-made millionaire, Cooper never endorsed the prevailing wisdom that the poor should be left to find their own salvation. He was convinced of the state's responsibility to alleviate misfortune, or failing that, the responsibility of the favored classes to engage in charitable activities. This philosophy was reflected in his dealings with labor, and the iron company he headed together with his son-in-law, Abram Hewitt, was noted for its progressive approach to the problem of labor-management relations.[1] In 1857, at the height of the panic of that year, Cooper established the Cooper Union in New York, a polytechnic institution concerned with job training and education in the manual arts. It became the one great and lasting monument to his liberalism, but it was not the last of his efforts to help the poor.[2]

In 1866, convinced that municipal corruption was depriving the working man of an opportunity to improve his station, Cooper and fourteen other men, including August Belmont, Hamilton Fish, and William E. Dodge, formed the Citizens' Association of New York.[3] In addition to its municipal reform program, the association also involved itself in a project to remove unemployed workers in the East to the free lands of the West. This seemed a natural solution to the problems of labor discontent, much more humane and responsible than strikes and boycotts. In 1868 Cooper, as secretary of the association, wrote to Governor Samuel Crawford of Kansas inquiring about settlement possibilities in that state. As Cooper put it, his group wanted to send surplus laborers in the East "to the grain fields of the West, which the Citizens' Association deems of great practical importance to the best interests of all parties concerned. . . . The vast surplus population of the East requires to be intelligently distributed."[4] Crawford could not have agreed more, nor could the railroads which served Kansas. According to one of them, the Santa Fe, emigration, not revolution, "is the panacea of the oppressed of the human family," and certainly Kansas stood ready to receive the oppressed whom Cooper might send.[5]

Cooper's effort to activate the safety valve by specific action was simply an extension of a commonly held belief. For almost 250 years escape to a near West, it was thought, had served to relieve the pressures of the American system. Now, however, the West was farther removed from the industrial centers of the nation, and a more systematic approach to population redistribution was necessary. The active promotion of emigration was one such approach.

1. See Allan Nevins, *Abram S. Hewitt with Some Account of Peter Cooper* (New York: Harper and Brothers, 1935), p. 267–91, and Edward C. Mack, *Peter Cooper, Citizen of New York* (New York: Duell, Sloan and Pearce, 1949), pp. 324–85.
2. Nevins, *Abram S. Hewitt*, pp. 169–91; Mack, *Peter Cooper*, pp. 243–77.
3. Mack, *Peter Cooper*, p. 345.
4. Cooper to Crawford, February 28, 1868, in Crawford Papers, KSHS.
5. *Star of Empire* (Santa Fe), July, 1869

Another was group migration, the formation of well-financed colonies with a specific destination. In this way the rigors of travel, the expense of land location, and the hardships of life on an isolated farm might be avoided. Unfortunately, the Homestead Law made no special provisions for this type of settlement. In 1870 Carl Wulsten, the president of the Chicago-based German Colonization Company, petitioned to Congress for the passage of a colony homestead act. The results of such a bill, he assured the legislators, would be little short of miraculous; the safety valve could be given real meaning. Wulsten asked the Congress to "look upon New York, Boston, Philadelphia, . . . Chicago, . . . and other large cities" and note the "amount of misery and wretchedness . . . hidden behind their marble palaces and cozy dwellings!" Literally thousands of poverty-stricken people crowded these cities, "scarce knowing how to find the wherewithal to still their hunger and thirst, or cover their nudity." [6] Wulsten had seen this misery and had determined that the overcrowded cities should be able to send their surplus inhabitants "to the broad acres of the West, where their miserable condition would be changed to a state of . . . comfort and happiness." [7] Like Cooper's, his was a beguilingly simple solution but one which must have commended itself to a number of Americans.

Seldom during the years immediately following the Civil War did people question the capacity of the Plains to absorb comfortably the discontent of eastern cities. It was simply taken for granted by people like Cooper and Wulsten that this newest frontier would prove as receptive to the poor as older frontiers had in years past. That the emigrant might find more misery and poverty on the Plains than he had known in the urban areas was unthinkable. Such an idea was contrary to tradition and faith, contrary as well to the expressed mission of American democracy after the war. And so the American people continued to believe that escape to the free lands of the West would supply a permanent remedy for their economic and social problems.

In 1873 they had ample opportunity to test this belief. Conditions prior to that date had been relatively good and, except among a few social tinkerers like Cooper, the possibility that the safety valve might close was of academic concern only. But in '73 a panic and depression, unprecedented in severity, struck the American economy. The poverty and despair which Wulsten had described three years earlier seemed as

6. U.S., Congress, Senate, *Petition of the German Colonization Company, January 18, 1870*, 41st Cong., 2d sess., 1870–71, S. Misc. Doc. 22, p. 2.

7. *Colorado Chieftain* (Pueblo), March 17, 1870.

nothing in comparison to conditions during the lean years of the mid- and late seventies. Obviously something had gone awry in the American economic system, and the safety valve began to assume more immediate and practical importance. There was a rush to implement it in the 1870s as more and more people sought solutions to the problems of unemployment, hunger, and suffering. Some saw the answer in lowering the tariff, others in raising it, and still others in monetary inflation or municipal reform. Many, however, looked for salvation to the broad empty acres of the West. Here, according to the industrial journal, *Age of Steel*, could be found an "outlet for idle people, for the surplus capital, the machinery, manufactures, and surplus products of the looms and shops of our region." But more was involved than just an "outlet." The safety valve did more than simply expel the poor, it admitted them to a freer and better life. Such was the case on the Great Plains. The *Age of Steel* told its readers of broad acres of grain and corn farmed by a prosperous and independent people. As for the Great American Desert, it had vanished as if the "hand of toil had touched it with a magic wand." [8]

The Plains states, eschewing false modesty, agreed. They endorsed emigration as the "True and Lasting Remedy" to industrial depression and they affirmed their ability to perform the job expected of all frontiers by promising "land for the landless, homes for the homeless, jobs for the jobless." [9] If a method could be found to expedite the removal of the unemployed of the East to these waiting lands of the West, economic prosperity would return. There was, of course, nothing new in this theory, but given the severity of the depression it came to possess a greater urgency.

Of all those in the East who embraced emigration as the safest solution to the problems of the depression, none did so with greater vigor than W. E. Webb. Webb was the author of one of the most popular gazettes of the era. Like all the others of that type, his gazette, *Buffalo Land*, contained glowing references to the potential of the western regions. As one of the editors of the *Star of Empire*, the promotional newspaper of the Santa Fe Railroad, he was well practiced in this type of literature.[10] Webb's gazette, however, was remarkable not for the

8. *Age of Steel*, in the *Kansas Farmer*, June 27, 1877.

9. *Omaha Republican*, September 14, 1877; S. F. Shaw to Silas Garber, November 4, 1875, Garber Papers, NSHS.

10. John Brainerd, "William Byers and the National Land Company" (Master's thesis, University of Denver, 1964), p. 15.

professionalism he brought to it but for its unqualified endorsement of the safety valve as an instrument of social control. Heretofore, Webb noted, the safety valve had been considered a natural consequence of the western movement and hence effective without any encouragement or regulation by the state. Now, for reasons not entirely clear to him, the valve seemed to have gone into disuse just when it was most needed. Tramps were roaming the streets of eastern cities while good land went begging on the western Plains. It was more than Webb could understand. In his mind there was no reason why people should starve while land was available for the taking, no reason why businessmen should be "besieged and worried with applications for positions."[11]

Webb had a simple solution for the "besieged" businessman; he had only to tack up a copy of the Homestead Law on the gates surrounding his plant and keep a good supply of copies of the law on hand for free distribution. This was answer enough for those who demanded non-existent jobs. Even the most vicious and ignorant of the unemployed could absorb the message it contained. But should they refuse to act upon it, Webb feared that laws might have to be passed compelling the cities "to drive from them the idle and vicious, and make them tillers of the soil in the wilds." This was harsh treatment, he admitted, but the results would be highly desirable. "Instead of brooding in the dark alleys, and breeding vice to be flung out at regular intervals upon the civilized thoroughfares, these germinators of disease and crime would be dragged forth from their purlieus and hiding places, and [placed] in the pure atmosphere of the large prairies and grand forests."

Webb allowed that the first to be sent away under this compulsory homestead act would have a difficult time of adjusting, but the chain of poverty in which they were trapped would be broken, the moral and physical disease which beset them would "not be propagated to suffocate their children." And all society would benefit. The rich would no longer be embarrassed or set upon by beggars. As Webb explained it, "There can be no excuse for begging in a country which offers every pauper a quarter-section of as rich land as the sun shines upon." Crime, drunkenness, and despair would be eliminated, and at considerable savings to the taxpayers. All the time, the morally diseased would be "disinfected" in the free, open spaces of the West. It was a grand scheme, and what it lacked in charity, Webb was convinced, it more

11. W. E. Webb, *Buffalo Land* (Philadelphia: Hubbard Brothers, 1872), p. 437. Quotations in the two following paragraphs are from the same source.

than made up in logic and practicality. As he put it: "It is more profitable to raise farmers than convicts."

There were many who agreed, though usually without the strident class prejudice which Webb betrayed. The idea of encouraging emigration out of the depressed cities, whether by legislative fiat or private action, had an understandable appeal, and a great many colonization schemes were started during the dark days of the 1870s. John Tice, author of the gazette *Over the Plains; on the Mountains*, wrote that there was scarcely a state east of the Mississippi that was not actively encouraging emigration.[12] The purpose behind these schemes was simple enough. The Co-operative Colony Aid Association of New York was typical in wanting "to promote the better distribution of labor in our country, and relieve the over crowded cities by stimulating and guiding a return to agricultural life."[13] They were joined in this wish by another depression-spawned emigration society, the Cosmo-American Colonization and General Improvement Bureau of Philadelphia. Again, the object was to relieve urban congestion and crime by stimulating immigration into the West.[14] The same motive guided the activity of the Irish Catholic Colonization Association. The founder of this group was Bishop John Spalding, a Ruskinesque Catholic prelate, whose burning ambition was to save the Irish from the baleful influences of the urban East and, it may be presumed, save the East from the Irish. In his mind, city life involved physical and moral degradation, insanity, and drunkenness. Were it not, in fact, "for the uninterrupted influx of healthy country blood the cities would become depopulated." By contrast, "happy is the country child. With bare head and bare feet he wanders through wood and field, or watches the grazing flocks . . . and all his dreams of peace and love gather round his mother and the home fireside."[15] Spalding's dreams extended principally to the plains of Nebraska. There he found the perfect home for his lost and wandering

12. John Tice, *Over the Plains; on the Mountains* (St. Louis: Industrial Age Printing Co., 1872), p. 146.

13. J. K. Ingalls, secretary, to Gov. J. P. St. John, June 27, 1879, St. John Papers, KSHS. E. V. Smalley, publicist for the Northern Pacific Railroad, was on the board of directors of the association.

14. A. J. Rogers to St. John, February 21, 1880, St. John Papers, KSHS. Letters of inquiry also arrived from individuals eager to escape depression conditions in the East. See, for example, James Dailey of New York to Gov. Silas Garber, February 18, 1878, and James Halder to Garber, January 23, 1878, Garber Papers, NSHS.

15. John L. Spalding, *The Religious Mission of the Irish People and Catholic Colonization* (New York: Catholic Publications Society, 1880), pp. 79, 95.

people, and a number of Irish colonies were established in the state in the 1880s.[16]

In addition to these private associations, a number of eastern newspapers had emigration columns in which the advantages of removal to the West were graphically depicted. E. O. L. Edholm, editor of one such column for the *Chicago Tribune*, was particularly enthusiastic about the prospects. In a letter to Governor Albinus Nance of Nebraska he outlined a "plan for inducing Emigration." It involved the inclusion of promotional material in eastern newspapers wherever conditions were particularly poor. Hopefully, the newspapers concerned would publish the material in an inconspicuous place and not as part of a general column relating to emigration. This would give it a certain detached quality unobtainable otherwise. Edholm even offered some suggestions as to what the promotional matter should contain. "Cases of individual prosperity," he commented, "must be sought out and given publicity, the railroad interests must not be neglected," and most important, "no section of the state must be slighted . . . but all given their due share of prominence." The last warning was particularly significant for, as Edholm mentioned, most eastern readers were convinced of the fertility of eastern Nebraska but the western regions were still considered a part of the Great American Desert.[17]

Edholm's scheme cannot be taken as typical of eastern journalistic promotion. Few of the papers were that systematic in their approach, the usual practice being the inclusion of a column or two in which different western states were featured. The *Chicago Tribune* had offered this service since the Civil War, although, according to one of its reporters, the effort had been stepped up considerably since the depression.[18] The *New York Tribune* was another journal that recognized that emigration was one form of relief from the depression, particularly for those not emigrating, and beginning in 1877 it carried a number of articles on emigration prospects under the lead "Homes for the Unemployed."

The value of this series suggested itself immediately to a number of

16. See James Shannon, *Catholic Colonization on the Western Frontier* (New Haven: Yale University Press, 1957); Mary Evangela Henthorne, *The Career of the Right Reverend John L. Spalding as President of the Irish-Catholic Colonization Association of the United States* (Urbana: University of Illinois Press, 1932).

17. E. O. L. Edholm to Gov. Albinus Nance, February 16, 1880, Nance Papers, NSHS.

18. Fred Perry Powers to Albinus Nance, February 17, 1880, ibid.

western promoters. A. E. Touzalin of the Burlington railroad was one of them. The *New York Tribune* was looking for homes; the Burlington had a more than ample supply. The problem became, then, one of advertising and marketing, and Touzalin appealed to Governor Silas Garber to meet this need by sending state promotional material for inclusion in the columns of the *Tribune*.[19]

Garber probably needed little convincing. Of all the high officials of the Plains states, he was undoubtedly the most interested in taking full promotional advantage of the depression in the East.[20] He recognized that many of the unemployed were eager to escape the urban centers and it seemed to him logical and practical that Nebraska serve as their refuge. He was joined in this belief by E. F. Test of the Union Pacific Railroad.

Few promoters were as opportunistic as this one; to Test, the depression was the most exciting development since the Kansas-Nebraska Act made the settlement of the Plains a moral imperative. Test recognized in Garber a kindred spirit, and in a series of remarkably candid letters he explained to the Nebraska governor the unlimited promotional possibilities presented by the colony and emigration drive in the East. Test left no doubt that this movement was an extensive one. The plan, as he described it, was to colonize in the West as many of the idle workingmen and their families as were willing to go. Test, furthermore, was convinced that the movement would soon be a general one as the depression deepened. The prospects for an immediate increase in Nebraska's population thus seemed to him excellent, but only if the state officials instituted a systematic movement to secure it. Nor would delay in the formation of such a campaign be advisable. The capitalists who were financing and directing this emigration were looking primarily to Kansas and Texas as future homes for their recruits. If Nebraska were to compete, she would have to abandon her customary modesty and convince these capitalists that she possessed unmatched resources and opportunities. Test admitted that even without any such systematic promotion Nebraska had fared well enough. Adam Smith,

19. A. E. Touzalin to Garber, March 30, 1878, Garber Papers, NSHS.
20. See, for example, J. F. Morton and Co. to Garber, November 4, 1876, in which Morton agreed to serve as Nebraska's agent in Massachusetts during the depression. Garber had also written on his own authority to the Altoona, Pennsylvania, emigration colony congratulating them on their prescience and mentioning the advantages Nebraska could offer them. Garber to M. B. Hunter, April 12, 1876, Garber Letter Press Books, NSHS.

for example, "an eminent financier of Chicago," had recently secured control of 140,000 acres in Boone County and was actively soliciting idle workers to form a colony and settle the land. This, of course, was an encouraging note, but as Test wrote to Garber, how much more extensive such development might be "if gentlemen of height and lofty character like yourself might be induced to participate."[21]

Presumably Garber's character was not sufficiently lofty to effect the desired results by itself; a month after he sent this first letter, Test was actively seeking out others of influence and means to aid him in his campaign. He had been led to believe that Jay Gould would be in Omaha sometime during the autumn of 1877. Here was a real possibility. If someone of importance could approach Gould, interest him in immigration, and ask him to hold out inducements to people settling along his line, the efforts would be well rewarded. After all, Test reminded Garber, "one word from Jay Gould to the press of New York and the eastern cities would give a prodigious influence to the movement." Test was positive that Gould would be receptive; indeed, he was somewhat surprised that the enterprising financier had not already noticed the opportunities presented him by the depression in the East. Here was a chance for him to "perpetuate his name for generations to come, by taking a personal and active interest in the matters of emigration."[22] If Garber could only enlist Gould's support, Test's plan for peopling Nebraska's plains would be assured of success. The poor in the East would then have "such inducements . . . held out to them that they [could] hardly consider remaining to suffer the ravages of poverty." Without his support, however, the state would have to await another depression, and no one, least of all Test, was willing to predict when the American economy would collapse next. It might be years, and Test was an impatient man. There was simply too much uncertainty in the boom-and-bust cycle to satisfy him completely, and he admitted a longing for a return to the days of Bleeding Kansas. "I often wish," he confessed somewhat wistfully, "that there were another Massachusetts Aid Society to people up our prairies."[23]

This was impossible, and so the Plains were forced to rely on the depression to stimulate immigration. It was not, of course, a wholly unacceptable arrangement. The East had manifested considerable

21. E. F. Test to Garber, August 21, 1877, Garber Papers, NSHS.
22. Test to Garber, September 21, 1877, ibid.
23. Test to Garber, September 17 and 21, 1877, ibid.

interest in using the West as a dumping ground for its unemployed, and the western states had no objection whatsoever to being so used. It was a comfortable position, being on the escape end of a safety valve. If operating efficiently the valve would deliver hordes of people with only the slightest effort on the part of the West. The fact that these people, almost by definition, would be poor was an object of only slight concern. Most of the boomers agreed with E. F. Test when he wrote, "locate the muscle here and it will *make money*."[24] All were welcome—almost.

There were people in the United States, possessing more muscle than most and less money than any, from whom this western hospitality was studiously withheld. These were the recently freed slaves. No one needed a safety valve more than they, yet no one found the avenues to the West more strewn with obstacles. Negro interest in emigration to the West began almost as soon as white rule was restored in the southern states. Benjamin Singleton, destined to be the prime mover in the Negro migration to Kansas, first wrote to Governor Thomas Osborne in 1876 asking for information on Kansas relative to colored immigration. There is no record of Osborne's reply, although it must not have been too discouraging. Within three years Singleton had succeeded in moving about seventeen thousand Negroes out of Tennessee, Texas, and Mississippi.[25]

The former slaves were understandably excited about coming to the land of Old John Brown; unfortunately, by the time they arrived the land was not excited about receiving them. There may never have been any great enthusiasm in the West for the coming of the Negro, but between 1876 and 1879 an attitude of toleration had become one of open hostility.[26] Albion Tourgee, carpetbag governor of North Carolina and later novelist of the Negro's condition during and after Reconstruction, was given a sample of this new western attitude in 1877 when he wrote to Governor George Anthony of Kansas inquiring about settlement possibilities for Negroes. Tourgee asked very little. The blacks of North Carolina desired simply "to go where they can find free schools and *be* free men."[27] Anthony's reply, sent through his

24 Test to Garber, September 18, 1877, ibid.

25. Singleton to Osborne, August 7, 1876, Osborne Papers, KSHS; Dick, *Sod House Frontier*, p. 196.

26. Everett Dick, in *Sod House Frontier*, p. 197, expresses the view that the Negroes were well received in Kansas.

27. Tourgee to Anthony, January 8, 1877, Anthony Papers, KSHS.

secretary, Benjamin Gray, was hardly enthusiastic. Usually letters of inquiry of this sort were answered with packets of promotional information, and Kansas took a particular pride in her schools and the independence of her citizens. Tourgee was sent a copy of the Centennial Report of the Kansas State Board of Agriculture. [28]

In spite of this rebuff (which was undoubtedly repeated in other Plains states), the Negroes continued to march into Kansas. By 1879 the movement had become a vast exodus and Kansas was becoming restive.[29] In part at least, the Kansans had only some of their own overzealous "promoters" to blame for the Negro migration. Scores of agents, allegedly representing Kansas, traveled the Negro areas of the South. These "agents" offered the prospective black immigrant the frequently promised forty acres and a mule as his reward for joining the parade to Kansas. It was an effective technique and not entirely out of character with promotional efforts in general. In this instance, however, it prompted a spirited response by Governor John St. John. The Governor denied that these agents represented anyone but themselves, and he deplored the fact that men would so misrepresent conditions in his state.[30] Needless to say, this issue had not troubled him particularly before. Misrepresentation of conditions in Kansas was accepted as a necessary requirement of effective promotion, and the Governor had acceded fully with this view.

A possible explanation for St. John's change of heart can be found in a letter he received from S. J. Gilmore, land commissioner for the Kansas Pacific Railroad. Gilmore had been "led to believe that the negro immigration has been an injury to us and the indications are that we will be over run with them next year." The injury, of course, was to the promotional campaign waged jointly by the Kansas Pacific and the State Board of Agriculture. The presence of the Negroes was proving particularly embarrassing to the railroad's agents in the Midwest, and Gilmore was convinced that white immigration to Kansas

28. Benjamin Gray to Tourgee, January 15, 1877, Governors' Letter Press Books, Anthony, KSHS.

29. See John Van Deusen, "The Exodus of 1879," *Journal of Negro History* 21 (April 1936): 111–29, and U.S., Congress, Senate, *Report and Testimony of the Select Committee to Investigate the Causes of the Removal of the Negroes from the Southern States*, 46th Cong., 2d sess., 1881–82, S. Rept. 693.

30. St. John to Cain Sartain, April 7, 1879, Governors' Letter Press Books, St. John, KSHS.

would suffer a serious setback if former slaves continued to be admitted to the state.[31]

A little over a month after the receipt of this letter, St. John indicated that he was willing to pursue a policy agreeable to the Kansas Pacific. As he suggested to F. A. Simmons, the leader of a group of Georgia Negroes, "you, as a leader among your people, should discourage any from coming here who have not the means to take care of themselves."[32] This warning in itself was not totally without precedent although it is unusual to find it in a governor's correspondence. The more common procedure in these instances was to encourage all to come, rich or poor, in the belief that prosperity would result as a matter of course. But St. John, in taking a pessimistic line, was simply echoing a similar warning given to all Negro applicants by Gilmore.

As land commissioner, Gilmore was the chief promotional officer of the Kansas Pacific, and hence was not a stranger to the use of hyperbole and misrepresentation. In his dealings with Negroes, however, Gilmore was considerably less effusive than usual. As he stated to all Negro applicants in a form letter, "We cannot advise persons to come to Kansas who have no money. There are more farm hands and ordinary laborers in the State now than can find employment. A large part of the farm work is done by machinery." Even this pronouncement, gloomy as it must have appeared to a southern freedman, was not considered discouragement enough. A few blacks might still accept the challenge, so Gilmore told them that "all the government land that is of any value has been taken, except in the Western one-fourth of the state," Of course, the Negro should also know that "there is no wood in Western Kansas except a few small trees along the banks of some creeks and this is owned by the early settlers." Lest some get the idea that those who controlled this timber supply were potential employers, Gilmore hastened to add that the settlers in western Kansas were "of very limited means . . . and they are unable to pay to have their work done, but must do it themselves." This closed off the possibility of farm labor and left the Negro back where St. John had left him, needing the means to take care of himself, at least until he had harvested his first crop. There was a strong possibility that there would be no first crop, given the lack of rainfall, trees, and good land in western Kansas, but

31. S. J. Gilmore to St. John, December 19, 1879, St. John Papers, KSHS.
32. St. John to Simmons, January 27, 1880, Governors' Letter Press Books, St. John, KSHS.

for those who might still wish to come, Gilmore was ready with an estimate concerning the minimum amount of money they should bring with them. The figure was $500 per family. He may as well have said $5,000.[33]

In 1879, about the time Gilmore was composing his form letter, A. C. Banks, a Negro from Georgia, wrote to Governor Albinus Nance of Nebraska, wanting to know "what privileges [the governor] could afford them as labors [*sic*] of America," He asked only for "one word of encouragement." There is no record of a reply.[34]

Thus did the Negro learn that the safety valve emitted whites only.[35] The discovery was made, however, only after they had moved in considerable numbers to the plains of Kansas. There were perhaps seventeen thousand blacks in the state by 1879 when St. John and Gilmore began their campaign of discouraging further entries. The principal Negro community was Nicodemus, located in Graham County in the northwestern part of the state. During their stay there the Negroes of Nicodemus supplied a touch of pathos and irony which serves as a fitting footnote to the great migration of '79. In 1886 the town newspaper, dubbed appropriately enough the *Western Cyclone*, attempted to refute those in eastern Kansas who continued to view the western part of the state as an uninhabitable desert. The editor of the *Cyclone* attributed this prejudice to the eastern Kansans' "inclination to cheat the poor man out of all but a bare and scanty existence." This explained the prejudice but it did not correct it, and so he continued with a description of the productive capacity of Graham County. "It may be set down as a verity," he wrote, "that industrious and intelligent farmers can produce as abundant crops of wheat, corn, oats, sorghum, broom corn, potatoes and vegetables . . . in this latitude, as in any other county in this wonderful state. Graham county is well adapted to . . . agriculture, . . . being well watered and a rich soil."[36] S. J. Gilmore could hardly have said it better—or more inaccurately.

Despite the unfavorable reception accorded the Negro poor, the notion that emigration was the surest method of relieving economic

33. Form letter sent by S. J. Gilmore to all inquiries by Negroes, 1879, copy in St. John Papers, KSHS.

34. Banks to Nance, October 16, 1879, Nance Papers, NSHS.

35. In 1877 a group of 200 Negroes, members of the North Carolina Freedmen's Emigration Aid Society, petitioned the Congress for a loan to allow them to settle in Liberia. No action was taken by the Congress (U.S., Congress, House, *Congressional Record*, 45th Cong., 1st sess., 1877), 6: 164.

36. *Western Cyclone*, May 13, 1886.

pressure in the East remained a persuasive one. And nowhere was it more popular than in the Plains states. Economic dislocation in the industrial centers seemed to promise an immediate increase in settlement, and the plainsmen looked on with undisguised delight as philanthropists and colonizers began to recruit new settlers from among the ranks of the unemployed. There was nothing callous or cynical in the western attempt to benefit from the distress in the East. This had been, in fact, a shared experience, each successive frontier benefiting in turn from depressions in the East, or so the theory went. Now it was the Plains' turn, and the people of that region were determined to make the most of the opportunities presented them by the panic and depression of 1873. Whatever aid they might receive from eastern emigration societies was, of course, sincerely appreciated. The plainsmen had no way of knowing how many people took advantage of the offers of these societies, but this in itself was not the only consideration. Eastern involvement in emigration, whether effective or not, was good publicity. It undoubtedly impressed upon people the advantage of western emigration, and the plainsmen were grateful not only because it might mean more settlement but because it implied an eastern acceptance of the basic principles of the boomers' frontier.

This acceptance, moreover, was not limited to private promotional agencies. The federal government also considered the possibility of implementing the safety valve. President Rutherford B. Hayes had given executive endorsement to the idea in 1878 when he stated that "it [was] a good policy, especially in times of depression and uncertainty in other business pursuits, with a vast area of uncultivated and hence unproductive, territory, wisely opened to homestead settlement, to encourage by every proper and legitimate means the occupation and tillage of the soil." [37]

Some congressmen, anticipating Hayes's remarks, had considered proper and legitimate encouragement to include grants of financial aid to those wishing to exercise their rights under the Homestead Act. In the period from 1877 to 1879 three bills were introduced, all by representatives of industrial centers, providing for some type of financial assistance to aid industrial workers in their escape to the West. Each was intended to relieve the pressure on the overburdened East.None of the proposals was given very serious consideration by the Congress; they were viewed, variously, as fiscally irresponsible, unconstitutional,

37. Second Annual Message, December 2, 1878, in *Messages and Papers of the Presidents*, ed. by Richardson, 6: 4457–58.

or discriminatory against the industrial sectors.[38] They were, perhaps, all that and more, but they were as well an expression of considerable unhappiness with the way the present system of land disposal was functioning.

This system, once thought the glory of the Union, had become unresponsive to the demands of the laboring class. The safety valve, long considered an automatic consequence of America's having a frontier, was effectively closed to those who most needed it. In a petition to Congress, more than twenty thousand Pennsylvania working men gave further expression to these beliefs. They first assured Congress of their readiness to work, a necessary gesture under the circumstances, and then they listed their grievances. Work was unavailable, personal savings were exhausted, "and hundreds and thousands of us are in a state of absolute want." Furthermore, they could see little prospect of an immediate change for the better. "The future is shrouded in gloom." Fortunately, it was not entirely shrouded. The Congress had already proven its generosity in land grants, mortgages, and construction loans to the railroads; surely it would not now ignore the "prayers of the laboring man for assistance in the dark hour of his necessity and pressing want."[39]

Armed with this petition, Congressman Hendrick Wright of Pennsylvania attempted to secure that assistance. His proposal called for a $500 loan, backed by a new greenback issue, to every family who wished to emigrate west. Wright was convinced that this legislation was necessary to the maintenance of economic harmony between management and labor. As he reminded his colleagues in the House Committee on Public Lands, there were over two million unemployed in the United States and many in that number were becoming increasingly restive. He for one was pleasantly surprised by the restraint they had displayed thus far, but he was not willing to commit himself on how much longer this restraint would last. The implication was obvious and ominous; if the Congress wished to prevent social revolution it had better find a way to encourage the unemployed to "settle down on God's great farm."[40]

38. For specific provisions of the bills, see Albert V. House, Jr., "Proposals of Government Aid to Agricultural Settlement during the Depression of 1873–1879," *Agricultural History* 12 (Jan. 1938): 47–50, 53–66.

39. U.S., Congress, House, *Congressional Record*, 45th Cong., 1st sess., 1877, 6: 164–65.

40. House, *Congressional Record*, 45th Cong., 2d sess., 1879, 8: 769.

Senator Ben Butler of Massachusetts introduced a similar proposal, though without Wright's ill-disguised threats. But the claims he made in behalf of the bill were no less promising. The purpose of the legislation was nothing less than the promotion of "the general interests and industries of the whole people." It would provide for the permanent welfare of the laboring class in all parts of the Union by affording them an opportunity to settle in the West "instead of remaining, as they now are, competitors for employment that cannot be furnished."[41]

None of the bills was given a favorable reception. Senator Thomas Ewing of Ohio, for example, in commenting on Wright's bill, remarked that most of the unemployed in the East were unsuited by training and disposition to be farmers. What was needed for recovery was not more farmers but monetary inflation.[42] A writer for the *Nation* was somewhat more flippant in dismissing the proposed bill. "The House," he said, "has good-naturedly extinguished the bill of Mr. Wright, the Pennsylvania Communist."[43]

Before it was "extinguished," the Wright bill occasioned considerable comment from some of the witnesses called to testify before a select House committee on the causes of the depression. The committee was chaired by Abram Hewitt of New York, son-in-law of Peter Cooper and a sympathetic spokesman for labor. As Hewitt explained it, one of the difficulties presented to the committee was that deserving families were being denied entrance to the West because of the cost of emigration. Hence they were forced to live out their lives in wretchedness and despair. Hewitt and many of those who testified at the hearings hoped that the government would do something to correct this condition.[44]

Among those who endorsed the notion of government aid for agricultural settlement were greenbackers, labor leaders, a representative

41. House, *Congressional Record*, 45th Cong., 2d sess., 1879, 7: 4380–81. The third bill was proposed by General N. P. Banks of Massachusetts in October, 1877. It was similar to the Wright and Butler bills in most details. See House, "Proposals of Government Aid," pp. 47–78.

42. U.S., Congress, Senate, *Congressional Record*, 45th Cong., 3d sess., 1879, 8, Appendix: 175.

43. *Nation* 28 (January 30, 1879): 75. Wright did have a long record of sympathy with greenback and labor causes. See House, "Proposals for Government Aid," p. 48.

44. U.S., Congress, House, Committee on Labor, *Investigation Relative to the Causes of the General Depression in Labor and Business*, 45th Cong., 3d sess., 1878–79. H. Misc. Doc. 29, p. 212.

of the Congress of Humanity, and a number of private citizens interested in airing their personal grievances. Their comments followed the established pattern. James Connally of the National Labor Greenback Party promised that if the Congress would "send our people off to the West, and secure them for a year, as it did the railroads, it could thereby relieve distressed cities." George Maddox of the Congress of Humanity looked forward to a diminution in crime as people were able to leave the vice-infested cities for the simple pleasures of a farm on the Plains. Neither of these comments pertained to the Wright bill specifically; Connally and Maddox simply wanted some form of relief. Patrick Logan, however, was more precise. The Wright bill seemed to him one of the most statesmanlike proposals to have been made in years, and it came at a time when statesmanship was in great demand. "Now, you have a homestead law to-day," he explained, "but what use is it? Hundreds in this city might as well say there was a splendid country on the moon. We can't go there, we can't get any place where the government land is, without having means to go there." Means meant $500 in cash and 100 acres of land. Another piece of interesting testimony came from one Jeremiah Thomas, an unemployed Negro from New York. Thomas's needs were simple—he wanted to have a farm, "live with a full stomach, and be as free as anybody else." He discovered, however, that he was unlikely to have any of these blessings unless the government supplied the requisite aid. If it did, Thomas was sure that a great many of his race would take advantage of the opportunity. In any event, that was "what he asked, and no more."[45]

It was all any of them asked, but the government answered with silence. Perhaps that was appropriate; many of the schemes, particularly Wright's, were vulnerable to considerable abuse, a fact noted by many critics of the bills. But this was not the only cause of opposition. Charles Francis Adams, Jr., who had a personal interest in transportation, felt that the railroads were already doing as much as could legitimately be done to move people to the western Plains. Alfred Atkinson, amateur economist and seer, insisted that the redistribution of population which these bills were expected to effect was already being accomplished by the railroads. What excess labor still existed would soon be redistributed intelligently and naturally. Carroll Wright, chief of the Bureau of Statistics for Massachusetts, was not as certain of this as Atkinson, but he was sure that the forced depopulation of one

45. Ibid., pp. 47, 61–62, 75–76, 145.

region to benefit another was not the correct path to lasting prosperity. In addition, he doubted that many of the unemployed in the East would be able to make the hard adjustments to agricultural life. "Some men," he believed, "must have their society. They are ill equipped to meet the isolation of life in the West." He cited the Negroes as an example, and in the process consigned them to a permanent place in the cities. "The colored man likes society; his society to him is important." That in itself would not necessarily disqualify him as a potential farmer, but more than just his social instincts were involved. It hardly needed saying, but Wright was moved to make one final remark. "A water-melon on the sunny side of the house is worth more to [the Negro] than any labor remuneration for his family." So ended the notion of forty acres and a mule.[46]

These objections to government-financed immigration did not imply a rejection of the theory of the safety valve, or a denial that removal to the West would benefit the unemployed. Wright commented favorably, for example, on the earlier use of indentures as a means of stimulating immigration, but he insisted throughout his testimony that any such scheme must be financed through private and not public agencies.

Joining him in this belief was one of the principal champions of the negative state, William Graham Sumner. In his remarks to the House committee, Sumner expressed no serious objection to private colonization, although he was not fully convinced of its usefulness. There might be a few so impoverished as to need this assistance, but for the most part, the problem was resolving itself quite naturally. Prompted by "common sense and right reason," he stated, the population has been redistributing itself ever since the hard times began. Obviously, however, everyone was not blessed with the same amount of common sense and right reason. There was an unemployment problem in the East, but that was hardly sufficient cause for the federal government to involve itself in affairs beyond its legitimate purview. Besides, Sumner did not think that American citizens needed or desired that kind of governmental aid. They were more than capable of effecting their own salvation by simply finding "some way to make their labor more productive or . . . getting out on new land."[47] Nor was this

46. See ibid., pp. 209, 435, 200, 201.

47. Ibid., p. 188. Sumner did mention that this would involve a difficult period of adjustment. All easterners were not prepared for the sacrifices necessary to life in the West. See ibid., p. 183, and "Sociology," in *War and Other Essays*, ed. by Albert Galloway Keller (New Haven: Yale University Press, 1911), p. 175, and "The Boon

an impossible dream. "We know," Sumner continued, "that there are only twelve persons to the square mile in a country which is rich and fertile and abundant in all the natural sources and things that men want to enjoy." The people knew it, too, and by following their "natural impulse" they could secure their own redemption.[48] In Sumner's mind, then, the safety valve was still working with all its old efficiency; there was no reason to interfere with its beneficent operation.

As better times were restored, interest in an enforced safety valve understandably waned. Few could be concerned with a problem which, from all indications, had resolved itself. Among those who were concerned, however, the question of how a poor man in the East was to finance a trip to the West remained a pressing one, particularly as labor became increasingly more militant in the late 1870s and 1880s. In 1883, a Senate committee met to look into the relations between labor and management. The committee discovered, not surprisingly, that they were not as healthy as they might have been. It also discovered that one of the causes of discontent was the workingman's inability to take advantage of the safety valve. Thomas O'Donnell, a mule spinner in the textile factories of Fall River, Massachusetts, was one of the witnesses who addressed the committee. It was established that he made about $150 a year and that with this sum he was expected to support his family of five. O'Donnell was understandably concerned about how he was to meet his responsibility, but the committee had a solution, as the following dialogue shows:

"Why do you not go West on a farm?"
"How could I go, walk it?"
"Well, I want to know why you do not go out West on a $2,000 farm, or take up a homestead and break it and work it up, and then have it for yourself and family?"
"I can't see how I could get out West. I have got nothing to go with."
"It would not cost you over $1,500."
"I never see over a $20 bill, and that is when I have been getting a month's pay at once. If someone would give me $1,500, I will go."[49]

As earlier experience had shown, no one was going to give him $1,500,

of Nature," in *Earth Hunger and Other Essays*, ed. by Albert Galloway Keller (New Haven: Yale University Press, 1913), p. 237.

48. *Causes of the General Depression*, pp. 188, 200.

49. U.S., Congress, Senate, *Report upon the Relations between Labor and Capital*, 48th Cong., 2d sess., 5 vols. (Washington, D.C.: GPO, 1885), 3: 453.

so the West lost another potential recruit and the East was burdened with another poverty-stricken family. That is not how the safety valve was expected to work.

An even more ominous warning was voiced during these same hearings by the land reformer, Henry George. George had written earlier in *Progress and Poverty* that escape to the West was becoming increasingly difficult because of corporate monopolization of the remaining land.[50] He had, of course, devised a remedy for this particular ill, but as he told the committee, corporate land ownership was not the only or even the most serious deterrent to successful implementation of the safety valve. First, he warned the senators that the extent of America's public domain was greatly exaggerated, but more important, the best part of it had been taken. What was left was "all deserts, all the mountain chains, all the poor land. . . . All through the western part of this continent water is scarce. . . . A great deal of that land . . . is not fitted by nature for agriculture." He then conjured up a frightening specter, one which most Americans had been wishing away for years. "There still exists," George stated, "'The Great American Desert,' although land-grant agents wipe it out of the maps."[51] Needless to say, this was not the type of testimony the committee members were anxious to hear. Like most Americans, they shrank from any reminders of desert sterility.

The deterrents to western immigration were considerable. It cost too much, the land was corporate owned, and most of it was unproductive. Yet in spite of these difficulties the westerners still clung to the belief that they were to be the chief beneficiaries of eastern discontent. And even more remarkably, many in the East continued to agree with them, continued to apologize for their wretched and vice-ridden cities and to proclaim the virtues of the rural life.[52] In New York the commissioner of emigration, charged with moving people out of the state, initiated an agreement with Kansas whereby his agency would distribute without charge all the promotional material Kansas could send him.[53]

---

50. Henry George, *Progress and Poverty: an Inquiry Into the Causes of Industrial Depressions and of Increase of Want with Increase of Wealth; The Remedy* (New York: Robert Schalkenback Foundation, 1942), p. 274.

51. *Report upon the Relations between Labor and Capital*, 1: 473.

52. See, for example, the *Address of the Honorable G. M. Lambertson at the Nebraska State Fair, Omaha, September 12, 1883* (Omaha: Herald Printing Co., 1883), p. 5.

53. H. J. Jackson to Gov. G. W. Glick, May 22, 1883, Glick Papers, KSHS.

Presumably a similar agreement was reached with the other Plains states. As late as 1889 the *New York Times* had a full-time correspondent who did nothing but tour the West and submit articles on immigration possibilities.[54] Appleton's *Encyclopedia* performed a similar function by advising its readers on the advantages of immigration and the best routes to follow to the various states.[55] Even Henry Norris Copp, whose *The American Settler's Guide* was usually a model of detached reporting, succumbed to the promotional fever. He assured all those in the Atlantic states who were discouraged with the "slow, tedious methods of reaching independence" that rich rewards awaited them on the public lands, assuming always that they possessed sufficient talent and energy.[56]

Few, of course, bothered to investigate the accuracy of their promises. They were little interested in the actual conditions on the Plains or whether the much-vaunted freehold farmer was really living the life of rural bliss assigned to him. Nor, obviously, did railroad and state promoters volunteer this information. Their literature was highly selective and emphasized the opportunities their region offered. Since these opportunities contrasted so vividly with the despair in the East, it was only natural that the West would hit hardest with its promotional appeals during times of distress in the older sections.

This was certainly true during the depression of 1873 and it continued during the boom of the 1880s and the depression of the '90s. Seldom, however, did the practice go as far as a notice in the *Irrigation Age* of December, 1897. The writer, not new to the game, urged western promoters to concentrate more of their attention on the South. Conditions in that region seemed to promise an abundant harvest of new immigrants—but only to those states and railroads willing to make the promotional effort to secure it. The condition he was referring to was an epidemic of yellow fever. It seemed the scourge was "turning many settlers our way."[57]

54. R. L. Lomax, U.P. Railroad, to Gov. Francis Warren, September 5, 1889, Warren Papers, WSHS.

55. Ernest Ingersol to Warren, October 28, 1889, ibid.

56. Henry Norris Copp, ed., *The American Settler's Guide* (Washington, D.C.: By the editor, 1880), p. 29.

57. *Irrigation Age* 12 (December 1897): 55–56.

CHAPTER FIVE

Implementing the Safety Valve: Promotion in Europe

The depression of 1873 and the subsequent attempts to relieve some of the suffering it caused gave ample evidence of the two sides of the safety valve theory. The East had been eager to be rid of its unproductive members; the West was just as eager to receive them. It was a very attractive arrangement and one which seemed to bode well for the future prosperity of both sections. It contained, of course, the standard inference that conditions on the frontier were significantly better than those in the older sections, but this contrast had been a part of the safety valve theory from the very beginning. When the theory was applied to Europe, however, the contrast became even more vivid, or so the promoters believed. The differences between East and West had never been as great as those between Europe and the United States, hence any promotion in the Old World carried with it the implication of escape. If nothing else, Europeans were expected to be overwhelmed by the sheer munificence of the Homestead Act. How could conditions not be better in a land where 160 acres was a gift of the government?

But it was not just free land which drew the Europeans. A House report on the causes of immigration to the United States set forth in considerable detail the circumstances which prompted them to leave. The report mentioned the "superior conditions of living," higher wages, fewer hours of labor, exemption from military duty, freedom from burdensome taxation, and most important, freedom from "regulations involving freedom of movement and personal liberty, together with the general belief that the United States presents better opportunities for rising to a higher level than are furnished at home."[1] It caused no

1. U.S., Congress, House, Commissioners of Immigration, *Report upon the Causes Which Incite Immigration to the United States*, 52d Cong., 1st sess., 1891,

surprise when one member of the investigatory commission noted that nine-tenths of the emigrants from Europe to the United States were drawn from country districts where employment opportunities were few, and where the poor "have not and can not expect to acquire at or near their old homes, real estate for themselves or their children."[2]

The United States, particularly during the Civil War when the North was suffering from a labor shortage, did nothing to discourage the notion that America was the land of plenty. The Republican party made the encouragement of immigration a part of its platform in the elections of 1860 and 1864, but even more revealing was the attitude of Secretary of State William Seward. In 1862 Seward wrote to consular and diplomatic officers and reminded them that "nowhere else can the industrious laboring man and artisan expect so liberal a recompense for his services as in the United States." The secretary hoped that the diplomats would "make these truths known in any quarter and in any way which may lead to the migration of such persons to this country." Seward hastened to add that his department could not offer financial assistance to those who decided to leave for the United States; the government's commitment to the encouragement of immigration did not extend that far. But then, too, the Homestead Act was at least as valuable an inducement as money could have been. It conferred on the immigrant the immediate status of freeholder, something he could hardly even aspire to in the Old World.[3] The federal government, therefore, felt under no obligation to do more.[4]

The diplomats responded handsomely to Seward's request that they assist in his promotional campaign. Many of them published the secretary's dispatches on immigration and the progress of the war effort in the North. Others delivered speeches and conferred regularly with officials of steamship companies and other parties interested in immigration.[5] The results of all this activity were encouraging. By the

---

pt. 1: 120. See also the report of Commissioner Joseph Powderly in which he dwells on the land question, ibid., p. 246.

2. Report of Commissioner Judson Cross, ibid., pt. 1: 235.

3. See Copp, ed., *The American Settlers' Guide*, p. 29.

4. There were a few critics of this laissez-faire policy. See, for example, the comments of the soil scientist Eugene Hilgard in "Progress in Agriculture by Education and Government Aid," *Atlantic Monthly* 49 (April 1882): 531. See also the Circular from Seward to Diplomatic and Consular Officers, August 8, 1862, in *Papers Relating to the Foreign Relations of the United States, 1862* (Washington, D.C.: GPO, 1863), p. 172.

5. See, for example, James Harvey to Seward, April 4, 1863, in *Foreign Relations*

time the war ended thousands of Europeans were prepared to leave their homes and join the ranks of newly minted Americans. The image of America had never been more glowing. United at last, with slavery abolished, it seemed to offer a fresh start to all who would come.

And many thousands came. One commentator reported that men who had managed to acquire a little property, often after years of sacrifice, were "literally throwing it upon the market . . . in order to . . . reach the inviting plains beyond the Mississippi."[6] Beret Holm, the tragic heroine of Ole Rölvaag's novel *Giants in the Earth*, sensed this same urge as she brooded:

> Men beheld in feverish dreams the endless plains, teeming with fruitfulness, glowing, . . . a Beulah Land of corn and wine! . . . People drifted about in a sort of delirium, like sea birds in mating time; then they flew toward the sunset, in small flocks and large—always toward Sunset Land. . . . Here on the trackless plains, the thousand-year-old hunger of the poor after human happiness had been unloosed![7]

That hunger, however, had been born in Europe. The Plains were expected to gratify it. The promoters reminded the poor of this hope and played upon it, but few European poor needed convincing. For many of them, escape to the United States had become the great desideratum of human fulfillment. Of course—and not just from a long tradition of self-congratulation—the Americans agreed. These new immigrants had a job to do. They were to take their place beside earlier pioneers who had stretched American institutions to the Pacific. They were to fill in the last empty spaces of the continent and help to erase forever from the maps the mocking inscription, Great American Desert. In the process they would be striking a blow not only for themselves, but also for American ideals as old as the Revolution. It seemed a heaven-made arrangement.

It was not, however, one which the western promoters were willing to leave to heaven for realization. Immigration was too important a

---

of the United States, 1863, pt. 2: 1203, and William Drayton to Seward, September 9, 1862, in *Foreign Relations of the United States, 1862*, p. 387. The American consul at Newcastle upon Tyne in England even published a promotional volume entitled *The Emigrant's Friend* (London, 1880) (Merle Curti and Kendall Birr, "The Immigrant and the American Image in Europe, 1860–1914," *Mississippi Valley Historical Review* 37 [September 1950]: 205).

6. Edward Self, "Why They Come," *North American Review* 134 (April 1882): 352.

7. Ole Rölvaag, *Giants in the Earth* (New York: Harper & Row, 1927), p. 220.

part of the development of their interests, and they set out to pursue the prospective immigrant, to track him down in his home if necessary, or on his farms and in his factories. Promotional agents were everywhere, delivering speeches and distributing handbills, all proclaiming the beauty and bounty of the Plains.

The agent's job was never a very difficult one, even when conditions in Europe were relatively good. The contrast afforded by the United States was still apparent enough. But the best promoters agreed that the time to advertise most forcefully was during periods of local or general unrest. This was a lesson they had learned from the Illinois Central Railroad, and the most minor local disturbance was enough to send hundreds of agents scurrying about the affected region to celebrate the opportunities of life on the Plains.[8]

Lewis F. Weise, the commissioner of immigration for Kansas, is a good example. In 1866 he wrote to Governor Crawford of the success he had enjoyed in the Tyrol region by exploiting the residents' understandable unhappiness with Austrian rule. He reminded the Tyrolians of the Homestead Act and of the unprecedented personal freedom they would enjoy in Kansas, and then, by his own admission, he allowed "immigration to take its natural course." Weise was convinced that this implied-comparison method would work equally well in the duchies of Schleswig and Holstein where Bismarck's expansionist policy in 1866 was disrupting old allegiances. Those two areas, he estimated, "would supply 10,000 persons with but a little prodding."[9] But these were not the only areas in and around Germany where the prospects for a large emigration were favorable. Weise consulted the statistical reports for most of Germany in order to determine which areas were economically depressed. These he considered the "most important tributaries of foreign immigration." After thanking Joseph A. Wright, America's minister plenipotentiary at the court of Prussia, for his assistance in this matter, Weise discussed these "tributaries":

> The Duchies of Schleswig and Holstein, Mecklenburg and Tyrol, are those sections which will make up the principal amount of immigration for Spring, 1867. Baden, Wurtenberg, and Bavaria, will also contribute their part, provided they are not combined with the leading northern power, Prussia, before Spring, 1867.

8. Gates, *The Illinois Central and Its Colonization Work*, p. 169.
9. Weise to Crawford, May 25, 1866, Crawford Papers, KSHS.

Incorporation into the Prussian-dominated North German Confederation was harmful to immigration prospects, for as Weise put it, "the internal affairs of [Prussia] have become more promising lately." This was an unwelcome development for a promoter. He worked more efficiently when the comparison between Old World and New could be more vividly drawn.[10]

Fortunately for the immigration interests of the West, Prussia's ambitions did not stop with the formation of the northern confederation. Bismarck's German policy required the political unification of all the states, which was realized in 1871 following the Franco-Prussian War. But, happily for the promoters, "internal order" was not the only consequence of this unification. Considerable tension was created by Bismarck's campaign, particularly in the former French provinces of Alsace and Lorraine. Officials of the Burlington Railroad recognized this fact in a promotional pamphlet of 1871. Directed primarily to the people of Alsace-Lorraine, they offered the usual inducements to immigration: the weather was kind, the crops good, the children happy. But they also promised that immigration to Nebraska offered a perfect "escape from the crushing heels of the German Empire's militarism." This must have struck a responsive note.[11]

Governor James Harvey of Kansas was another who saw in Bismarck's expansionism an opportunity to increase the population of the Plains. In November of 1870 Harvey was invited to attend an immigration convention, called to deal with the problems of the middle passage together with those encountered upon first landing.[12] The convention made clear that these problems were likely to become particularly pressing in the next few years. The Franco-Prussian War was expected to drive a number of Germans toward America, and provisions had to be made to ensure that they would not be misled or swindled. Harvey absorbed this message with detachment. He deferred to no man in his devotion to the immigrants' welfare, but what really concerned him was the reference to the Franco-Prussian War. Europe was once again ripe for promotion. In his annual message of January, 1871, he suggested that the state take immediate advantage of European distress by mounting a new and more aggressive promotional campaign. He also proposed the commission of a sort of watch-dog agency to keep the

10. Weise to Crawford, August 4, 1866, ibid.
11. Quoted in Overton, *Burlington West*, p. 366.
12. Lucius Fairchild, governor of Wisconsin, to Harvey, September 24, 1870, Harvey Papers, KSHS.

state promoters alert to changing conditions in Europe—especially if the changes were for the worse.[13]

Soon after Harvey offered his suggestions a book appeared entitled *Kansas: Her Resources and Development,* by Dr. Wayne Griswold. Whether Griswold was acting on Harvey's recommendations is unknown but certainly he displayed a similar attitude toward promotion. Millions of laboring men and women all over Europe, he wrote, "are struggling for a mere living, with little hope of bettering their condition." For those unfortunates, "emigration presented a certain guarantee for good, cheap homes for themselves and families, and that in a free country, where liberty rests upon constitutional law, giving to all equal rights." The contrast was thus clearly drawn.[14]

Another interested observer of the distress in Europe was E. F. Test. Considering his excitement during the depression of 1873 in the United States, this is no surprise. In another of the series of letters he wrote to Governor Silas Garber of Nebraska, Test outlined his plan. There was, he noted happily, "appalling distress" among the working-men and middle classes of Great Britain. Some of the more desperate of these classes were actually stealing their fares by stowing themselves in the holds of vessels bound for America. Germany, Test continued, was also suffering, though unfortunately, "in a less degree than Great Britain." If this were not enough, he had noticed that morning that "the distress is now spreading into Sweden." It was almost more than a promoter could absorb at one sitting, and Test was fairly panting by the time he got to the crux of his letter. "It seems to me *this is our golden opportunity* to build up a great State, and we may depend upon it, if the legislature does not put forth some organized movement to occupy the field other states will." If Nebraska should fail to act, the Swedish immigration would go to Minnesota, the German to Kansas. This was intolerable and Test had made up his mind that "*now* was the time to *work* and the state ought to *advertise* and have its *drummers* broadcast its opportunities" to the oppressed of Europe.[15]

The jobs of "drummers," or agents, must have been pleasant ones; certainly the Plains states never suffered from any paucity of applicants for such positions. But these agents, after all, were the advance troops

13. Annual Message of Gov. James M. Harvey, January 10, 1871, in *Messages of Kansas Governors*, 1: 15–17.

14. Wayne Griswold, *Kansas: Her Resources and Development* (Cincinnati: Robert Clark & Co., 1871), p. 85.

15. E. F. Test to Garber, December 19, 1878, Garber Papers, NSHS.

of any promotional campaign; they carried the message to the people, and few of them underestimated their value or their talents. One wrote to Governor Samuel Crawford of Kansas that "people [in Europe] are thinking of Kansas as the driest and poorest state in the Union;" an intolerable condition obviously, but one easily corrected. Just "give me the office," the letter continued, "and be sure a stream of Emigrants shall flow in to you[r] stat[e] next summer."[16] Similar promises were made by every applicant. The Reverend A. O. Sheldon assured Governor Silas Garber of Nebraska that he would "literally make known [the state's] claims to attention." In return for this favor Sheldon asked only for "contributions from patriotic friends and buyers and sellers."[17] John O'Neill was similarly confident that he could do the state a good turn by encouraging immigration from abroad.[18] Another petitioner, one S. Stamford Parry, added credence to his application by claiming to be an employee of Jay Gould. He was about to open an emigration department in Antwerp with the aim of directing the stream of emigration to Nebraska and neighboring states. A letter appointing him the official agent of the state would "make my job easier and more productive for you."[19] Of all the prospective agents, however, none was so candid or so revealing as John Williams, the "General Bureau Chief of the Emigration America Company of New York." Williams desired appointment as official emigration agent for Kansas, and as evidence of the devotion he would bring to his work, he made an extraordinary offer. "We can supply," he promised, "several thousand Swedes to be furnished *if ordered now*, during the ensuing summer." This type of service was unusual even in the business of promotion.[20]

In at least some instances, these agents seem not to have exaggerated their talents. It was reported that Cornelius Schaller, a Burlington agent in England, had managed in the short space of three weeks to secure a boatload of immigrants from Liverpool, all bound for Nebraska.[21] C. D. Nelson, Nebraska's agent in Denmark, Norway, and Sweden, wrote back that he had personally convinced ten thousand Scandinavian farmers to emigrate to Nebraska.[22] Colorado, meanwhile,

16. John P. Swensson to Crawford, February 6, 1865, Crawford Papers, KSHS.
17. A. O. Sheldon to Garber, March 9, 1875, Garber Papers, NSHS.
18. O'Neill to Garber, March 21, 1877, ibid.
19. Parry to "The Governor of Nebraska," July 15, 1892, Boyd Papers, NSHS.
20. John Williams to Samuel Crawford, March 14, 1865, Crawford Papers, KSHS.
21. In Overton, *Burlington West*, p. 363.
22. *Dakota City Mail*, September 1, 1871, WPA Writers' Project, NSHS.

had retained the services of Edward Reed of the United States Emigration and Banking agency in London. Reed was sent fifteen hundred copies of the pamphlets of the Territorial Board of Immigration for use as promotional ammunition in his new role as "agent of immigration." [23] Two years later it was noted with favor that Reed had done the territory great service in "forwarding emigrants." He had expended $3,000 in advertising and issued over ten thousand copies of promotional literature, and the results were more than enough to justify the time and labor. [24]

Reed, obviously, was a hard-working promoter, dedicated and thorough, but even he did not approach his assignment with quite the same fervor as an unidentified Nebraska agent in Scandinavia. In a letter to an Omaha newspaper this zealous campaigner rejoiced in his successes. He reported total "Victory! The battle is won for our state." But lest there be any misunderstanding, he added that it had been a "hard fought battle; a great deal harder than [he had] imagined." Fortunately his next assignment was somewhat easier. "I go to Sweden," he wrote, "and will have easy work there. I shall try my best to beat the agent for Minnesota." Should this prove unexpectedly difficult, he had one final weapon. "I may have to face them by threatening to lecture publicly about Nebraska—a step I hope will be unnecessary." [25]

Such self-effacement was not a common characteristic. Most of the agents delighted in lecturing and grasped every opportunity to deliver their well-rehearsed addresses on the glories of the Plains. Public speaking, however, was only one of their myriad talents. The agents were equally adept at evading the various European laws prohibiting promotional activity, a task that demanded a high degree of resourcefulness. The House report on the causes which incited immigration took special note of this activity. Commissioner H. J. Schulteis, a man vitally interested in immigration restriction, spent a frustrating year trailing agents as they went about their work of attracting even more Europeans to American shores. According to Schulteis, the agents circumvented the antipromotion laws by "procuring advertisements, posters, boom town circulars, railroad circulars, and books giving descriptions of all the States." Judson Cross, another member of the commission, commented similarly on the remarkable ease with which

23. George Clark to Reed, June 11, 1872, CTBI, CSHS.
24. Colorado Territorial Board of Immigration, *Report . . . 1874* (Denver, 1874), pp. 8–9.
25. *Nebraska Statesman* (Nebraska City), July 29, 1871.

railroad pamphlets and folders could be obtained; indeed, the railroad agents were the most active promoters in Europe. To the despair of the commission, they "scattered their handbills quite freely." [26]

According to the commission, these agents spoke often and well; they were, in addition, elusive and mobile. But even this did not exhaust their list of skills; they also displayed a striking talent for misrepresentation. Schulteis mentioned a promotional pamphlet which was "full of preposterous statements." Joseph Powderly reported that the railroad literature he saw was always "temptingly displayed. . . . The alkali beds of the West and Northwest, look as well on paper as if made up of the most fertile lands in the United States." This was obviously an injustice, not only to the Europeans, but to the Americans as well. Powderly, like all of the commissioners, favored some type of immigration restriction. His particular concern was the effect of unrestricted immigration on the labor market, and it was here that the misleading counsel of the promoters was most pernicious. As Powderly put it, "On reaching the United States and discovering the real nature of the swindle, there is but one thing left to the emigrant to do—turn to the already crowded manufacturing centers to look for employment." Schulteis mentioned yet another consequence of the promoters' "highly colored" reports. "We know," he wrote, "that Congress recently passed an appropriation to aid our own settlers in the Dakotas to procure seed wheat, because they were destitute." The logic was inescapable. If American settlers, supposedly inured to the hardships of the frontier, were in need of federal assistance, how could the European immigrant be expected to prosper, and more to the point, how long could the solvent American taxpayer be expected to support that immigrant in his futile struggle with the Plains? "Eight million farm mortgages," Schulteis continued, "cannot be explained in such a manner as to harmonize with these . . . railroad and land syndicate circulars." [27]

Though compiled in the 1890s, this report undoubtedly could have been written at any time during the promotional fever of the '70s and '80s. The commissioners displayed a definite anti-immigration bias, but that in no way detracts from the relevance of their remarks concerning the extent of the promotional effort in Europe. Indeed, they were probably in a better frame of mind to evaluate that effort than an earlier commission would have been. By the 1890s a number of people had come to doubt the ability of the United States in general and the

26. *Report upon the Causes Which Incite Immigration*, pt. 1: 283, 187, 14.
27. Ibid., p. 289, 248, 283.

Plains specifically to serve as a refuge for Europeans. The commission reflected that pessimistic mood. But no such doubts troubled the easy consciences of the earlier decades. The encouragement of immigration was then considered an essential element of American growth and the promoters were able to apply their talents with relative impunity. What difficulties they faced, and there were some, had more to do with the nature of their profession than with any interference by federal authorities.

Promotion in Germany is a good example. The boomers were in the business of selling, and as in any such enterprise, there were inevitable problems. First of all, they were attempting to sell an idea, a notoriously bad product and one that demands a certain amount of sales vigilance. Usually the product caused no embarrassment. The idea that the good life was available on the Plains was generally well received. Here, of course, it enjoyed a built-in sales appeal. The Edenic image, coincident with the discovery and settlement of the New World, had conditioned the Europeans to accept this notion. But occasionally the product would cause a promoter no little discomfort. The experience of C. B. Schmidt is a case in point. Schmidt was a foreign agent for the Santa Fe Railroad and a most persuasive spokesman for Kansas. He was instrumental in securing the majority of the Mennonites who came to America for the Jayhawk State and was considered to be especially effective when dealing with German peoples. Schmidt, like the other promoters, emphasized the freedom from restraint which emigration to the Plains would bring. So successful was he that the name of Kansas "soon became as familiar to the households of the German peasant as that of Canaan was to the Israelites in bondage." Almost sixty thousand Germans had made their homes along the line of the Santa Fe because of his good work. Only one thing was holding that number down—the state's insistence on retaining its prohibition laws. Many Germans were of the impression that such laws were necessary only in a state which "was populated chiefly by outlaws, gamblers, and drunkards." In addition, as a steamship company official reported to Schmidt, those laws were "an unbearable encroachment on personal liberty," particularly for the beer-loving Germans, and totally out of character with the image of Kansas as "a new found Eden." Schmidt could only nod in solemn agreement and await, in vain as it developed, a liberalization of the laws.[28]

28. Schmidt's lament appears in the *Daily Commonwealth* (Topeka), July 23, 1881. The German-American Volks Verein was in full agreement. They told Gov.

A second problem confronting the promoters in Germany was the language of advertising. Though temptingly displayed and containing promises of great rewards, the promotional literature had also to make its message intelligible to the German reader. Communication was no very great difficulty for the agents, most of whom were German-speaking; but those agents were also required to distribute pamphlets and newspapers from the United States, most of which were written with a dictionary in one hand and a German grammar in the other. The German-American Volks Verein of Kansas, an emigration club in Hamburg, brought this use of incorrect German to the attention of Governor G. W. Glick of Kansas. Usually the errors in word choice or grammar were harmless, but occasionally a mistake was made which destroyed the effectiveness of an entire article. The club noted particularly the use of the word *haide* in an article of the *Topeka Telegraph*. The *Telegraph*, by using the word to describe the plains of central Kansas, had undoubtedly intended to conjure up images of a soft, rolling heath. But *haide*, as the Volks Verein pointed out, was used in Germany to describe a marshy gorse, a thicket-filled region of negligible fertility. It represented "to every German peasant a horror beyond description." [29]

This, however, was not the only communication obstacle confronted by the promoters. Fred Hedde, an agent for Nebraska in addition to his work for the Union Pacific, complained that the only newspapers that would agree to publish his advertising were directed more to the intellectual class and were seldom seen by the laboring men. It was, of course, the latter group which Hedde had hoped to convert. Even more serious was the inability of the Nebraska promotional pamphlets to make comprehensible the one central fact about settling the Plains. "The German," Hedde implored, "*must* be made to understand that the land is *free!*" [30] Such a gift was so alien to them that considerable emphasis had to be placed on the precise terms of the Homestead Act. Robert Schaller, another of Nebraska's overseas agents, was faced with the same problem. "It was with difficulty," he wrote from Germany in 1871, "that I could get them to believe that they could get 160 acres of land FREE in Nebraska." [31]

G. W. Glick that prohibition was unquestionably the principal deterrent to German immigration (L. Rohr to Glick, July 23, 1883, Glick Papers, KSHS).

29. L. Rohr to G. W. Glick, July 23, 1883, Glick Papers, KSHS.

30. *Omaha Republican*, February 4, 1873.

31. *West Point Republican*, May 12, 1871, WPA Writers' Project, NSHS. Most of the promotional literature had a copy of the Homestead Act appended.

Once this point was firmly established, and once the language and communication barriers were broken, the western promoters were able to proceed with their customary lack of caution. In fact they discovered that if words like *haide* might prejudice their case, others equally incorrect in certain contexts might just as likely aid it. They also discovered that though the idea of free land was alien and incomprehensible and needed constant emphasis, there were other promises that were far more relevant to German conditions than American. Both lessons were used extensively and to good effect.

In 1883 the Northern Pacific Railroad published a descriptive booklet advertising its lands in North Dakota. It contained the usual promotional information, including a drawing of a panoramic view of the Dakota countryside. The picture showed hard-working farmers laboring in a land of obviously great abundance. The house and out-buildings were immaculate and commodious, the fields well tilled and bursting with grains. A river, lined with trees, wound its way languorously through the length of the farm. It was all very pastoral, rounded and soft in appearance. The promoters of the Northern Pacific identified this idyllic spot as *"Ein Gut* in Dakota." They did not call it *ein Heimstaette*, literally, a homestead; nor did they call it *ein Hof*, the more familiar German translation for farm. Instead they chose to use *Gut*, which inspired in every German peasant illusions of aristocratic grandeur. *Ein Gut* is presided over by *ein Gutsherr*, naturally. He might well be a Junker, but at the very least he is a "gentleman farmer, lord of the manor, or landed proprietor." He is not a yeoman, certainly he is not a peasant; nor, it might be added, would he ever be a Dakota farmer, unless he could bring his aristocratic, manorial trappings with him.[32]

None of the states or railroads of the central Great Plains seem to have displayed such ingenuity, but they were almost as reckless in some of the literature they directed toward the Germans. Nebraska, for example, issued a pamphlet in 1871 in which it claimed that the state had none of that "new, half-developed American appearance about it." Instead the German immigrant would find a country remarkably like his own, or at least that part of it where the inhabitants had "been swept away by the war."[33] The reference to the war was neither acci-

32. *Die Nord Pacific Eisenbahn, der Staat Dakota, Mittheilungen fuer Landbauer und Alle, die ein eigenes Heim suchen* (New York: Love & Alden, 1883), p. 14.

33. "Diese Gegend hat wenig von dem neuen halb entwickelten Amerikanischen Aussehen an sich: sondern man denkt sich unwillkuerlich in irgend eine Landschaft

dental nor pointless. Nebraska, it was claimed, was relatively uninhabited, yet so great was its natural bounty that it possessed many of the developments which were usually considered products of a large population. Germany was in a similar state owing to the war. The land was developed but many of those responsible for this, including, it was fervently hoped, those to whom this message was directed, had been forced away. Now these emigrants had an opportunity to find a new home without having to endure the rigors of pioneering. Little wonder, then, that in Nebraska a "person begins to feel his full worth as a free man, his chest is expanded just like the great prairies around him and his soul soars up in a feeling of . . . worship of the Creator of such magnificent country."[34]

The Burlington Railroad confirmed the basic argument of this appeal in a pamphlet published in 1880. The Burlington added, however, a note of class consciousness which the earlier appeal had only implied. Until recently, the road confessed, only the poorer classes of people had moved into Nebraska. This was to be expected, given the frontier conditions then prevailing. Fortunately all that had changed. The affluent well-bred German need no longer fear association with lower types, even of his own people, since by 1880 only "the best and most solid class of immigrants" were being admitted. Nebraska could by then afford the luxury of receiving and rejecting immigrants, according to the dictates of reason and good taste.[35] Needless to say, such an argument was not usually addressed to the Americans. They were told that civilization had preceded them on the Plains but never that a well-structured class system was evolving. That was a feature of German society and hence was reserved for a German audience.

The emphasis here given to promotions in Germany, though admittedly disproportionate, is not misplaced. The conventional wisdom held

---

in Europa versetzt, von welcher der Krieg die Einwohner weggesegt hat" (Nebraska Bureau of Immigration, *Eine Wortheile und Huelfsquellen; oder, Wohin soll Man auswandern und warum?* [Lincoln, 1871], p. 5).

34. "Hier fuehlt der Mensch in der That seine volle Wuerde als ein Freier Mann, seine Brust dehnt sich aus wie die grossen Prairien um ihn und seine Seele erhebt sich im Gefuehle der Dankbarkeit und Anbetung zu dem Schoepfer eines so herrlichen Landes" (ibid., p. 4).

35. "Mit der besten und solidesten Klasse von Einwanderen" (Burlington Railroad, *Länd in Nebraska, 600,000 Aker, des besten Landes . . . in Nebraska* [Lincoln, 1880]).This same pamphlet referred to the remarkably low number of policemen in the state. Law and order were so well entrenched that there was little need for enforcement officers.

that certain European nationalities were better adapted to agriculture than others, either through training, disposition, or racial characteristics. The English were included among this select group; so too were the Welsh, Scots, and Scandinavians. But of all the Europeans the Germans were unanimously adjudged the finest farming people anywhere. The state or railroad able to coax a German family to its borders was considered fortunate indeed. Most of the other Europeans suffered by comparison, though some were poor agriculturists by any standards. W. C. Harris of the Burlington admitted in 1870 that he had such "a poor opinion of the French and Italian immigrants for agriculturists that [he did] not issue any circulars in their languages." Instead he confined his European promotional campaign to Germans, Scandinavians, English, Welsh, and Scots, "as they make good farmers."[36] N. B. Falconer, a Nebraska agent, was similarly disposed. "I have done what little I could," he reported, "to advance the honor and interests of Nebraska, but the French are not a colonizing people and little can be done with them to advance our material interest." Like Harris, Falconer left France to concentrate his promotional energies on more productive areas. Scotland seemed promising in this regard and he informed Garber of his intention to "induce the capital and population [of that country] to settle with us." He then paid his respects to the safety valve theory, adding that he hoped to "do both them and ourselves good."[37]

The verdict that the French were ill-suited to agriculture was not universally accepted. A Nebraska promotional pamphlet called them "fiery Frenchmen" and invited them to join the "hardy Swedes, economical Canadians, and industrious Germans" in conquering the Nebraska plains.[38] At least three French families may have been influenced by this attitude. In 1882, Governor Albinus Nance received a letter inquiring about the possibility of establishing a French colony.[39] Likewise, the Santa Fe Railroad had no objection to the French. In an undated pamphlet, reissued many times, the road described in glowing French the incredible beauties of Kansas.[40]

Generally, however, the belief persisted that men of certain nationali-

36. Quoted in Overton, *Burlington West*, p. 303.
37. N. B. Falconer to Garber, June 24, 1878, Garber Papers, NSHS.
38. J. H. Noteware, *The State of Nebraska* (Lincoln, 1873), p. 10.
39. U. Douot to Nance, May 20, 1882, Nance Papers, NSHS.
40. Santa Fe, *Le Kansas . . . sa situation, ses ressources et ses produits: Le chemin de fer d'Atchison, Topeka, et Santa Fe* (Topeka, n.d.).

ties made better farmers than others, and quite naturally the boomers saved their most vigorous promotion for a select group. Nowhere is this better shown than in the promotional campaign launched by the western states to secure the immigration of the Russian Mennonites—in spite of the fact that the Mennonites made some rather stiff demands as conditions of that immigration. They wanted the right to live in closed communities with their own local government, plus the right to use the German language in all matters, public and private. In addition, they insisted upon complete religious freedom, exemption from all military service, and land of good quality at a moderate price and on easy terms. They also reminded the Plains states that Canada had offered to pay all transportation costs, and although this was not an essential condition, it would be greatly appreciated.[41] (Usually immigrants were less demanding. The Homestead bill to most of them was an act of such overwhelming generosity that little else was needed to secure both their gratitude and their allegiance.) The promoters, however, were undeterred by the Mennonite demands. They were dealing with a remarkable people. President Grant, in his annual message of 1873, called them "a superior class, . . . industrious, intelligent, and wealthy."[42] Needless to say, presidents did not commonly refer to specific groups of immigrants in their State of the Union messages, but then it was not often that this caliber of people evinced a desire to immigrate. Eugene Schuyler, a United States diplomatic official in Saint Petersburg, was even more effusive than Grant. The Mennonites were, in his mind, "intelligent, industrious, and persevering, in addition they [were] very clean, orderly, moral, temperate, and economical." They were also "extremely religious," but considering their other virtues they could easily be forgiven an occasional excess.[43]

But the Mennonites had even more to commend them than purity of mind and heart. They had over the years proven themselves capable of growing grains on "steppes that were formerly perfectly bare."[44] It was this recommendation that excited the interest of the promoters, for much as they might hate to admit it, that was a fair description of the

41. Charles H. Smith, *The Coming of the Russian Mennonites* (Berne, Ind.: Mennonite Book Concern, 1927), p. 58.

42. U.S. Grant, Fifth Annual Message, December 1, 1873, in *Messages and Papers of the Presidents*, ed. by Richardson, 6: 4207.

43. Eugene Schuyler to Hamilton Fish, March 30, 1872, in *Foreign Relations of the United States, 1872*, p. 487.

44. Ibid.

Plains. If the Mennonites could grow things on treeless steppes, they could be dirty, immoral, intemperate, and prodigal in their habits and still be worthy of recruitment. The fact that they were none of these things was simply an added bonus. They warranted whatever promotional effort was required to secure them, and that effort was considerable.

Three states, Minnesota, Nebraska, and Kansas, in a doubtful exercise of states' rights, passed laws exempting the Mennonites from military duty, a necessary condition since Canada had already granted them such immunity.[45] Even so, the Mennonites were still not entirely satisfied. As they explained in a petition to the Congress, they wished to be free "for at least fifty years from everything that concerns war," including any taxation for support of military activity. The assurances of the states that they would not have to serve in the capacity of combatants were of no value to them in this regard. But the prediction of Secretary of State Hamilton Fish must have given them great comfort. Fish, in a display of divination unusual in secretaries of state, assured the Mennonites that "for the next fifty years we will not be entangled in another war." He further stated that should the impossible come to pass and the United States find itself involved in a war, Congress would probably not "find justification in freeing them from duties which are asked of other citizens," but this could hardly have dampened the Mennonites' enthusiasm. They had no reason to be concerned with what had suddenly become a purely academic consideration.[46]

With that kind of promotional support from the State Department, the western boomers cannot be too seriously faulted for their own promotional excesses. Canadian officials, for example, were forced to take extreme precautionary measures to guard Canadian-bound Mennonites from American agents.[47] So serious did such promotional larceny become that the American Mennonites formed a board of guardians to watch over their European coreligionists. The board never suffered from inactivity, but Nebraska land agents must have been

45. Smith, *Coming of the Russian Mennonites*, pp. 114–15. See also Annual Message of Gov. Thomas A. Osborne, January 11, 1874, *Messages of Kansas Governors* (1857–77), p. 19, and Osborne to John F. Funk, May 2, 1873, Governors' Letter Press Books, Osborne, KSHS.

46. Petition of Mennonites Paul Tschetter and Lorenz Tschetter to the President, July 26, 1873, and Hamilton Fish to the Tschetters, September 5, 1873, quoted in Smith, *Coming of the Russian Mennonites*, pp. 72, 74.

47. Ibid., pp. 103, 105–6.

Courtesy of the Kansas State Historical Society

Promotional piece advertising Santa Fe Railroad lands on the plains of Kansas

Railroad literature distributed in Germany

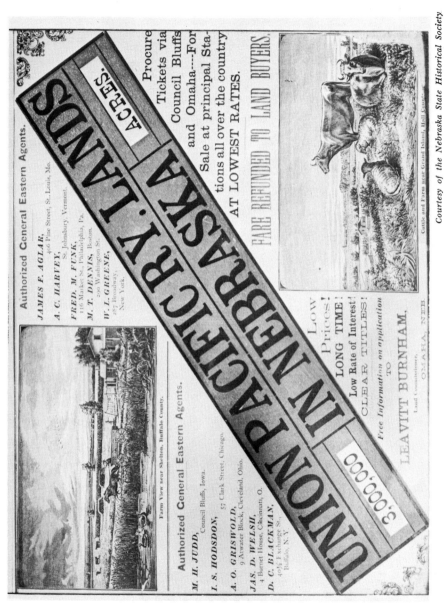

Union Pacific promotional piece

EMIGRANTS' GUIDE

TO THE

KANSAS PACIFIC RAILWAY LANDS.

Best and Cheapest Farming and Grazing Lands
in America.

6,000,000 ACRES FOR SALE

BY THE

KANSAS PACIFIC RAILWAY CO.

—"Ours shall be the forest and the prairie,
And boundless meadows ripe with golden grain."

LAND DEPARTMENT, KANSAS PACIFIC RAILWAY CO.,

LAWRENCE, KANSAS, APRIL, 1871.

JOHN P. DEVEREUX,
Land Commissioner.

SAM'L J. GILMORE,
Sec'y Land Department.

Kansas Pacific Railway pamphlet, 1871

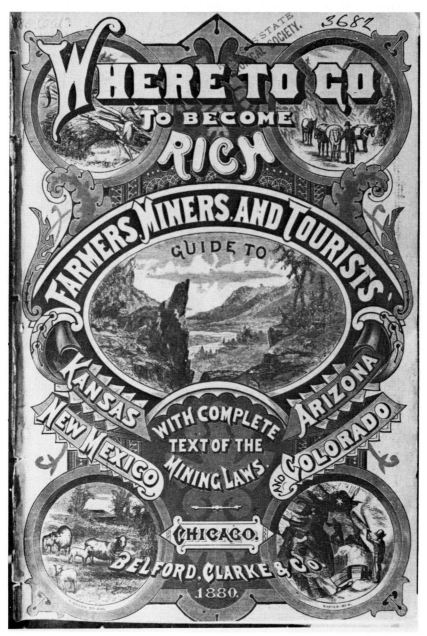

Santa Fe Railroad promotional pamphlet, 1880

THE prime object of this publication is to present truthful illustrations of that rich and beautiful section of country traversed by the **Burlington & Missouri River Railroad,** and to give, in connection with them, such reliable information concerning the lands along the **BURLINGTON ROUTE**, now offered for sale by this Company, as will satisfy all the inquiries which an intelligent person would make, in anticipation of removing thence to find his future home and fortune.

It will be found worthy of careful examination.

"I hear the tread of pioneers
Of nations yet to be;
The first low wash of waves where soon
Shall roll a human sea.

The rudiments of empire here
Are plastic yet and warm;
The chaos of a mighty world
Is rour ᶦnto form.
[WHITTIER.

From a Burlington brochure

"Modern Farming," from Linus Brockett's *Our Western Empire* (1882)

"The Emigrant's Dream of Kansas," from J. H. Beadle's *The Undeveloped West; or, Five Years in the Territories* (1873)

particularly trying.[48] Some of them, upon discovering that most of the Mennonites were bound for Kansas, tried to delay their luggage in Lincoln and in that manner force them to remain in the Nebraska capital at least long enough to be escorted on a tour of the state. After much persuasion a delegation of Mennonites agreed to the tour—in exchange for their luggage, presumably. It must have been a whirlwind experience. They were escorted by the state land commissioner and by a number of representatives of the Burlington Railroad, including A. E. Touzalin, who had recently resigned from the Santa Fe and was particularly eager to defeat his former employer in the competition for this rich harvest of immigrants.[49]

In spite of the Nebraskans' best efforts, the Mennonites remained unimpressed with the state. They still preferred Kansas. Touzalin, though obviously disappointed, did not abandon the campaign. Since the Mennonites liked the grass of Kansas better than that of Nebraska, the Burlington agreed to furnish them hay through the winter free of charge; since the water in Kansas was nearer the surface than in Nebraska, the Burlington was prepared to build pumps and windmills for every section; since Nebraska's sandy soils made transportation difficult, the Burlington offered to build plank roads between Mennonite farms. These were extraordinary inducements but they were little more than preliminaries to Touzalin's final promise. The Mennonites had earlier petitioned for the right to hold lands in common as a necessary condition of group settlement. The Homestead Act, unfortunately, did not allow for this type of communal filing, but once again the Burlington stood ready to offer assistance. Touzalin reminded the Mennonite delegation that the railroad's lands were not so encumbered and he offered them free of charge as much land as they could reasonably absorb, organized and distributed in any manner they might choose. Despite this unprecedented display of generosity, Touzalin gained only one important convert. Cornelius Jansen, a noted Mennonite lecturer and author, was persuaded that Nebraska was the best farming area on the Plains. Kansas, he added, was assuredly the worst.[50]

This was convincing testimony, but it was not enough to deflect the Mennonites toward Nebraska. Kansas and the Santa Fe continued to be the chief beneficiary of their immigration.[51] The principal reason

48. Dick, *Sod House Frontier*, p. 189.
49. Smith, *Coming of the Russian Mennonites*, pp. 161, 64.
50. Ibid., pp. 67–69, 84, 120–21.
51. Six hundred Mennonite families immigrated to Kansas as contrasted with

for Kansas's success seems to have been the activities of C. B. Schmidt, agent for the Santa Fe and one of the most effective promoters on the Plains. Schmidt had two undoubted advantages: he spoke fluent and persuasive German and he was able to visit Russia and advertise Kansas lands directly and personally before the Mennonites left for the United States. Many of the first impressions Schmidt left with the Mennonites must have remained when they reached their new home.[52]

Why the majority of the Mennonites chose Kansas was irrelevant; that they did, however, was a source of considerable pride to the Santa Fe. The company was convinced that the Mennonites had chosen well —so convinced, in fact, that its officials were determined that the world should know of this decision and the success which followed it. As promoters of the company revealed in a well-used pamphlet, "many of them began with nothing but all are well off now." Then, never forgetting the Nebraska bid, they mentioned the "extensive traveling and thorough investigations of many localities" which preceded the Mennonites' choice of the Arkansas Valley "as the place for their people; and they chose wisely." Indeed, what more convincing testimony could be offered of the fertility and adaptability of Kansas soil than that the finest farmers in Europe had chosen it above all others, "unless it be the uniform success which has followed that decision?"[53] Not only were the Mennonites good farmers and hence a most welcome addition to the Kansas population, but they also supplied the state with considerable promotional ammunition.

The response in Russia to the American promotional campaign was understandably unfavorable. The Russian government had stripped the Mennonites of their military exemptions but it hardly suspected that such action in itself would precipitate a mass exodus.[54] Obviously the Americans were not the only ones to recognize the agricultural talents of the group and the Russians were at least as eager to keep them as the Americans were to obtain them. C. B. Schmidt, for example, was forcibly removed from Russia, but only after he had accomplished his

---

eighty to Nebraska. Two hundred families went to the Dakota Territory and 230 more to Manitoba. Ibid., p. 106.

52. Ibid., p. 111; Dick, *Sod House Frontier*, p. 189; Alberta Pantle, "Settlement of the Krimmer Mennonite Brethren at Gnadenau, Marion County," *Kansas Historical Quarterly* 13 (February 1945): 259–85.

53. A. C. Tewksbury [Santa Fe], *The Kansas Picture Book* (Topeka: A. S. Johnson, 1883), p. 61.

54. Smith, *Coming of the Russian Mennonites*, p. 38.

proselytizing mission.[55] The real Russian counteroffensive, however, began in the spring of 1874 when the czarist government sent Adjutant General von Todtleben to dissuade the Mennonites from leaving. Von Todtleben brought word that performance of certain civil functions could be substituted for military duty, but more important, he warned the intending emigrants that conditions in the United States were universally unfavorable for an agricultural people. He used a rather curious argument to illustrate the latter point. The Mennonite emigration took them to the Dakotas, Nebraska, and Kansas, yet von Todtleben seemed totally ignorant of conditions in these states. The American "pioneer settlers," he told his listeners, "[are] compelled to spend much time and labor in draining swamps and cutting forests before the land be fit for cultivation."[56] By 1874 these warnings were not enough to counter the barrage of propaganda laid down by the American promoters. The Mennonites were determined to leave; a kind of land hunger had overtaken them and no amount of Russian concessions or warnings could deter their emigration.

The Russian attitude was not necessarily typical of European sentiment in general. Some nations at certain times actively aided the American recruiters; others just as actively opposed them. In few European nations, however, were the officials unaware of the significance, whether for good or ill, of emigration. Most recognized, at least tacitly, the basic relevance of the safety valve theory and, depending on the situation in their nation and the talents of the prospective emigrants, tried to act upon it according to their own best interests. One response was to cooperate with the American promoters in implementing the safety valve to the benefit of all concerned. Nowhere is this better illustrated than in England.

As early as 1870, the English Parliament engaged in a rather heated debate on the advisability of encouraging emigration out of Britain as a remedy for economic distress. The arguments in favor of such a policy were based on the safety valve theory. One member of Parliament, for example, lamented the fact that Nova Scotia and New Zealand were so far removed from the main islands of the empire. If only they could be interposed between Great Britain and Ireland, he claimed, England's economic problems, present and future, would be immediately relieved.[57] The whims of geography prevented so easy a

---

55. Dick, *Sod House Frontier*, p. 189.
56. Smith, *Coming of the Russian Mennonites*, p. 95.
57. *Hansard's Parliamentary Debates*, 199 (3d Series, 1870), in *Historical Aspects*

solution, but that in itself did not seem cause for despair. The New World was a considerable distance away but it could still supply relief from overcrowding and economic dislocation. All that was needed was a determined effort, whether official or private, to lead the English poor to more favored locations.

The consequences of not making this effort could well prove disastrous. An English newspaper reported in 1872 that it was the duty of "every philanthropist, in these days of strikes and 'Internationals' to encourage emigration on the part of industrious workingmen ... out of the home country, where the struggle between labour and capital is daily becoming more and more embittered." By so doing the philanthropists would be conferring a benefit not only on England but on the United States and Canada as well. The two nations were to be the chief recipients of these "industrious workingmen," and the author of this particular article was confident that both would be grateful for the service England was offering them. It is instructive to note that the notice from the English newspaper was reprinted in the *Sterling* (Nebraska) *Observer and Midland County Advertiser* and that a copy of the reprinted story appeared in the promotional files of the Burlington Railroad—ample evidence that the western boomers were interested in this type of news, and that England was directing at least some of its emigrants to the Plains.[58]

By the 1880s England had developed a rather elaborate system of agencies designed to direct the poor and criminal elements to newer and hopefully better worlds. Of these agencies the most common were prisoners' aid societies. Judson Cross, one of the commissioners appointed to look into the causes of immigration to the United States, described their method. A few days before a convict was discharged, Cross wrote, an officer from one of the societies visited him in prison and discussed plans for the prisoner to "go to the United States." The society then arranged for financial aid, secured passage on a ship, and offered a not overly fond farewell. It was a very simple system, but to the Immigration Commission it represented a grave threat to America's free institutions. H. J. Schulteis, another of the commissioners, reported that there were more than seventy of these discharged prisoners' societies in Great Britain and that by their own accounting they had managed to

---

of the Immigration Problem, ed. by Edith Abbott (Chicago: University of Chicago Press, 1923), p. 172.

58. Curti and Birr, "The Immigrant and the American Image in Europe, 1860–1914," p. 226 and note.

direct over half of the criminals in the empire to the United States. This in itself was injurious enough, but what made the policy even more baneful in Schulteis's mind was the involvement of the English government. As he pointed out, "The annual cost [to the British government] per criminal is 35 pounds, and the saving . . . in this connection . . . is the cause of the popularity of this exportation system." The popularity of the practice, moreover, extended to official London. Schulteis explained: The prisoners' aid societies were "quasi governmental, and receive money for work done by prisoners while in captivity." [59]

The United States commissioners were hardly pleased with this arrangement, but the English, fearful of their ability to absorb their poor, embraced it as an ideal solution to the problems of overcrowding and poverty. As one of Schulteis's English correspondents remarked, the "great method whereby the over-competition in the labor market can be relieved . . . is emigration." Lord Leigh, another advocate of directed emigration, mentioned an additional advantage. "The diminution of crime in this country," he told Commissioner Joseph Powderly, "is due in a great measure to the Discharged Prisoners' Aid Society." Powderly, with one eye on the rising crime statistics in the United States, ruefully agreed.[60]

Criminals, however, were not the only class of people sent abroad by the English. The British clergy had long been active in directing orphaned and destitute children to Canada and the United States.[61] There was also a group called the Self Help Emigration Society of London whose object was the relocation of deserving Englishmen, not necessarily criminal in background. As the name of the organization implies, it was closely attuned to the image of the New World; and as one of its pamphlets makes abundantly clear, it was founded on the theory of the safety valve. England, the author of this pamphlet reminded his readers, was a nation of 121,000 square miles on which there lived, in varying degrees of comfort, 36 million people. It seemed obvious then that with a population increasing at the rate of two million a year, competition would yearly become more intense and work more difficult to obtain. It was equally clear what the solution to this problem might be. "Emigration . . . from the overcrowded country" to less well developed areas "is recognized as one of the best remedies of the poverty . . . now existing." And, needless to add, the United States

59. *Report upon the Causes Which Incite Immigration*, pt. 1: 238, 283, 284.
60. Ibid., pp. 270, 254.
61. Ibid., p. 10.

offered abundant opportunities in this regard.[62] Another organization of similar purpose was the so-called Tuke Fund, established in the late 1870s. Between 1882 and 1884, this fund spent over £69,500 in assisting almost ten thousand emigrants, most of whom went to the United States.[63]

These are rather conventional examples of directed emigration in comparison with the Jewish Colonization Association, which Schulteis called the single "most collossal plan for assisting pauper emigrants" in England. This association was formed by Baron Hirsch, an Englishman of Jewish descent, and included among its stockholders Baron Rothschild and other prominent members of English Jewry. The society, according to Schulteis, enabled Hirsch to organize "all associations of Jews everywhere into a vast reservoir of effluent population, most if not all of which is to overflow into the United States."[64] The truly remarkable thing about the experiment, at least in the minds of the American commissioners, was that Hirsch was trying to establish his recruits in agricultural colonies. The Jew, as the commissioners assumed everyone knew, was notoriously unsuited to this type of work, and Schulteis expressed considerable doubt that the efforts of Baron Hirsch to make farmers out of his coreligionists would prove successful. All such experiments in the past, he noted, had shown themselves to be "unqualified failures."[65]

The "threat" from England, then, seemed to be that forced emigration would swell the American labor force, although the Hirsch scheme seems indication enough that England was not necessarily limiting its emigration quotas to industrial workers only. There is no reason to assume, therefore, that many of the emigrants from Great Britain did not make their way to agricultural regions, including the Great Plains.[66] In the case of the other European nations the possibility that emigration involved people of agrarian habits was even greater, and, as was apparent to every observer, those countries were often as active as England in encouraging emigration.

62. Report of Commissioner Joseph Powderly, ibid., p. 248.

63. *Foreign Relations of the United States, 1886*, pp. 841–42.

64. *Report upon the Causes Which Incite Immigration*, pt. 1: 270–71.

65. Ibid., p. 307. See also p. 172 ff. for a discussion of previous attempts at Jewish colonization.

66. See, for example, the description of rural America in the English guide book by William Saunders, *Through the Light Continent; or, The United States in 1877–78* (London: 1879), p. 293 ff., cited in Curti and Birr, "The Immigrant and the American Image in Europe, 1860–1914," p. 216 and note.

A German commentator, Wilhelm Roscher, had recognized as early as 1856 that emigration was considered the "safest cure for the ills of over-population from which so many parts of our fatherland suffer." Roscher did not necessarily endorse this notion—he felt personally that the German states should unite and develop their own colonial empire—but he was fully aware of the depths of feeling which accompanied theories of emigration. He recognized as well the safety valve implications of those theories. "Emigration," he went on to say, "has at the present time become so immensely the fashion that millions of Germans believe not only that the immigrants themselves profit by it but also that *those whom they leave behind* will have room for a comfortable increase themselves."[67]

It would be very difficult to determine just how extensively the German states pursued any official policy of directed emigration. Bavaria was said to be practicing it "at an exorbitant rate" in 1868, and it was reported that same year that Westphalia was sending discharged prisoners to New York where they were met by railroad agents and sent into the interior.[68] Lewis F. Weise, the Kansas boomer, mentioned that he had received considerable help not only from German newspapers but from various German officials. Three of the leading papers had agreed to publish his promotional circulars, but more important, the circulars, together with any other promotional material deemed pertinent, were read to the people by a representative of the local mayor. This service involved the sanction of the provincial governor but this, too, was readily granted.[69] It should be noted, however, that as a general rule the governments of the German states and later the government of the unified German nation did not encourage emigration quite so openly. At times, in fact, they opposed it, although as Schulteis reported, they placed few "obstacles . . . in the way of paupers who seek a home abroad."[70]

Certainly they must have placed few obstacles in the way of the many private emigration agencies which were active in Germany in the sixties and seventies. These groups usually had some connection with promoters in the United States and hence their motives were considerably

67. William Roscher, "Kolonien, Kolonialpolitik und Auswanderung," 1856, in *Historical Aspects of the Immigration Problem*, ed. by Abbott, pp. 314–15.
68. George Bancroft to William Seward, January 23, 1868, *Foreign Relations of the United States, 1868*, pt. 2: 42–43.
69. Weise to Samuel Crawford, August 4, 1866, Crawford Papers, KSHS.
70. *Report upon the Causes Which Incite Immigration*, pt. 1: 288.

less than philanthropic. But they supplied, nevertheless, a significant service to the western boomers by educating the citizens of their region in the Edenic image of America. The German-American Volks Verein of Kansas was one such agency. Another, the German-American League, included among its board of directors the vice-president of the Hamburg House of Representatives. The league also published a promotional newspaper entitled the *International German American Advertiser*, and in the words of the United States consul in Hamburg, Samuel Williams (whose own involvement was of questionable propriety), this paper "promised to be of great service in promoting emigration to America." He, therefore, urged Governor Crawford of Kansas to take advantage of such service by advertising in its columns. The cost was nominal, only $1,200 a year, and the rewards of increased immigration were worth much more.[71] Fred Sommerschu, a partner in the enterprise, offered Crawford even more convincing evidence of the effectiveness of this type of advertising. The *German American Advertiser*, he assured the governor, was published in good German— unlike some of the pamphlets sent out by railroads which had the "lamentable effect of prejudicing very many intelligent persons against America." That was an important service, but Sommerschu also assured Crawford that the *Advertiser* would stay within the German anti- promotion laws by not "seducing to emigrate."[72] Theirs would be purely an educational venture.

Some of the other private emigration agencies in Germany were equally circumspect. One of them, the German Humboldt Association, was particularly active in the Halle and Saxony areas. The group published a journal entitled *Nature* and generally seemed to have dis- guised its promotionalism by professing its abiding interest in the flora and fauna of other lands. Fred Hedde, Nebraska's agent in Hamburg, considered the association to be of incalculable benefit to the state. It agreed to publish in *Nature* a number of Hedde's articles entitled "Nebraska: The Immigration State," in addition to a continuing series of articles concerning United States land laws.[73]

71. Samuel Williams to Gov. Samuel Crawford, June 15, 1867, Crawford Papers, KSHS.

72. Sommerschu to Crawford, June 15, 1867, ibid. Whether Crawford ever took advantage of this offer is unknown, although the penuriousness of the Kansas legislature at this time would seem to have worked against it.

73. *Omaha Republican*, February 4, 1873.

Hedde did not receive the same kind of cooperation from the German steamship companies, although they too were active in the promotion of emigration. Hedde reported that the steamship companies had a complete system of agents all over Germany. These agents were the only ones who had regular communication with those classes who were good candidates for emigration, and as Hedde pointed out, "It is in the interests of these men to induce as many people to emigrate as they possibly can." Obviously, here were people in a perfect position to help Nebraska, either by distributing its handbills and pamphlets, or better yet, by guiding the emigrants directly to the state. They must have realized the importance of their position, for Hedde mentioned that he had to rely on their natural interest in emigration in order to have them distribute his pamphlets. "Monetary inducements," a much more effective method, he could not offer.[74]

Other Europeans, though less active in the field than the Germans, also engaged in this type of promotion. In Hungary, Paul D'Esterhazy presided over the First Hungarian-American Colonization Company, a private concern committed to finding better homes for that nation's poor. Better, in this case, meant rural, for D'Esterhazy refused to allow his people to become members of an industrial working class so long as agricultural possibilities were open to them. Thus, as he explained to Governor Albinus Nance of Nebraska, "what we need is thorough information as to the extent of available lands—either public, private or cooperative [and] . . . the nature of the climate and soil."[75]

In Switzerland, a similar kind of promotion was conducted under more official auspices. In the town of Gersau, for example, the local government gave each unemployed family $37.97 to cover passage to the United States. That sum, according to Nicholas Fish, American ambassador to Switzerland, left the immigrant with less than $10.00 upon arrival. Unless they had supplementary funds, most would become wards of the government—an unhappy situation, Fish allowed, but one which would arise with greater frequency as other Swiss villages began to follow the example of Gersau.[76] In Sweden and Denmark there were discharged prisoners' aid societies similar in most respects

74. Ibid.
75. Paul D'Esterhazy to Nance, April 8, 1882, Nance Papers, NSHS.
76. Nicholas Fish to William Evarts, January 24, 1881, *Foreign Relations of the United States, 1881*, p. 1111. The Swiss assured Fish that all the emigrants were able-bodied, but Fish doubted this.

to those in England. One essential difference was the emphasis the Scandinavian groups placed on settlement in agricultural areas.[77]

A number of Europeans, then, gave considerable aid to American promoters in the matter of immigration. More often than not, their cooperation was dictated by expediency: the Europeans wanted to be rid of some of the more burdensome members of their society. But whatever concern was expressed as to the character of these directed immigrants was limited to the eastern United States. Ultimately, this concern led to a State Department communique which termed all such behavior "positive acts of discourtesy on the part of foreign Governments."[78] Although the diplomatic language was rather strong, it obviously did not have the desired effect, and it became H. J. Schulteis's dreary duty to prepare the American people for "an army of paupers . . . drilled to invade this country." Europe, Schulteis went on to say, expected the United States "to absorb the weakness of their lands and to decrease in greatness and in general welfare in inverse ratio to the increase in population."[79] The western regions, however, were not so sensitive about the background of the new arrivals. Theirs was a land especially created for the poor, and few western promoters were in a position to exercise great discrimination about whom they would and would not accept. To them, European participation in their promotional projects, whatever the motive, was simply further confirmation that their campaign to implement the safety valve had more than just local support.

With some exceptions, most notably Great Britain, foreign support came from private sources. Some local officials in Germany also lent encouragement, but the more common official response to American promotional efforts appears to have been one of opposition. The reason for official unhappiness is not difficult to find. The American promoters, though they were not averse to accepting the poorer members of European society, were primarily interested in recruiting the more talented and well trained. But this class was the one the European states were most eager to keep. The United States expressed some official displeasure over the efforts of private European groups to send surplus popula-

77. Sidney Cooper to James D. Porter, November 26, 1885, *Foreign Relations of the United States, 1886*, p. 840; Rufus Magee to James A. Bayard, January 26, 1886, ibid., pp. 841–42.

78. John Davis to Henry Ryder, January 23, 1883, *Foreign Relations of the United States, 1883*, pp. 251–52.

79. *Report upon the Causes Which Incite Immigration*, pt. 1: 274.

tion to America; likewise, some Old World countries protested the behavior of certain American promoters for trying to tempt Europeans to the United States. Sometimes this protest was indirect, as when the Scandinavian press tried to arrest the large emigration from the region by reciting stories of alleged poverty and brutality in the United States.[80] Emphasis in these anti-American accounts varied according to time and place. During the Civil War and Reconstruction period it was on militarism, corruption, or the "arrogance" of Negroes. Later, as the Gilded Age reached full flower, it was on political and moral degeneracy, or the excesses of the idle rich.[81]

The champions of the pan-Slav movement were particularly bitter about American attempts to lure their conationalists away from the fatherland. Indeed, the movement sponsored the publication of a book entitled *The Land of Promise* in which innocent Slavs were swindled by promoters into coming to the United States and then left to perish from hunger, thirst, and exposure on an American desert.[82]

More direct means of opposition were employed by some of the German states. As early as 1867, H. N. Congar, the United States Commissioner of Immigration, had sent a circular to various American consuls warning them not to contravene the emigration restriction laws of the nation in which they were stationed.[83] Seven years later Secretary of State Hamilton Fish made the warning more explicit. Fish told Governor Thomas Osborne of Nebraska that some of the European governments, especially those of Germany and France, had displayed such hostility to the presence of American promoters that the State Department "desires to remain divested of any participation in . . . agencies of that nature." Fish went on to say that this washing of the hands was "not from any insensibility to the importance of immigration as an element of our . . . development"—a needless

80. See, for example, Hans Mattson, *Reminiscences: The Story of an Emigrant* (St. Paul: D. D. Merrill Co., 1891), p. 301; Overton, *Burlington West*, p. 368; James Campbell to William Seward, April 30, 1865, *Foreign Relations of the United States, 1865*, pt. 3: 196–98.

81. Curti and Birr, "The Immigrant and the American Image in Europe, 1860–1914," p. 227. C. F. Adams to William Seward, March 18, 1864, *Foreign Relations of the United States, 1864*, pt. 1: 327–28, has an account of English attempts to forestall emigration by recounting alleged horror stories coming from the Civil War.

82. Cited in Curti and Birr, "The Immigrant and the American Image in Europe, 1860–1914," p. 222. Curti and Birr mention a number of other works of similar intent.

83. Copy in Samuel Crawford Papers, KSHS.

addition, in view of his own involvement in the Mennonite promotion —but rather from a desire to avoid embarrassment. He respectfully asked that the agents be cautioned "against any enticement or solicitation of individuals to emigrate, and . . . directed to confine their labors to affording accurate and reliable information."[84] In spite of this reproof, American agents continued to violate the antipromotion laws, and European governments were forced to take more direct action. In Hamburg, for example, it was reported that ten thousand copies of Texas promotional literature had been confiscated,[85] while in Austria all promotional activity, including the printing and distribution of pamphlets, was prohibited by law.[86]

Whatever the extent of European antagonism, it could not have been more than a nuisance to the American promoters. A number of observers, here and abroad, commented on the ease with which the antipromotion regulations could be evaded; and, of course, so long as there were European poor and private agencies committed to their relocation, the American boomers had little need of official support. Their own promotional network was extensive and mobile. At any given time and in any given place, state and railroad agents could lay down a barrage of promotional literature, but should these agents overlook anyone, the boomers could fall back on other sources. Newspapers and private land developers also indulged their talents for promotional misrepresentation, and some of the finest descriptive prose of that generation came from those agencies. The boomers had recourse as well to the various fairs and expositions which became in time little more than promotional extravaganzas. The federal government even lent a hand with the passage of land laws designed frankly to stimulate interest in the western country and then make it easy to satisfy that interest. And when easterners and Europeans began to participate in the boom by encouraging emigration, the western promoter's dream of rushing torrents of people descending on the Plains

84. Fish to Osborne, September 15, 1874, Osborne Papers, NSHS. Four years later the State Department denied a recommendation to one Ferdinand Lechleitner. Lechleitner had asked for diplomatic clearance that he might promote for Nebraska (Lechleitner to Gov. Silas Garber, September 24, 1878, Garber Papers, NSHS; W. H. Hunter to Lechleitner, September 20, 1878, copy in Garber Papers, NSHS).

85. Heinrich Lemcke to Gov. G. W. Glick, October 6, 1883, Glick Papers, KSHS. The enterprising Lemcke had an alternative method of promotion. As he told Glick, the newspaper he had projected could easily evade the laws, and for a slight monthly fee, Lemcke could keep the name of Kansas before the German people.

86. *Report upon the Causes Which Incite Immigration*, pt. 1: 123.

was almost complete. But these were not the boomers' only advantages. Their methods were efficient, their promises calculated to appeal to certain universal drives. All that was needed was a theory which would make those promises realizable, and a catch phrase to capture the attention and calm the doubts of the prospective immigrants. They found both in one stroke of imaginative sloganeering. The theory dealt with the increase of rainfall consequent upon cultivation. The slogan which expressed it was "rain follows the plow."

CHAPTER SIX

Rain Follows the Plow

The Plains boomer fervently believed that his prosperity and that of his region bore a direct relationship to the number of people he could attract. It was essentially a quantitative approach, but in an area of sparse population and undeveloped resources it was a perfectly natural one. The Plains could be developed in no other way, and an entire profession arose to meet one central purpose: convincing people that their future and that of their children were secure on the Plains. The boomers were zealous in the effort. Prospective settlers were promised everything from good health to guaranteed crop prices. The soil was rich, the yields prodigious, the prospects unlimited—and all of this from an area once condemned as a great sterile desert.

The boomers mocked the desert theory, they attacked it with sophistry and bombast, and in their rhetoric they destroyed it. Nor did they doubt that their victory was complete, for the promoters had developed a theory which removed the final and most stubborn deterrent to successful settlement. The older wisdom had held that it did not rain enough on the Plains, that it never had and never would. This was, admittedly, a difficult image to change, but it gave the boomers only slight pause. They reasoned that man, particularly in America, had met and overcome every obstacle in the path of his expansion. Obviously the alleged lack of rainfall on the Great Plains would succumb to the conqueror as easily as all the earlier hazards. It was the ultimate weapon of this conquest, however, which made their theory so appealing. The plow, symbol of the American farmer, was to give life to the Plains, not just by breaking them, but by producing conditions which would lead to increased rainfall. In short, rain follows the plow. The slogan was the perfect promotional device. It had a nice rhythmic sound and it contained reference to the two most treasured symbols of the American farmer. The boomers could use it as the feature attraction of their promotional campaigns; but equally important, they could use it to buoy their own sagging confidence during hard times. Both an appeal and a source of comfort, the slogan was the single most important promotional device to come out of the boomers' frontier. Without it, in fact, that frontier could scarcely have been sustained.

The notion that rain follows the plow was preceded by theories which identified other objects of civilization as the agents of climatic change. There were those who thought rain followed railroad tracks and telegraph wires, trees and cannon fire.[1] But the most popular agent, probably because it involved no extra effort, was the plow.

Before discussing that theory, however, a question must be asked: How could the plainsmen prove so susceptible to a theory which appears to have contained nothing more substantial than a mixture of superstition and wishful thinking? In part, of course, the notion of increased rainfall was simply one manifestation of man's alleged dominion over nature. God had created man superior to his natural environment and man was exercising that superiority. In part, too, it represents the belief that the civilizing influences of the "American way" were manifestly destined to sweep aside all obstacles to the expansion of that culture. Deserts were doomed to quick extinction. But the theory of increased rainfall was too specific a product of both of these beliefs to fit comfortably within any generalized definition. A more specific explanation is thus required.

In 1891 Colonel W. E. Tweeddale of Kansas attempted to account for the acceptance of the theory by reference to the belief in divine intervention. He emphasized the credence given the Biblical account of the land of Canaan where the direct interposition of God had converted a once sterile desert into a land of milk and honey. With such knowledge and belief, Tweeddale concluded, it was only natural for settlers on the Plains to expect that fertility would follow settlement, and since the only cause of infertility was inadequate moisture, they could also expect increased rainfall. Tweeddale was the only near contemporary to attempt to interpret the early acceptance of the notion

1. For examples of each, see Hutchinson, *Resources of Kansas*, pp. 35, 37, 38; Richardson, *Beyond the Mississippi*, p. 79; Richard Smith Elliott, *Notes Taken in Sixty Years* (St. Louis: R. P. Studley & Co., 1883), pp. 302–8; Robert Dyrenforth and Simon Newcomb, "Can We Make It Rain?" *North American Review* 153 (October 1891): 387.

of increased precipitation. His theory, though not entirely convincing, commands a certain respect.[2]

A more plausible explanation, however, involves the Americans' experience with earlier frontiers, particularly the prairie region. It was widely assumed at the time that Americans began to enter this tall grass country that a land incapable of sustaining forests would prove incapable of producing corn. The soil was obviously infertile and the rainfall inadequate. Consequently, farmers avoided the open, treeless sections of the prairie states. They selected the wooded regions instead and there undertook the back-breaking labor of clearing the timber to prepare the ground for cultivation. When the wooded areas were exhausted, the prairie farmer was forced to move into the treeless areas convinced, it may be assumed, that failure would be the probable result. These areas, however, proved more fertile, more productive than the best timbered land, and with considerably less labor. But the farmer refused to admit the error of his original belief. An absence of trees still meant poor soil and insufficient rain. Apparently some change had taken place, the soil had somehow been improved, the rain somehow increased. The agent of that change was easily identifiable. Man had altered the natural conditions and made them good. If the prairies, parts of which had also been included in the Great American Desert, could be reclaimed, so also could the Plains. At least there seemed no reason to dismiss the latter regions without first challenging the accepted notions of permanent aridity.[3]

By the 1860s a variety of scientists and politicians became convinced that the rainfall of the Plains could be increased. In the 1870s this belief was widespread and still growing. The theory of increased rainfall offers a perfect example of a people believing what they most urgently wanted to believe, but the support of trained scientists certainly added a comforting respectability to their theory.

One of these scientists, Ferdinand V. Hayden, offered more than reassurances alone. He was the first of the notable rain-follows-the-plow men, and as one of the four commissioned explorers of the trans-Mississippi West, Hayden was in a unique position to have his theories heard. But more important, he was in total agreement with the guiding

2. W. E. Tweeddale, "Irrigation for Homesteaders in Western Kansas," KSBA, *Report for the Quarter Ending March 31, 1891* (Topeka, 1891), p. 79.

3. See Gates, *The Illinois Central*, p. 11; Robbins, *Our Landed Heritage*, p. 186; Dick, *Sod House Frontier*, p. 487; and V. E. Shelford, "Deciduous Forest Man and the Grassland Fauna," *Science* 100 (August 18, 1944): 135.

philosophy of the western promoter. William Goetzmann called him "the businessman's geologist," and Hayden richly deserved the title, for in his mind the work he did for the United States Geological Survey of the Territories was little more than an extension of the boomers' frontier.[4]

This does not mean that he had any direct or personal interest in the growth and development of the West, only that his sympathies lay with those who did. As he once wrote, "it is my earnest wish at all times to report that which will be most pleasing to the people of the West." On another occasion he admitted his desire to hasten the day when the western territories achieved full maturity and were admitted to the Union. Indeed, he was prepared to spend "the remainder of the working days of [his] life" in the pursuit of that goal.[5] This is hardly accepted scientific method, nor is it altogether consistent with Hayden's own disclaimer of personal interest in the results of his work. "Scientific men who are truly devoted to their calling," he had written with just the proper amount of majesty, "cannot be speculators or ardently given to pecuniary gains. . . . I am obliged to speak the truth as I read it in the great book of nature."[6] Too often he wrote the book to fit his purposes, but this is evidence not of duplicity but of a shared faith in the simple theories of his generation.

Regardless of motive, the results were the same. People read his reports, accepted them as scientific truth, and immigrated on the basis of the promises they made. Cyrus Thomas, one of Hayden's chief assistants, congratulated him on the fact that the sections of the West described most fully in his reports had received the greatest portion of the immigration. Thomas thought it safe to assume that Hayden's scientific surveys had had something to do with this.[7] Richard Smith Elliott, a railroad promoter, was another who recognized the important contribution Hayden was making in furthering immigration interests. "Your labors," he wrote, "have certainly been of immense benefit

4. William Goetzmann, *Exploration and Empire* (New York: Alfred Knopf, 1966), p. 498.

5. F. V. Hayden, *Preliminary Report of the United States Geological Survey of the Territories . . . 1871* (Washington, D.C.: GPO, 1871), p. 7; and U.S. Geological Survey, *Fourth Annual Report of the Survey of the Territories, 1873* (Washington, D.C.: GPO, 1873), p. 7.

6. U.S. Geological Survey, *Third Annual Report of the . . . Survey of the Territories . . . 1872* (Washington, D.C.: GPO, 1872), p. 7.

7. In U.S. Geological Survey, *Second Annual Report of the . . . Survey of the Territories . . . 1871* (Washington, D.C.: GPO, 1871), p. 209.

to us. . . . Your reports have the rare merit of grouping facts of great interest to the scientific world, and at the same time affording light and knowledge to the plain and unlearned classes."[8]

Elliott and Thomas may have been referring to Hayden's discussion of the High Plains. Hayden had written that that area had often been identified as the Great American Desert: no longer, however, for "every year, as we know, . . . this belt becomes narrower and narrower, and as a continuous area it has already ceased to exist, even in imagination."[9] The light and knowledge which Hayden supplied was pretty conventional stuff; it was the source alone which distinguished it.

More significant than Hayden's own theories on increased rainfall were those of some of the contributors to his reports. Hayden offered his name and that of his government to a number of trained and amateur scientists. The two most important were the aforementioned Thomas, an entomologist, and Elliott, a promotional agent for the Kansas Pacific Railroad. Thomas was a conscientious man who felt an obligation to expose certain of the promoters as "too sanguine" in their belief in the future of the Plains. Such overconfidence resulted in "suffering and hardships," the inevitable consequences, Thomas thought, of the exaggerated and glowing descriptions of the promoters.[10] Having thus established his own scientific purity, Thomas was free to contribute to that same misrepresentation, suffering, and hardship.

He admitted that he was somewhat disappointed by his first impression of the Plains—promotional distortion had conditioned him to expect something better. But nonetheless he found there a bread-producing area "surpassed by none on the continent."[11] He had explained why four years earlier, when he offered as his "firm conviction that the increase [in rainfall] is of a permanent nature." So convinced was he of this fact that he suggested in all seriousness that settlements be established on the far western edge of the Plains and then proceed eastward. As they progressed, these settlements would produce more rain; the streams draining eastward would, as a result, never run dry

8. R. S. Elliott to Hayden, April 16, 1872 in Elliott, Letter Press Books, Missouri Historical Society, St. Louis, hereafter cited as Elliott LPB.

9. U.S. Geological Survey, *Third Annual Report of the . . . Survey of the Territories . . . 1872* (Washington, D.C.: GPO, 1872), p. 16.

10. Cyrus Thomas, "Physical Geography and Agricultural Resources of Minnesota, Dakota, and Nebraska," in *Sixth Annual Report of the United States Geological Survey of the Territories Embracing Portions of Montana, Idaho, Wyoming and Utah,* by F. V. Hayden (Washington, D.C.: GPO, 1873), pp. 276, 278.

11. Ibid., p. 278.

and irrigation would be possible throughout the year. But Thomas was no typical irrigationist. Settlement was also moving westward, and farming under ditch would be required only until these two converging, rainbearing flanks of settlement, one coming from the east, one from the west, rendered it unnecessary.[12]

Thomas chose rather curious sources of information to confirm this remarkable theory. In 1873 he submitted to the Burlington and other railroads a series of questions dealing with the agricultural potential of the Plains. The answers were predictable. Burlington officials did confess an earlier uneasiness regarding the cultivability of their western Nebraska lands, but their fears, happily, had been put entirely to rest by the miraculous workings of natural law. "As settlement proceeds," they told Thomas, "the annual rainfall will become increasingly larger." This was the lesson they had learned from the settlement of eastern Nebraska and they had no reason to doubt its continued applicability. Thomas admitted that some might challenge the objectivity of the report. After all, he wrote, "the railroads are deeply interested in this matter." But in this instance Thomas had no reason to doubt the accuracy of their theory. "I may safely state," he concluded, "that it is correct."[13]

Richard Smith Elliott, the other noteworthy contributor to Hayden's reports, was the industrial agent for the Kansas Pacific Railroad. His job was to attract immigrants to Kansas Pacific lands but to do that he had first to find suitable outlets for his promotional material. Publications of the federal government seemed ideal for this purpose, and Elliott began actively to cultivate the good wishes of various federal officials. As he explained to C. S. Lanborn of the K.P., "It is my intention to make use of the Dept. [of Agriculture], particularly as an advertising machine, and as I want to use the Commissioner, I must of course ask his *opinion*."[14]

Whether he practiced this form of flattery on Hayden is unknown. He did congratulate him for his contribution to the recruitment of immigrants and perhaps that was considered recognition enough. In either event, Hayden proved to be a loyal partner by publishing two

12. Cyrus Thomas, "Agriculture in Colorado," in *Preliminary Field Report of the United States Geological Survey of Colorado and New Mexico* . . . , by F. V. Hayden (Washington, D.C.: GPO, 1869), p. 141.

13. Thomas, "Physical Geography and Agricultural Resources of Minnesota, Dakota, and Nebraska," pp. 309–10.

14. Elliott to Lanborn, September 18, 1870, Elliott, LPB.

pieces of blatantly promotional literature. Even Elliott had no illusions about their scientific worth. As he confessed jokingly to a Kansas Pacific official, "I have made up a 'learned' report for Dr. Hayden to be published next year."[15] In both of these reports Elliott offered the assurance that the rain was increasing and that western Kansas and eastern Colorado were unmatched for agricultural production anywhere in the world.[16] Indeed, the only remarkable thing about either paper was that Hayden would give them an audience, and that he would offer this service knowing that each had been closely edited by President John Perry of the Kansas Pacific.[17] This was rather curious behavior for a man who read closely from the book of nature and deplored the suffering and hardships which resulted from its misreading.

Offering his pages to promoters like Elliott was not Hayden's only abuse of his official position; he was no more circumspect in his off-duty hours. In 1880 he lent his name and his reputation to a massive gazette entitled *The Great West*. The book itself was little more than a compilation of reports on the resources and opportunities of the region it purported to describe. But Hayden was named as its author and the gazette no doubt benefited from this association. Among other things, it contained Longfellow's poem "The Far West," with its references to "billowy waves of grass ever rolling in the shadow and sunshine." It endorsed the ideas of Professor Samuel Aughey, the Nebraska boomer, and Robert Strahorn, a noted publicist for the transcontinental railroads. A quotation from Dr. James Butler, the undercover promoter of the Burlington, appears in its pages, as do a number of passages from the Kansas State Board of Agriculture. Hayden's own comments are almost superfluous, although they do illuminate the general nature of the volume. He used, for example, the rainfall statistics of Dr. A. L. Childs of Plattsmouth, Nebraska, and reached the same conclusion Childs had: rainfall was increasing

15. Elliott to George Hale, January 9, 1871, ibid.

16. Richard Smith Elliott, "Report on the Industrial Resources of Western Kansas and Colorado," in *Preliminary Report of the United States Geological Survey of Wyoming and Portions of Contiguous Territories . . . 1871* (Washington, D.C.: GPO, 1872), pp. 442–58. This report was also published as U.S., Congress, House, *Material Resources of Western Kansas and Eastern Colorado*, 42d Cong., 2d sess., 1872, pp. 442–56. The other paper was Richard Smith Elliott's "Experiments in Cultivating the Plains along the Line of the Kansas Pacific Railway," in *Preliminary Report of the United States Geological Survey of Montana and Adjacent Territories*, by F. V. Hayden (Washington, D.C.: GPO, 1872), pp. 274–79.

17. Elliott to Hayden, January 9, 1871, Elliott, LPB.

appreciably throughout the state. In Hayden's words, "the agricultural area [of Nebraska] extends almost to the western boundary of the State; and, indeed, in what is now the grazing-region the processes which have made the eastern half arable are in rapid progress." A similar change, Hayden noted, was "going on along the eastern border of the whole arid region from Montana down to Mexico."[18] Thus Hayden gave a kind of pseudoscientific status to the theory of increased rainfall. He accomplished this not so much through his own profound discoveries—he still was unsure about what caused the increase—but rather because of his national reputation as a geologist and explorer. He was the publicist of the theory, not its philosopher.[19]

The latter honor belongs jointly to two men, Samuel Aughey and C. D. Wilber, both of Nebraska. In 1873, Aughey, then a professor of biology at the state university, presented an address to the legislature entitled "Geology of Nebraska." In it he first expressed some of the ideas which were later to coalesce around the fetching slogan "rain follows the plow." As he put it, "One of the most interesting of the meteorological facts which affect this region is this—that as civilization extends westward the fall of rain increases from year to year."[20] As this change progressed the climate of Nebraska would begin to approach the "wonderful conditions of the Tertiary epoch." That sounded promising, even to those whose knowledge of geological epochs was shaky. Later, when Aughey described those conditions, his listeners began to understand the true significance of the theory. "In this . . . age," he said, "Nebraska possessed a semitropical climate. . . . Magnificent forests reared themselves on the borders of the lakes. . . . This section of country must have been enjoying the delightful climate and the balmy breezes we now . . . associate with Mexico and Cuba." To the grizzled Nebraska farmer who had fought drought, grasshoppers, and wind, this was a heartening piece of news, as it must have been to the prospective immigrant who looked to Nebraska as a future home. But to Oscar Mullon, Burlington promoter and interested spectator at Aughey's address, it was a statement of such profound significance

18. F. V. Hayden, *The Great West: Its Attractions and Resources* (Philadelphia: Franklin Publishing Co., 1880), pp. 15, 117, 176, 179, 183–84, 268, 276.

19. For a slightly different view see Henry Nash Smith, "Rain Follows the Plow: The Notion of Increased Rainfall for the Great Plains, 1844–1880," *Huntington Library Quarterly* 10 (February 1947): 169–93.

20. Samuel Aughey, *The Geology of Nebraska: A Lecture Delivered in the Representative Hall at Lincoln . . . January 20, 1873* (Lincoln, 1873), p. 14.

that it had to be shared with the world, particularly, it must be assumed, that part of it whose Tertiary past was irreclaimable.[21]

Of equal importance to the Nebraskans was Aughey's assurance that they did not have long to wait for the expected changes to occur. Aughey, in fact, had noticed as early as 1872 that significant changes had taken place in the vegatative cover of the Sand Hills. No longer did they resemble the barren and desolate region described by Hayden himself only four years before. Some of them had become grass-covered, and even the most barren had a few new grasses struggling to survive. This was remarkable enough, but according to Aughey, "the change since then is even greater."[22]

Eight years later, in 1880, Aughey was even more convinced that something truly miraculous was happening to the Sand Hills. By that date there was "no doubt" in his mind that this once condemned region was not only capable of cultivation but would "someday be cultivated." Nor was Aughey's prediction a superfluous addition to his statement, for by 1880 he had fully developed the theory that rain follows the plow. What he was saying, in effect, was that sufficient climatic change had taken place in the state generally to permit successful though limited cultivation of the Sand Hills. This would cause local rainfall to increase, which would lead in turn to more settlement, more culti-vation, and still more rain. For those who would follow the progression to its conclusion, more rain would produce more trees which would themselves increase not only the rainfall but the number and extent of lakes and springs, creating in the process a greater evaporative surface and more rain. Fortunately for meteorological sanity, Aughey brought his progression to an end when Tertiary conditions were reached.[23]

What was truly remarkable, however, was that by this time the genera-tive force behind the change was thought to be the plow. Never had a more humble implement been considered capable of effecting such cataclysmic change. The plow worked its miracle by breaking up the

21. To this end Mullon took notes of Aughey's entire address and secured their publication in the report of the State Board of Agriculture and in various Burlington promotional pamphlets (Aughey, "'Geology of Nebraska', Notes taken by Oscar Mullon of the B & M Railroad," NSBA, *Fourth Annual Report . . . 1873* [Lincoln, 1874], pp. 67, 83–84).

22. Aughey, *Geology of Nebraska*, p. 22.

23. Samuel Aughey, *Sketches of the Physical Geography and Geology of Nebraska* (Omaha: Daily Republican Book and Job Office, 1880). The quotations in this and the following three paragraphs were taken from pp. 44, 45, 46, 50, 52, 85, 139, 140, 141, 153–55, 300.

impervious sod of the Plains. This greatly increased the absorptive power of the soil and the moisture which once ran off in tiny rivulets was now retained. "Thus," wrote Aughey, "year by year as cultivation of the soil is extended, more of the rain that falls is absorbed and retained to be given off in evaporation, or to produce springs. This, of course, must give increased moisture and rainfall.'" Aughey confessed that the change might take longer in western Nebraska than it had in eastern, but that it would occur was beyond question.

The social and economic consequences of increased rainfall were momentous. More was involved than simply better and more regular crops. The future of the race, for example, depended in large measure upon the ability of the United States to supply its population with farms. With the rain steadily increasing in Nebraska a whole new agricultural empire was opened up. Here on the Plains "a healthy, vigorous and beautiful race of men and women" would take their places alongside America's earlier pioneers. In fact, the Nebraska settlers would be of slightly higher station than earlier frontiersmen. Aughey explained why: "In the older States the families that live on . . . naturally barren soil are inferior in culture and social life to those that live in the fertile valleys." Once Nebraska had been transformed into one vast fertile valley the prospects for further cultural development would be unlimited. Music, painting, sculpture, and art would flourish in direct proportion to increased rainfall. But Nebraskans would be more than just cultured; they would be robustly healthy. For proof Aughey suggested that his readers contrast the sallow complexions evident in the older regions with the "hue of health and glow of spirits found in Nebraska." The reason for the strikingly good health of the Nebraskans lay in the ozone content of the air. The presence of ozone could cure almost anything—malaria, consumption, asthma, bronchitis, indigestion, inflammation of the lungs, even heaves in horses. The conclusion was inescapable: "Nebraska must sooner or later become a health resort."

Even this did not exhaust the benefits to accrue from increased rainfall. The shortage of wood, which Aughey admitted was a serious problem, was soon to be solved by the lush forest growth which would accompany the rain. The grasshoppers, which Aughey denied were a serious problem, would soon disappear, the most potent agency "against their increase and destructiveness [being] the increasing rainfall of the State."

The empire of Nebraska was thus beginning to take shape. The annual increase in rainfall was preparing it to take its proper place as an immigrant state. This involved a great responsibility, as Aughey recognized. Nebraska had to prove itself capable of receiving and supporting the overflow population of the eastern states. Like other and older frontiers, Nebraska was to serve these purposes, and Aughey welcomed the challenge and the opportunity to show that the safety valve never worked better than when it opened on Nebraska. He became in the process the state's most active and persuasive promoter.

Aughey's reputation as a boomer was secured in his speeches and books. It was publicly admitted by railroad authorities that his "geological papers on soil, etc., of Nebraska have been a most important factor in securing so large an immigration into the State." This was not entirely accidental.[24] The railroads obviously recognized that Aughey's work, in spite of its scientific trappings, was an important contribution to their promotional campaigns; likewise, Aughey could not have been ignorant of the use to which his articles were to be put. He realized their value and so he consciously strove to secure for them the widest possible audience.

Aughey played an important role in the boomers' frontier. He lent a certain scientific credence to a theory which motivated the entire promotional effort and for this he earned the genuine appreciation of a number of interested parties. It is unfair, however, to attribute to him motives entirely base. Though his methods may have lacked the clinical detachment usually associated with geology and botany, there is every reason to assume that he believed what he said. This may explain what he did, but it hardly justifies it. His theories were based on deductive and selective experimentation. They were designed less to enlighten than to seduce. Nor can ignorance or superstition be used in his defense. Aughey's theories were not simply wrong, his methods and purposes were wrong as well. He was not only a mistaken scientist; he was no scientist at all. Perhaps the best description of him came from Roscoe Pound, best known as a jurist, but before then, a practicing and highly respected botanist. Pound knew Aughey personally. His own degree was from the University of Nebraska and he had had occasion to study some of Aughey's work. He was singularly unimpressed. Dr. Aughey, according to Pound, was a "first class charlatan."[25]

24. A. T. Andreas, *History of Nebraska* (Chicago: A. T. Andreas, 1882), pp. 1057–58.

25. Robert Manley, "Samuel Aughey: Nebraska's Scientific Promoter," *Journal of the West* 6 (January 1967): 117.

Aughey's chief assistant in formulating the theory that rain follows the plow was Charles Dana Wilber. Wilber was an amateur. His promotionalism was more open if less sophisticated than Aughey's. It was also more defensive and more given to romantic musings. His belief that rain follows the plow was based not so much on scientific investigation as on his assumption that nature was meant to obey man's will. He was a typical boomer, imaginative, energetic, and totally uncorrupted by the facts.

In 1879, a year before Aughey announced that rain follows the plow, Wilber made the following comments before the Nebraska State Horticultural Society. A desert, he assured his audience, is not the result of any divine perversity. On the contrary, it is the "result of conditions that can be controlled by the genius and industry of man." He then explained how in a characteristic passage. "With a logic that cannot rest we are forced to this conclusion, that the agencies of civilization now in action are such as will secure a complete victory over the wilderness and waste places of western territory." The conquest of the wilderness had always been uppermost in the minds of Americans, particularly the stubborn wilderness which was the Great Plains. But Wilber gave them a new weapon with which to fight an old war. "The plow will go forward," he said. "God speed the plow. . . . By this wonderful provision, which is only man's mastery over nature, the clouds are dispersing copious rains." The plow was a marvelous tool, "more powerful in peace than the sword in war, . . . the instrument which separates civilization from savagery; and . . . converts a desert into a farm or garden."[26]

Two years after making this speech Wilber wrote a book which gave fuller expression to his theory. In it he quoted some of the rainfall statistics compiled by Dr. A. L. Childs of Plattsmouth, the same statistics used to such good effect by Hayden. Wilber was particularly interested in the years from 1855 to 1872. He divided these years into two nine-year and three six-year periods. The important figures were these: During the first nine-year period the average rainfall for the state as a whole had been 25.75 inches; during the first six-year period, it was only 23.70; but during the last six-year period (1867–72) 38.18 inches had fallen on Nebraska's by then well-plowed soil. "As will be seen," Wilber concluded, "each period gives an increased rainfall."[27]

26. C. D. Wilber, "The Relations of Geology to Horticulture," Nebraska State Horticultural Society, *Annual Reports . . . 1878 and 1879* (Lincoln, 1879), pp. 91, 92.
27. Charles Wilber, *The Great Valleys and Prairies of Nebraska and the Northwest*

The reason for this was so logical that only someone with an advanced case of myopia could fail to see it. But Wilber was a man of inexhaustible patience. He would explain it, simply and clearly, that all might understand. "Suppose now," he wrote, "that a new army of frontier farmers . . . could, acting in concert, turn over the prairie sod . . . and present a new surface of green, growing crops instead of the dry, hardbaked earth." The consequences would be immediately apparent. A "cool" landscape would replace a "hot" one. The land would be green, the hills softened and more rolling in appearance. A pastoral scene would be substituted for the once harsh and forbidding surface of the Plains. And no one, Wilber contended, could contest the inevitable effect of this surface upon the moisture in the atmosphere. A reduction of temperature had to occur; the clouds would then release their moisture and Nebraska would receive more rain. "The chief agency in this transformation," Wilber reminded his readers, "is agriculture. To be more concise, *Rain follows the plow.*"

Here was a system of development so perfect that it seemed to Wilber almost divinely ordained. Overeagerness was the only thing that could possibly defeat it, and Wilber paused long enough to warn of that hazard. What worried him was that the rush for land would proceed too fast, that isolated groups of people would move too far in advance of existing settlements and hence beyond the line of increasing rainfall. Climatic change required relatively dense settlement. A few scattered and isolated communities could not work the desired change, and so it was important that the line of immigration move forward slowly and not push out in detached settlements. If Wilber's warning were heeded the "wild prairie" would disappear soon enough, "and lo! the new farm and forest would brighten in its stead."

Wilber was enraptured by the prospect. Everywhere, he wrote, under these changed conditions, "the clouds will gather into larger clouds, and overspread the heavens; and the impending shower will fall upon the farm and garden, not by grace of fortuity, but by an eternal law." Wilber was overwhelmed, the English language was barely able to express his vision. As he put it,

> In this miracle of progress, the plow is the avant courier—the unerring prophet—the procuring cause. Not by any magic or enchantment, nor by incantations or offerings but instead in the sweat of his face, toiling with his hands, man can persuade the heavens to yield their treasures of dew

(Omaha: Daily Republican Printing Company, 1881). The quotations in this and the following three paragraphs were taken from pp. 52–53, 68, 70, 91, 137.

and rain upon the land he has chosen for a dwelling place. It is indeed a grand consent, or, rather, concert of forces—the human energy or toil, the vital seed, and the polished raindrop that never fails to fall in answer to the imploring power of prayer and labor.

Such was the power of man over nature.

A new theory had been born as Americans sought to make the Plains habitable for themselves and for all others acceptable to them. Their search led them to many strange theories, but few as strange or as scientifically aberrant as that of increased rainfall. The belief that the rainfall could be increased through cultivation was hardly worth the support of the most unbalanced alchemist. It was little more than a fervent dream which constant incantation was expected to make real. That it enjoyed the endorsement of some reputable men is evidence not of its scientific credibility but of the urgency with which the American people approached the settlement of the Plains. They could, in their rhetoric, make these Plains almost anything they wished: a haven for the oppressed, a bountiful garden, a Beulah Land of milk and honey. But until Hayden and Thomas, Aughey and Wilber, the Americans could not make the Plains humid, and so long as the region remained semiarid it was capable of frustrating all the promises made in its name. Once converted, however, the boomers' frontier could continue without pause. The theories of increased rainfall, particularly those of Aughey and Wilber, supplied that conversion factor.

The railroads listened to Aughey's and Wilber's discussions of the rain-follows-the-plow theory with considerable interest. The roads had fought unceasingly against the idea of the Great American Desert for years, but with limited weapons and limited success. The two Nebraskans supplied them with a counter theory to the desert which was perfect in every detail and they quickly seized upon it. The railroads, of course, were not ignorant of the earlier theories of increased rainfall. Indeed they had used some of them in their promotional campaigns. But until the appearance of rain-follows-the-plow they had only been able to present various accounts of increased rainfall, none of which contained the simplicity of argument which distinguished those of Aughey and Wilber. This does not mean that the the railroads' use of earlier theories was unimportant in the total context of the boomers' frontier. Many of them were imaginative; all of them were at least as scientific as Aughey's and Wilber's.

Particularly is this true of the theories of Richard Smith Elliott, until the mid-1870s one of the chief theoreticians of increased rainfall and the man upon whom the railroads depended for much of their promotional material. As industrial agent for the Kansas Pacific Railway from 1870 to 1873, he exemplifies the early interest of the railroads in increased rainfall. At one time or another, Elliott was a farmer, printer, newspaper editor, sub-agent for the Indian Bureau, member of Doniphan's expedition, real estate promoter, and insurance agent. He was also the inventor of a hydraulic dredging machine designed to widen and improve the Mississippi River. With this machine Saint Louis, his native city, could expect to surpass Chicago in the competition for industry and commerce. He was no more correct in this evaluation than in some of his others.[28]

Such endeavors were of trifling importance, however, when compared with the grand scheme of his life: the reclamation of the entire Plains region. Here, too, his solicitous concern with the welfare of Saint Louis was partly responsible for his interest. Saint Louis was, in effect, the eastern terminus of the Kansas Pacific Railroad. A share of any rewards which accompanied the development of the Kansas Pacific land grant would necessarily accrue to that city. In Elliott's opinion, however, the Kansas Pacific was seriously underestimating the potential of the western half of its grant, and in the process depriving Saint Louis of an important source of revenue.[29] In order to correct this deficiency he published a short pamphlet in March, 1870, entitled *Climate of the Plains*. It was both a correction and a job application. Elliott emphasized the seasonal distribution of rainfall on the Plains and made some rather flattering comparisons between the wheat-producing regions of Russia and the grasslands of Kansas.[30] He was not prepared as yet to state definitively that the rainfall was increasing, but there seemed to him solid evidence to suggest that possibility. It was a possibility he was eager to explore.

He was confident, moreover, that the Kansas Pacific would share his enthusiasm. With considerable accuracy he reminded John D. Perry, president of the line, of the central difference between building a railroad on the Plains and building one in more favored localities. "Most railroads in America," he wrote to Perry, "have been built through regions of good repute and no effort or but little has been needed to attract population. Such is the case in the Eastern half of your road in Kansas." Such, unhappily, was not the case in the western

28. Elliott, *Notes*. Elliott to Charles Mason, January 24, 1870, Elliott LPB.
29. Elliott, *Notes*, pp. 303–4.
30. Reprinted in ibid., pp. 302–8.

half. There the line traversed "a country reputed unfit for anything but pastoral industry. Such a region can have but a sparse population, and but a limited business for the road." But, Elliott continued, if it could be shown that agriculture could be profitably pursued in the western half of the Kansas Pacific grant, a number of deserving people, Perry not the least of them, would benefit immeasurably. Elliott was sure he could perform the necessary demonstration. Once again he made only the most oblique and cautious reference to increased rainfall. Diversification, he insisted, was the key to success.[31]

By the summer of 1870 he was fully cured of such diffidence. He had become a convert to the theory of increased rainfall. Granted, his commitment appeared to grow in direct proportion to his need of a job, but it seemed to have been no weaker for all that. By then, too, he had secured the endorsement of Joseph Henry of the Smithsonian Institution, whose support could only have impressed certain of the Kansas Pacific officials. As Elliott wrote to C. B. Lamborn, secretary of the road, in regard to Henry, "I think I can *prove* by him—and he is a good authority in Meteorology—*that not only is the climate changing, but from causes in operation a great change is to be expected.*"[32] Two days later he wrote from an outpost in western Kansas that "enough moisture [had] floated over . . . to make the plains the garden of the world." With Henry's help he was sure he could make this moisture fall.[33]

Thus did Elliott give expression to one of the most common observations of those who would make it rain: the Plains had as many rainy days and as many cloudy days as the prairies to the east. Surely some of that water could be precipitated before it passed eastward. The slightest push would seem enough to start torrential downpours, whether that push be administered by cannons, trees, railroad tracks, telegraph wires, or plows. The Kansas Pacific officials must have thought so too, for in September, 1870, they appointed Elliott industrial agent and agreed to finance three agricultural experiment stations which he was to conduct on the plains of western Kansas. All of them were designed to prove that the rainfall was increasing.

These stations were located at Wilson's Creek, the town of Ellis, and Pond Creek, respectively 239, 302, and 425 miles from the eastern

31. Elliott to John D. Perry, April, 1870, Elliott LPB.
32. Elliott to Lamborn, September 16, 1870, ibid. See also Elliott to Daniel Witter, May 25, 1870, ibid.
33. Elliott to Lamborn, September 18, 1870, ibid; Elliott to Henry, September 22, 1870, ibid.

border of the state. Pond Creek, being the farthest west, was considered by Elliott "one of the worst spots on all the Plains." If crops could be made to grow there, he reasoned, they could be grown anywhere.[34] But Elliott had immense confidence, not only in his own wonder-working abilities, but in the land itself. The Plains had been unfairly categorized as often by those favorably disposed toward them as by the desert theorists. "Even the grand ideas of William Gilpin," Elliott wrote, "are short of the value of that . . . region between the west line of Missouri and the mountains of Colorado." Gilpin had consigned the Plains to pastoral use only; Elliott would prove their agricultural value.[35]

He had few illusions about the purpose of his assignment. He was to inform the world of his experiments, not necessarily as a gesture of humanity, but "as a means of advertising the road!" Success, moreover, was inevitable. Even if he should fail to prove the wealth of the country, he could "at least demonstrate that it had a railway in it!"[36] Here, then, was the man the Kansas Pacific officials turned loose on an unsuspecting public. They employed him to conduct agricultural experiments which only the most skilled agronomist should have attempted. He masqueraded as a scientist and his unfounded theories were called truth.

Every one of these theories came to the same conclusion: Kansas was about to experience more rain than she had ever known before. This prediction in itself was not new. What distinguished Elliott from the other theorists of increased rainfall was his almost total lack of scientific discrimination. He endorsed at various times every theory ever put forward to explain climatic change. He accepted many different and often contradictory ideas, which is to say that he had no idea at all. His own theory as he explained it to the Kansas Pacific was a confused and jumbled combination of all those which preceded it. Rain followed plows and trees, surely, but it also followed telegraph wires, railroad tracks, irrigation ditches, streams and rivers, colony town sites, roads, and fire prevention.[37]

34. Elliott to R. E. Carr, November 15, 1872, ibid.

35. Elliott, *Notes*, p. 303.

36. Ibid., p. 304.

37. At one time or another Elliott endorsed all of the conceivable rainmaking agents. See Elliott, *Industrial Resources of Western Kansas and Eastern Colorado* (St. Louis: Levison and Blythe, 1871), p. 24; Elliott, *Notes*, pp. 299–300, 310; "Forest Trees in Kansas," in *Annual Report . . . 1872* of KSBA (Topeka, 1874),

The officials of the Kansas Pacific must have looked on with bewilderment at this assortment of rain producers. The garden had not bypassed Kansas after all. But Elliott was indefatigable in his researches. He proceeded with reckless dedication, and in 1871 came to the disquieting conclusion that snow also followed rails, and wire, and plows, and all the other accompaniments of civilization. But snow, as Robert Carr, the new president of the line, reminded Elliott, held up trains and forced delays in freight service. Elliott was sympathetic but adamant. If Carr wanted rain he must also accept snow—that was the natural order of things. But at least he could take comfort in the fact that increased snowfall was "not an unmixed evil." It meant that the rainfall too was increasing, that settlers were coming, that the railroad was making money.[38] Carr, presumably, was appeased.

Elliott tended his experimental stations with almost maternal care. He visited them frequently to check on the progress of the wheat, corn, rye, and barley which he had planted in expectation of increased rainfall. In the summer of 1872, he seemed to one sympathetic reporter on the way to "the realization of his fondest hope, namely: That of abolishing the 'Great American Desert.'"[39]

The officers of the Kansas Pacific would be pleased with such progress. The desert had been a source of embarrassment to them for years, and Elliott never lost sight of the fact that his principal mission was to promote the settlement of K.P. land by eliminating from it any lingering traces of that desert. It would be an oversimplification, however, to assume that that was his only motivation. Elliott was a promoter but like most of that breed he was aware of the larger implications of proving the Plains habitable. He was also an American of the late nineteenth century, which in itself presupposes a concerned interest in the future possibilities for national growth. The fact that that growth must soon fill the Plains with happy yeomen and happier Kansas Pacific officials was indeed fortuitous, for it allowed men like Elliott to combine more practical considerations with idealism. In Elliott's case, idealism meant the maintenance of the safety valve.

As early as 1868, even before he began to consider a position with the Kansas Pacific, Elliott expressed his concern that the overflow

---

p. 258; *Republican Daily Journal* (Lawrence, Kans.), March 9 to April 14, 1871; Elliott to Robert Carr, November 9, 1872, Elliott to Joseph Wilson, September 21, 1870, and Elliott to John Perry, January 7, 1871, all in Elliott LPB.

38. Elliott to Carr, November 20, 1871, Elliott LPB.

39. Tice, *Over the Plains; on the Mountains*, p. 250.

population of the eastern cities be allowed to drain off to the West.[40]
Two years later he repeated the idea, this time in connection with
the experiments he hoped to lead for the railroad. These experiments,
he told General John Pope, must be "in advance of that peopling of the
Plains . . . which the census of 1870 *will show must soon be necessary.*"
His belief, of course, added a degree of urgency to Elliott's fumbling
attempts to make corn grow at Pond Creek. More was at stake than
the sale of Kansas Pacific land, for until "the popular estimate of the
value of the great plains was changed, the necessary settlement of that
region would be by a desperate people searching for any alternative to
urban life."[41] There was some question in Elliott's mind whether
American institutions could stand the strain. Kansas would be settled;
by whom, when, and under what circumstances were still at stake. But
until some settlement changed the climate the popular estimate of the
Plains would remain the same. Here was where God could "make good
use . . . of the railroad promoter in His great work to provide homes for
future generations." The promoter could activate simultaneously both
the safety valve and the theory of increased rainfall. According to
Elliott, the process was going on over a very large region, "and every
encroachment of the 'frontier' upon the open, arid plains . . . is so
much gained, . . . [for] as the march continues the desert narrows its
bounds." In a few years it was to have disappeared, and with it the
"popular estimate."[42] Promotion had thus become its own reward.
The railroads attracted the people, the people brought the rain, the rain
attracted more people. Surely the gods were smiling upon the Americans.

By 1873 they no longer smiled on Elliott. His project to make the
Plains blossom had been discontinued. The drought and panic of 1873
had prevented the Kansas Pacific from meeting its bonds, and its
industrial agent, once the handmaiden of God in the settlement of the
Plains, was suddenly dispensable.[43] In his brief tenure, however,
Elliott had done much to further the theory of increased rainfall. He
had endorsed it so completely, so unquestioningly, and he had imparted
so much of his faith to others, that not until the 1890s would the

40. Elliott to S. W. Pike, August 22, 1868, Elliott LPB. See also Elliott to Horace
Greeley, February 22, 1870, and Elliott to Whitelaw Reid, March 5, 1870, ibid.
41. Elliott to Pope, June 29, 1870, ibid.
42. Elliott, *Notes*, p. 324.
43. Elliott, however, remained forever the promoter. His book, *Notes Taken in
Sixty Years*, was by his own admission a promotional effort (Elliott to C. B. Schmidt,
April 23, 1884, Elliott LPB).

boomers' frontier begin to reexamine the premises upon which it was based. Until then the railroads would continue to promote on the promise of increased rainfall and immigrants would continue to respond to that promise.

Though Elliott was dismissed as industrial agent and resident rainmaker, boomers for the Kansas Pacific continued to promote on the basis of his theories. They were joined eventually by almost every road which went in or near the western half of the Plains. All were confident, as Elliott had been, that increased rainfall would be one of the rewards of settlement. In June, 1875, the Union Pacific carried an article by Samuel Aughey in its promotion newspaper, the *Pioneer*. It was written before Aughey had settled upon the plow as the agent of increased rainfall, but the promise was nonetheless explicit. No such uncertainty as to the principal cause of this climatic change was apparent in the comments of A. C. Wheeler, unofficial boomer for the Santa Fe. Wheeler directed his attention to the railroad's lands west of Fort Dodge. According to his account, these lands, which had once been thought unproductive, were then yielding prodigious crops. The cause of the change was clear. "All that the great plains need to redeem them—if the conversion of the finest grazing lands into farms may be called redemption—is the plow." [44]

By the 1880s few railroad men would disagree that such a conversion was indeed redemptive. Carrying cows was profitable enough for the railroads only so long as there was nothing else to carry. The railroads never considered the cattle industry a permanent part of their development program for the Plains, and once the agricultural frontier began to encroach on grazing lands, they were quick to promise that rain was following it. The eighties, then, were the decade of greatest activity in railroad promotion. The roads struck hard and often in their campaign to attract new immigrants. And invariably their promises made reference to increased rainfall.

In 1880 the Burlington promoters gave an indication of the general tone this promotional flurry was to take. "The old proverbial drought of the Far West," they assured their readers, "is a thing of history. The causes which produced long seasons of drought in the early years, no longer exist." They had been replaced by new forces which worked in new and wondrous ways to make it rain. Among these were cultivation, tree planting, railway, telegraph, and town building, "and

44. A. C. Wheeler, *The Iron Trail* (New York: F. B. Patterson, 1876), p. 22. See also Santa Fe, *How and Where to Get a Living* (Topeka, 1876), p. 7.

other causes of atmospheric disturbances attendant upon civilization."[45]
The Santa Fe promoters were somewhat less eclectic in their approach.
One of their promotional pamphlets contained an illustrated rendition
of the rain-follows-the-plow theory. The pamphlet was entitled *The
Kansas Picture Book*, and it appears to have been designed for intending
immigrants with little time for reading long promotional tracts. The
caption on a picture of a Kansas farmer using a steel plow asks, "Who
killed the Great American Desert?" The sturdy yeoman depicted
answers assertively, "I did, with my team and plow."[46]

How many prospective immigrants believed the moral of that picture
story is unknown, but officials of the Union Pacific Railroad certainly
did. In Nebraska, they reported that their lands had experienced a
remarkable increase of rainfall since the first settlement of the state.
In the process western Nebraska had been converted from a stock-
growing region to "one combining both stock and grain."[47] A similar
change was evident in Kansas where "the effect of general settlement
... will be to produce a marked increase in the annual rain-fall."[48]
Eventually, when the entire region came under cultivation, it would
become "one great absorbent body, that may be likened truthfully to a
sponge." Having established this fact, the promoters for the U.P.
were obligated to explain this spongy land of theirs. They accepted
the responsibility happily. "The more moisture," they reported, "the
more vegetation; the more vegetation, the better is the moisture retained
and given off to evaporation to make more moisture, and so on in an
endless circle." Here was a theory with enormous, if dizzying, implications. The Plains were progressing from desert wilderness to grazing
domain, to agricultural garden, to subhumid grassland, to forest, to
swamp.[49]

Once the Union Pacific accepted this progression, it was an easy
step to an admission that the first explorers might have been right in

45. Burlington, *Nebraska, B & M Lands* (Omaha, 1880).

46. Tewksbury, *The Kansas Picture Book*, pp. 56–57. For the proper effect the
picture on the following page shows an African native working his land with a crude
wooden plow. It is captioned simply, "I didn't."

47. Union Pacific, *Guide to the Lands of the Union Pacific R'y Co. in Nebraska*
(Omaha, 1882), p. 13. See also *Pioneer*, December, 1883.

48. Union Pacific, *Kansas: The Golden Belt Lands* (Omaha, 1882), p. 10.

49. Union Pacific, *The Resources and Attractions of Nebraska* ... (Omaha, 1893),
p. 25; *Nebraska: A Complete and Comprehensive Description of the Agricultural
Resources, the Stock Raising, Commercial and Manufacturing Interests*, 3d ed
(Omaha, 1897), p. 11.

describing the Plains as a desert. To do so did not involve a repudiation of the garden image; in fact it sustained it by affirming that the creator of that garden was man. Not only that, it allowed the promoters to proclaim their objectivity by giving them an opportunity to speak negatively of the Plains. Surely no one could doubt the honesty and detachment of the Union Pacific promoter who wrote in 1893 of the "Great American Desert [spreading] its arid, lifeless mantle of sand over thousands of square miles of the great western basin of the Mississippi. . . . The superheated air rising from the parched and lifeless clays and sands of this American Sahara, withered the verdure and stifled the creatures around its borders." But then, he continued, settlers entered this hellish region and gradually the desert began to recede. By 1893 it had moved beyond the limits of Nebraska. "Little by little the Great American Desert [had] faded away." [50]

That the desert had disappeared seemed evident to the promoters of the 1890s. A decade earlier, however, the issue was still in doubt, and for the identical reason mentioned by Wilber—the insatiable desire for land which led settlers beyond the rain line. The Santa Fe warned of this danger in 1880 while at the same time promoting their lands. The settler, according to the railroad, "should not go too far west," particularly since the Santa Fe had so much good land at reasonable terms farther east. The advantage to the settler in taking up these lands was considerable, for he would then remain within the "rain limits." As the Santa Fe explained, "The rainline . . . has moved steadily, year by year, at the rate of about 18 miles per annum, keeping just ahead and propelled by the advancing population. It is to the interest of the settler, therefore, to keep behind this line." [51] The Union Pacific and the Rock Island agreed, though they failed to include in their warning a time table which could be used to determine a safe time for moving on. [52]

This was an inspired piece of promotion. It incorporated a number of different objects dear to the railroads while at the same time giving an impression of studious concern for the welfare of the settlers. The

50. Union Pacific, *The Resources and Attractions of Nebraska*, p. 8. The Santa Fe also promoted on this basis. See "Effects of Civilization on the Climate and Rain Supply of Kansas," in *Guide to the Arkansas Valley*, by Santa Fe (Topeka, 1881), pp. 1–3; Santa Fe, *How and Where to Get a Living*, p. 36.

51. Santa Fe, *How and Where to Get a Living*, p. 36.

52. Union Pacific, *Five Million Acres: The Union Pacific Guide; Homes and Farms in Kansas and Colorado at Low Prices and Eleven Years' Credit* (Kansas City, Mo., 1882), p. 6; *Western Trail*, July, 1886.

new arrivals were kept from scattering and moving too far west, which greatly facilitated the railroads' freight scheduling. They were also encouraged to settle in colonies, which accomplished the same thing and allowed the roads to dispose of their lands in larger quantities. And it gave the impression that increased rainfall was now taken for granted as part of life on the Plains. In fact, so sophisticated had science become that it could predict the rate at which the rain line was moving and thus instruct the immigrant on precisely where to settle in order to achieve the maximum precipitation in his particular rainfall zone. It was all a routine matter.

Like so much of the promotional material to come out of the boomers' frontier, this device was probably the product of an obscure employee's imagination. Hopefully he was sufficiently rewarded. But minor functionaries in the promotional division were not the only railroaders to endorse the theory of increased rainfall. On at least two occasions presidents of railroad corporations announced publicly their acceptance of the theory. Sidney Dillon of the Union Pacific stated simply that the railroads brought the people, the people brought the plows, and the plows brought the rain. Charles Francis Adams of the same road was somewhat less simplistic, explaining that the plow broke the impervious sod, which permitted the soil to retain more moisture, which increased the evaporation, which produced the rain.[53]

Vernon Louis Parrington defined the late nineteenth century as an era in which frontier values were accepted as standards for the entire nation.[54] His thesis receives partial confirmation in the acceptance of the various notions of increased rainfall by federal officials, railroad executives, eastern scientists, and gazetteers.[55] But, as Parrington's interpretation suggests, the theory of increased rainfall was a peculiarly western product. In no section of the country was it embraced with greater fervor or publicized with greater anticipation. The plains-

53. Sidney Dillon, "The West and the Railroads," *North American Review* 152 (April 1891): 445; Charles F. Adams, "The Rainfall on the Plains," *The Nation* 45 (November 24, 1887): 417.

54. V. L. Parrington, *Main Currents in American Thought*, vol. 3, *The Beginnings of Critical Realism in America: 1860–1920* (New York: Harcourt, Brace & World, 1958), pp. 9–10.

55. For examples of gazetteers, see Brockett, *Our Western Empire*, pp. 82, 98, 208, 366, 730–31, 736, 862, 863, 907; William Thayer, *Marvels of the New West* (Norwich, Conn.: Henry Publishing Co., 1890), p. 657; Samuel Bowles, *Across the Continent* (New York: Hurd and Houghton, 1869), p. 138; Webb, *Buffalo Land*, p. 485.

man looked upon it as a means of attracting neighbors, but he used it also to sustain his own efforts in farming a semiarid region. Eventually "rain follows the plow" became for him a kind of incantation. If chanted often enough and believed fervently enough, it might be made to come true. And so the westerner believed it, not only because he wanted to but because he had to.

This was particularly true in Nebraska and Kansas where irrigation was originally considered the last resort of a defeated farmer and not to be engaged in by American yeomen. It was, as well, a defilement of the land, an admission that the rainfall was inadequate and had to be supplemented by means of ditches and canals. Attitudes were to change in both states but not until the potency of the plow as the agent of increased rainfall had been exposed as a myth.

Nebraska's great contribution to the theory was the team of Aughey and Wilber. These two concluded the issue as far as the state was concerned and seldom did Nebraska promoters depart far from their teachings in the conduct of promotional campaigns. The editors of the leading agricultural newspaper in the state recognized the value of Aughey's theory as early as 1878 and from that time forward seldom neglected to reaffirm their faith.[56] Following this lead, every promotional agency in the state by the 1880s was actively publicizing Aughey's and Wilber's theory to what they hoped was a receptive immigrant audience. The State Land Commissioner said that rain followed the plow and so did the State Board of Agriculture.[57] The State Horticultural Society agreed, one of its members adding further sanction to Aughey's theory by reminding his colleagues of the passage in Genesis "where it is said that there was no rain because there was not a man upon the the earth to till the ground."[58]

It is doubtful that this remark reached a very large audience, but such cannot be said regarding the address Orange Judd delivered at the

56. *Nebraska Farmer*, May, 1878. Subsequent issues to about 1893 almost always contained some reference to increased rainfall.

57. F. M. Davis [state land commissioner], *Nebraska: Its Advantages and Resources* (Lincoln, 1880), p. 9; NSBA, *Transactions . . . from September, 1876, to September, 1879* (Lincoln, 1880), p. 99. Even Charles Bessey, one of the most respected botanists of the nineteenth century, was influenced by Aughey's and Wilber's work. See NSBA, *Annual Report . . . 1885* (Lincoln, 1886), p. 81. L. W. Hicks, the state geologist, was yet another scientist who succumbed. See "Report of the State Geologist," in *Annual Report . . . 1892* of NSBA (Lincoln, 1892), pp. 182–89.

58. Nebraska State Horticultural Society, *Annual Report . . . 1883* (Lincoln, 1885), p. 23.

Nebraska State Fair in 1885. Judd was the editor and publisher of the *Prairie Farmer*, a well-known midwestern journal, and Nebraska obtained full promotional value from his presence by reprinting the text of his address and distributing it as part of its advertising campaign. Judd acknowledged his debt to Aughey and Wilber, praising their experiments as among the most important ever conducted in agricultural science. He then added to their theory a corollary of his own, one which must have delighted the gathered Nebraskans. "As soon as ... Kansas settles up and breaks its prairie sod," he said, "those parching winds that formerly came up into Nebraska, and still come at some points, will be heard no more." [59]

While Orange Judd was reminding Nebraskans of their debt to Aughey, Robert Furnas was in New Orleans trying to recruit more farmers and their plows at the World's Industrial and Cotton Centennial Exposition. The official Nebraska publication for the exposition, put together by Furnas, contained three pages on increased rainfall. According to Furnas, rain was following a variety of objects in his state, plows and trees being the most important leaders. "Professor Aughey" was his source and his inspiration. "Judging from the past," Furnas told his readers, "we may confidently expect a continued increase in rainfall." As a result, "the most enthusiastic believer in the western movement of agriculture might be astonished to-day and not be surprised if the whole slope from the base of the mountains eastward could be made an agricultural region." If there were any who were not enthusiastic believers in the westward movement of agriculture, they remained well hidden, and Furnas, by using that phrase, made the necessary connections among the desert, the garden, and America's cultural mission. [60]

Eight years and two droughts after the New Orleans show, Nebraska was presented with another opportunity to parade her resources at a national exposition. The Chicago World's Fair and Columbian Exposition was the event and rain-follows-the-plow was again the theme. This time, however, there was some equivocation on the part of the Nebraska representative. There seemed "little reason to doubt that the annual precipitation will perceptibly increase ... [for] rain is said to

59. *Address of Mr. Orange Judd at the Nebraska State Fair, Lincoln, Sept. 16, 1885* (Lincoln, 1886), pp. 9–12.

60. Robert Furnas, *Nebraska: Her Resources, Advantages, Advancements, and Promises; World's Industrial and Cotton Centennial Exposition* (New Orleans: E. A. Brandon & Co., 1885), pp. 20–22.

follow the plow." This was uncommon restraint for Nebraska, but time and much suffering had deprived Aughey and the other prophets of the millennium of some of their infallibility.[61]

Kansas never produced a publicist as significant as Aughey or Wilber, but the state did not suffer from a lack of rain-follows-the-plow theorists. In fact, in the early 1870s, a number of Kansas promoters came to conclusions remarkably similar to those of Aughey. F. G. Adams, in a privately published guide, the *Great Homestead Region of Kansas*, wrote in 1873 that the rainfall of the Plains was steadily increasing. This in itself was not remarkable but the author attributed the increase to cultivation, tree planting, and the elimination of Indians, buffaloes, and prairie fires.[62] The *Daily Commonwealth* of Topeka was less certain about the specific origins of the increased rainfall but it did agree with Adams that the substitution of "American" for Indian culture would have much to do with it.[63]

By the late 1870s the notion of increased rainfall was widely accepted in Kansas. Aughey had announced his discovery and the state had the services of a philosopher to explain the phenomenon. The *Chronoscope* of Larned carried an account of Aughey's theory in eight long installments; such detail was necessary, presumably, to avoid confusion and misunderstanding. Certainly there could be no mistaking the consequences of the theory: "The 'Great American Desert,'" the series concluded, "has disappeared, and in its place is presented a system of agriculture such as the world scarcely ever dreamed of." [64]

That was encouraging news to those who farmed or hoped to farm the plains of Kansas. But they were not the only ones affected. The money lenders also remembered "when the whole region of this state was 'The Great American Desert'" so well that one of them, J. B. Watkins, had established a geographical limit west of which he would not loan money. Fortunately, the limit was receding. Watkins was confident that "the rainless belt has retreated before the march of civilization

61. *Nebraska: Her Resources, Advantages and Development*, prepared and comp. by Joseph Garneau (Omaha, 1893), p. 5.

62. F. G. Adams, *The Homestead Guide, Describing the Great Homestead Region in Kansas* . . . (Waterville, Kans., 1873), pp. 39, 41.

63. March 26, 1873.

64. March 12 to April 30, 1879. See also Henry Inman, "On Climatic Changes in the Prairie Region of the United States," *The Kansas City Review of Science and Industry* 2 (July 1878): 232; and L. T. Bodine, *Kansas, Illustrated: An Accurate and Reliable Description of This Marvellous State* . . . (Kansas City, Mo.: Ramsey, Mollet & Hudson, 1879), pp. 3–4.

and that wherever civilization has pressed hardest there the limit is farthest west." Looser money, in other words, also followed the plow.[65]

It seems reasonable to assume that a loan company would be among the last enterprises to accept the slogans of railroad and state promoters. Such was not the case in Kansas. Kansans, however, were always more sensitive to being called desert dwellers than were the other residents of the Plains and they tended to endorse every notion which could be used to confute the desert theorists. Rain-follows-the-plow was the best counter theory they had ever had and they embraced it with considerable enthusiasm. It became eventually the only way they could explain their presence in the state. That a loan company official dealing in Kansas lands should endorse it was not overly remarkable. It would have been difficult, in fact, to have found anyone in the state in the seventies and early eighties who did not.

In 1880 one of the leading newspapers in the state, trying to bolster the spirits of the drought-stricken farmers of western Kansas, reminded them that drought was the one common experience which bound all Kansans together. It was not, of course, an experience which any of them had enjoyed; it was just one of the features of life in Kansas. In fact, the paper continued, "It is not unreasonable to assume that there will continue to be [destitution] until the State shall have been all settled and reduced to cultivation." At that time the rain would increase and agriculture would flourish. But until then western Kansans would have to accept their role as rainmakers without complaint. This was a new frontier hardship, making it rain, but once successfully endured the rewards were sweet. Then the good times could begin.[66]

Whether that particular story pacified western Kansas is unknown, but certainly the promoters of the region accepted its basic lesson. In 1883 the *Garden City Herald* indulged its gift of prophecy by forecasting the town's future prospects. It asked its readers to project a hundred years hence: the year is 1983 and "in place of the red man and buffalo, now extinct" stands Garden City with its hundred thousand people, the metropolis of southwestern Kansas. Tributary to it, five hundred thousand farmers' homes dot the plains. "Through a wise policy of cultivation and tree planting the old northern gave way to gentle zephyrs. Kindly rains visit us, without disastrous floods, or dreaded droughts."[67] In 1960 the population of Garden City was

65. Allan Bogue, *Money at Interest* (Ithaca, N.Y.: Cornell University Press, 1955), p. 86.

66. *Daily Commonwealth* (Topeka), June 3, 1880.

67. *Garden City Herald*, March 24, 1883.

11,811, but the *Herald* was right about one thing: even with this population the town did become the agricultural metropolis of southwestern Kansas—and northwestern as well.

Five years later, in 1888, the town of Liberal challenged the Garden City prediction. Southwestern Kansas would have its metropolis but location (the town was named because of the water supply it hoped to control) definitely favored Liberal's bid. This confidence was inspired by the same belief which moved Garden City. "The course of immigration tending in our direction," the town's newspaper reported, "with the increase of cultivation . . . attendant thereupon, will induce a greater amount of rainfall each succeeding year." Within five years, the story continued, southwestern Kansas would produce more corn to the acre than the counties along the Missouri river, and inside of that time Liberal would have a population of ten thousand.[68]

In spite of Liberal's disclaimer that it had wearied of "this blatant 'boom town' business," the people of Liberal and Garden City can be forgiven their own boom-town enthusiasm. It was a natural reaction, particularly since so many men in Kansas joined them in their excesses. The *Garden City Herald*, for example, just six years after its ill-fated prediction, reported that A. C. Dodge of the U.S. Department of Agriculture had expressed amazement at how far the rain belt had moved west since he last saw it. Within ten years, Dodge guessed, it would be at the Rocky Mountains.[69] G. H. Allen, a trained agronomist, wrote in 1888 that western Kansas would one day have more rain than the eastern or central part of the state. The soil, he explained, was more friable and hence better able to absorb the ever-increasing rainfall.[70] Dr. W. A. Yingling did not comment on this possibility, but he did believe that "the Rain Belt moves westward apace with the Star of Empire, [and] . . . may now be considered extended to, or about, the Colorado line."[71] Even Professor Frank H. Snow, later chancellor of the state university at Lawrence, and a man who should have known better, was a believer. He first announced his support of the theory of increased rainfall in 1872 and from that time until 1888, though he occasionally doubted his own wisdom, he continued that support.[72]

68. *Liberal Leader*, May 3, 1888.

69. November 14, 1889.

70. Quoted in the *Kansas Farmer*, April 5, 1888.

71. W. A. Yingling, *Westward; or, Central and Western Kansas* (Ness City: Star Printing Co., 1890), p. 13.

72. See Snow, "Climate of Kansas," in *Annual Report . . . 1872* of KSBA (Topeka, 1873), pp. 397–407; and "Climate of Kansas," in *Second Biennial Report . . . 1879–1880* of KSBA (Topeka, 1881), p. 467.

Some of Snow's articles appeared in the various publications of the Kansas State Board of Agriculture, originally an educational agency but after 1877 the principal promotional organ of the state. In the 1880s the board adopted the theory of increased rainfall and began to promote almost exclusively on the promises it offered. These promises were considerable, as an article by Martin Mohler showed. Mohler was the secretary of the board, and in 1886 he delegated to himself the responsibility of presenting a summary brief in defense of the rain-follows-the-plow theory. It was a masterful performance. "The rapid and unparalleled progress of Kansas in agriculture," he wrote, "is due largely to that climatic change which has been brought about by the settlement and improvement of the country." Nor was this truth known only to westerners. It was "an established fact, known and understood by intelligent people everywhere." The most important of these intelligent people, for Mohler's purpose, resided in the East, and he was pleased to report that the theory of increasing rainfall had been accepted there and was bringing thousands of people to Kansas every year. As these thousands pushed their way into the western part of the state, their "magic touch" would change that once sterile region "to a garden spot of great beauty."[73] Though directed to the other members of the board, Mohler's report was obviously intended for more than just home consumption. He had confirmed, in typically routine language, that rain followed the plow and that all who immigrated would be both the agents and the beneficiaries of that change. The board thus showed again that its interests far transcended lessons in scientific agriculture and the organization of county fairs.

In 1889 it published an article which demonstrated that it had even more diverse interests than just promotion. The author of the article, John Hay, was a geologist for the United States Geological Survey, a position which obviously did not inhibit his imagination. Hay attempted to explain the universal importance attached to the settlement of the Plains.

We feel that in our endeavors to extend the present boundaries of the habitable portion of our globe, bringing to our use and service the elements and forces of nature by which we are surrounded in order to surmount the obstacles in our pathway and ameliorate the conditions of our fellow man,

73. Martin Mohler, "Kansas Agriculture, Prospectively Considered," in *Report . . . for the Quarter Ending March 31, 1888* of KSBA (Topeka, 1888), pp. 9, 13–15.

we are but following the pathway marked out by that Eternal Mind which "planned and built and still upholds the world."[74]

Americans, in their westward movement, were never guilty of not taking themselves seriously enough but this piece of rhetoric is high-blown by any standards.

Hay was equally clear as to how the Americans were to go about extending the boundaries of the habitable portion of the globe. Actually little conscious action on their part was necessary. They had simply to do what they had always done—plow the soil. The consequences in Kansas alone would be astounding. "Simply as an agricultural state," Hay predicted, "with one family of five persons per 160 acres," it could support 1,600,000 people. This is what increased rainfall meant for the state but, as Hay had tried to make clear, it meant even more for humanity.[75]

In Colorado the theory of increased rainfall was not endorsed as enthusiastically as it had been in Kansas and Nebraska. The reason is not difficult to see. The usual theory held that rainfall increased in direct proportion to the density of settlement. Since Colorado was on the western edge of the Plains it would be the last to receive this influx of settlers and therefore the last to receive the rainfall they brought with them. The theory also held that it was self-defeating for a homesteader to move out beyond the established rainfall line and therefore Coloradans had to wait for Kansas and Nebrasks to be fully settled before they could begin to claim that rain was following the plow. And that, as they recognized, might take years. In the meantime they emphasized the irrigation possibilities of their state, only occasionally mixing the two promotional claims by insisting that rain followed the reservoirs.[76]

By the late 1880s the time for waiting had passed. Kansas and Nebraska had just experienced five years of boom—by the standards of the 1870s they were almost overcrowded. Surely, settlers could now come into Colorado secure in the knowledge that the rainfall line had

74. John Hay, "Prevention of Drought and Hot Winds," in *Proceedings of the Eighteenth Annual Meeting . . . 1889* of KSBA (Topeka, 1889), p. 105.

75. John Hay, "Atmospheric Absorption and Its Effect Upon Agriculture," in *Proceedings of the Nineteenth Annual Meeting . . . 1890* of KSBA (Topeka, 1890), pp. 123–29. See also John Hay, "The Central State, Its Physical Features and Resources," *Harper's New Monthly Magazine* 77 (June 1888): 46.

76. Gov. Edward McCook told an audience that irrigation produced more rain and hence "as the amount of irrigation increases, the necessity for it apparently decreases." Reprinted in *A Colony Pamphlet, Longmont, July 1, 1871*, in *Experiments in Colorado Colonization*, ed. by Willard, p. 152.

not been passed. *Field and Farm*, an agricultural journal published in Denver, announced the good news in 1886. Rain was definitely increasing in the eastern part of the state, and it would continue to increase, as the precedent of Kansas and Nebraska showed. In addition, the paper continued, a full 75 percent of the state's new recruits had once lived in Nebraska. Obviously they knew what they were doing, and they came to Colorado, the editors of the paper insisted, "with the belief that rain [would] follow them." They even knew how fast. "Compute the time it has taken to bring this result in Nebraska," they wrote, "and then follow the rainbelt as it travels westward, and you can readily see what Colorado will have to contend with fifteen years hence. If we don't have a continuous deluge we will at least have enough rain to get along comfortably."[77] The possibilities of agriculture in Colorado without irrigation were just becoming known and, predictably, the state was determined to share the news with the world.[78]

The State Board of Immigration, which enjoyed a brief revival in 1889, assured the incoming settler that within the previous five years the "rainbelt" had extended far enough to reduce the need for irrigation in the eastern part of the state. A similar argument was made four years later at the Chicago World's Fair and Columbian Exposition. The director of the Colorado exhibit, C. S. Faurot, emphasized the fact that most of the settlers in the rainbelt counties of the state were originally from Kansas and Nebraska and hence were well aware of the miraculous changes a plow was capable of effecting. Particularly was this true in the far eastern tier of counties where distance from the mountains made irrigation impossible but proximity to Kansas and Nebraska made increased rainfall inevitable.[79]

Such an argument was standard promotional procedure. In most instances, if a county or region could not be irrigated it became immediately eligible for admission to what Colorado promoters called the "Rain Belt." This was a dubious honor—most Coloradans preferring

---

77. *Field and Farm*, May 29, 1886; see also ibid., November 12, 1887, and June 22, 1889, where reference is again made to the experience of Kansas and Nebraska.

78. Ibid., April 16, 1887.

79. Colorado State Bureau of Immigration and Statistics, *Natural Resources and Industrial Development and Condition of Colorado* (Denver, 1889), pp. 7, 20, 58; C. S. Faurot, *A Report on the Resources and Industrial Development of Colorado, 1893 . . . Colorado Exhibit, World's Columbian Exposition* (Denver, 1893), p. 21; see also C. S. Faurot, "The Resources of Colorado," *Colorado Magazine* 1 (August 1893), p. 441. This *Colorado Magazine* is not to be confused with the historical journal of the same name.

irrigation where possible—but it did great service to the cause of promotion. Now the whole of eastern Colorado could be boomed for agricultural settlement.

Among the private agencies that endorsed the rain-follows-the-plow theory was the Greeley Board of Trade, a boomer organization that, by its own admission, had once rejected the validity of all notions of increased rainfall in order to promote on the basis of irrigation. By 1887 the members of the board were convinced of the error in their earlier thinking. They wrote of the annual increase in rainfall caused by the cultivation of the soil and the consequent condensation of the moisture which was continually floating over the Plains from the mountains. This increase was making a "huge garden out of the once Great American Desert." [80] Another private group which renounced its earlier devotion to irrigation was the Colorado Homestead Company, a Denver-based firm with extensive land holdings throughout the eastern half of the state. The land in question was located in "what is known as the Rain Belt of East Central Colorado. . . . NO IRRIGATION IS NECESSARY as the rainfall is now sufficient to raise abundant crops and is still increasing." [81] The Syndicate Land and Irrigation Company was even more effusive as it attempted to market its lands in the southwestern corner of the state. The title of the company is evidence of its earlier commitment to irrigation, but fortunately the need for ditches and canals had been removed. As one of their pamphlets put it, "in the eastern part of the State lies the most fertile valley in America; its excellence can not be spoken of in terms too glowing." Those terms were already too glowing, but the company proceeded to even greater misrepresentation. Much of its land was located in Baca County, a high (4,400 feet), wind-swept, semiarid section which forms the southwestern corner of the state. A good part of it was to be blown away in the Dust Bowl storms of the 1930s, but to the Syndicate Land and Irrigation Company, Baca County was part of "what is known as the 'Rain Belt,' or non-irrigated area of eastern Colorado where successful agriculture without irrigation is an established fact." [82] The tragicomedy of the boomers' frontier was still in season.

80. Greeley Board of Trade, *Farming in Colorado . . . With a Short Review of the Climate and Resources of Weld County* (Greeley, 1887), pp. 3–4.

81. Colorado Homestead Company, *Prosperity in Colorado, and Health to Enjoy It* (Denver, n.d.), p. 5.

82. Syndicate Land and Irrigation Company, *Valuable Data* (Denver, n.d.), pp. 42, 43.

The same spirit was displayed by the newspapers of eastern Colorado, as the example of the *Cheyenne Wells Gazette* shows. Cheyenne Wells is located in east central Colorado near the Kansas line. It is in a region where elevation and distance from the major rivers make irrigation all but impossible, and hence, in the lexicon of the Colorado promoters, it was chosen to be in the "Rain Belt." The editors of the *Gazette* had no quarrel with the decision. Indeed, they seem rather to have enjoyed it. They were placed in the same category as western Kansas, and since the rainfall had increased, western Kansas was indistinguishable from eastern Kansas, which in turn was indistinguishable from Illinois.[83] Little wonder then that Cheyenne Wells considered itself "the Kismet City; the Child of Destiny; the Ward of Fate." The very sight of 160 acres of eastern Colorado sod was enough "to make one mad with gladness."[84]

All of this, the editors contended, was the result of the constantly increasing rain. It had removed the need for irrigation and thrown open to a waiting world the once sterile lands around Cheyenne Wells. As evidence of the truth of this contention they cited statements of Charles Francis Adams, Mark W. Harrington, editor of the *American Meteorological Journal*, and Professor A. J. Bent of the State Agricultural College.[85] All confirmed that rain had followed the plow all the way to Colorado. The *Gazette*, seemingly never satisfied, also carried a story from the *Caddoa* (Colorado) *Times*. The Caddoans were equally convinced that cultivation brought more rain but they were unwilling to leave it at that. "The increase of railroads," they thought, ". . . and also the increase of activity on the roads has the same effect of producing more showers. . . . The concussion of the air and rapid movement produced by railroad trains and engines affects the electrical conditions of the atmosphere."[86] This comment was made in 1887, long after the theorists of increased rainfall had settled on the plow as the principal agent of climatic change. But Coloradans had waited a long time for the theory to have relevance in their section and they were determined to use every feature of it.

The same determination was not apparent in Wyoming. While the cattle interests were still in control of the territory there were few plows for rain to follow. Once they had surrendered their control, per-

83. *Cheyenne Wells Gazette*, June 4 and September 17, 1887.
84. Ibid., June 11 and December 31, 1887.
85. Ibid., December 10, 1887, June 23, 1888, and August 27, 1888.
86. *Caddoa Times* in ibid., December 3, 1887.

iodic droughts had made it clear that irrigation was necessary for successful agriculture in most sections of the state. There was one reference to the possibility of increased rainfall in Territorial Governor Thomas Campbell's 1869 message to the legislature, and this reference was repeated in an 1870 report of the United States Commissioner of Agriculture.[87] No attempt was made to promote on the basis of either of these comments, however, until 1888 when Governor Thomas Moonlight expressed an interest in the formation of an immigration bureau to take advantage of the increased rainfall expected to reach Wyoming soon. And even then, trees were to be the agent of that increase. As Moonlight put it, "Every argument in favor of tree planting in Nebraska, Kansas, and Colorado will apply with greater force in Wyoming."[88] Regardless of the accuracy of this forecast, Wyoming would not begin to promote agricultural settlement until the 1890s, and then only on the promises held out by irrigation. In large measure, then, it missed the boomers' frontier, for that frontier, to an overwhelming degree, was founded on theories of increased rainfall.

Those theories, especially that which held that rain followed the plow, provided the promoters with a perfect recruiting device. As such the theories were much more than just quaint pieces of Western folklore. The promise of increased rainfall made the boomers' frontier possible; and that frontier, far from being merely an expression of local chauvinism, was an attempt to sustain the garden image of the American West. That image might have been shattered by the desert myth had Americans not been assured of the meteorological potency of the plow.

87. Message of Governor Thomas Campbell to the First Legislative Assembly of Wyoming Territory ... 1869, typed copy in the WSHS library; "Agricultural Resources of Wyoming Territory," in *Report of the Commissioner of Agriculture for the Year 1870*, by Frederick Watts (Washington: GPO, 1871), p. 551.

88. *Message of Governor Thomas Moonlight to the Tenth Legislative Assembly of Wyoming Territory ... 1888* (Cheyenne, 1888), pp. 10, 11.

CHAPTER SEVEN

Dissenters and Defenders

Generally speaking, by the 1880s promotional excesses were tolerated, even encouraged, by the plainsmen. This was true because once the rain-follows-the-plow theory became a part of the effort, promotion became its own reward. People were the agents of climatic change and a little misrepresentation in attracting them could easily be excused. The plainsmen, then, looked at the boomer with reverence and gratitude. To question his word or his function was to deny the future of the region, an unpardonable sin on any frontier. But the West was not the only section to praise the boomer; the East joined in the applause, and the promoters no doubt took pride in the fact that their performance was given nearly unanimous assent. Perhaps this explains why they reacted with such vehemence when challenged, and why every expression of dissent, regardless of how mild, was interpreted as a libel on the land and its people.

There were dissenters, however—men east and west who for one reason or another felt an obligation to dispute some of the more grandiose of the promoters' claims. These men were significant not only for their ability to remain rational in the midst of frenzy but for the response they elicited from those whose motives and judgment they called into question. One of the first to challenge the prevailing mood was J. H. Beadle. Beadle was a gazetteer, one of that fraternity of travelers and writers who toured the West after the Civil War. Most of these men were highly optimistic in their reports, but according to Beadle the future of the Plains was anything but bright. The entire area from Canada to Mexico and from the Missouri River to the coastal ranges he described as a "Mauvaises Terres, a complete desert." Those seeking the yeoman's paradise of the Jeffersonian imagination were thus well advised to look elsewhere.[1] Beadle, moreover, was not

1. J. H. Beadle, *The Undeveloped West; or, Five Years in the Territories* (Philadelphia: National Publishing Co., 1873), pp. 50–51, 233, 234. Beadle also denied that

alone; Robert Louis Stevenson was another traveler who was struck by the disparity between the promoters' accounts of this land and the reality of conditions. Indeed, like Beadle, he wondered how civilized man could live in this "God-forsaken country." It offered neither spiritual solace nor physical sustenance, only gauntness and space.[2]

Beadle and Stevenson, for reasons unknown, were spared the wrath of the plainsmen. Their criticisms went unanswered, a courtesy not extended to General William Babcock Hazen. In 1875, Hazen published an article in the *North American Review* entitled "The Great Middle Region of the United States, and Its Limited Space of Arable Land." In it he insisted that rain did not follow trees, a serious enough charge in itself; but he went on to deny the notions that transcontinental railroads should precede settlement, particularly on marginal lands, and that promoters were capable of objective description.[3] Hazen directed his criticism at the promotional activities of the Northern Pacific Railroad and it was from that source that most of the response came. E. V. Smalley, publicist for the N.P. and later its court historian, countered Hazen's article with a report from Governor Isaac Stevens that the entire northern route was suitable for cultivation and that "there was no such thing as a desert" anywhere along the path of the line.[4] Linus Brockett, whose gazette *Our Western Empire* was the most complete in its field, also called attention to Hazen's irreverence. In Brockett's mind, Hazen's was a "crushing article," a slanderous attempt to defame an entire region.[5]

---

the American farmer was eligible for admission to a paradise if one could be found. He was more a soil miner than the sturdy yeoman of legend.

2. Robert Louis Stevenson, *Across the Plains, with Other Memories and Essays* (New York: Charles Scribner's Sons, 1892), pp. 44–45.

3. W. B. Hazen, "The Great Middle Region of the United States and Its Limited Space of Arable Land," *North American Review* 120 (January 1875): 33, 27, 25. Hazen also wrote a short pamphlet dealing with the same themes, *Our Barren Lands: The Interior of the United States West of the One-Hundredth Meridian and East of the Sierra Nevadas* (Cincinnati: R. Clarke & Co., 1875). For a recent compilation of the reports and articles in the Hazen affair, see Edgar I. Stewart, ed. and comp., *Penny-An-Acre Empire in the West* (Norman: University of Oklahoma Press, 1968).

4. E. V. Smalley, *History of the Northern Pacific Railroad* (New York: G. P. Putnam's Sons, 1883), p. 86. Smalley later changed his mind. In 1895 he wrote an article confirming Hazen's original theories ("The Future of the Great Arid West," *Forum* 19 [June 1895]: 466–75).

5. Brockett, *Our Western Empire*, p. 740. If this was his purpose, Hazen succeeded fully. Northern Pacific bonds fell to $10 after the publication of his article (ibid.).

Brockett was unable to account for Hazen's perfidy except to note that his motives must have been deep and perverse. Charles Dana Wilber, however, offered one explanation, predictable in its defensiveness, for Hazen's betrayal of the boomer spirit. Easterners, Wilber wrote, craved desert literature. They seemed to have some unconscious need for self-flagellation. It was, in fact, the same demonic need which drove them to drink, and Hazen, insensitive to the canons of responsible literature, catered to this need, pandering to the East's craving for deserts even where none existed.[6]

In the spring of 1879, another naysayer joined the attack against the boomers' frontier. Landon, or Professor Eli Perkins, as he preferred to be known, warned that a trap was being set for credulous emigrants and that they were being deceived and pushed "into a famine region."[7] Included in this famine area was all the country west of the 100th meridian, including most of the central Great Plains. Spokesmen for that region responded immediately to the "Eli Perkins school of 'scientist.'" Brockett excoriated him, accusing him of ignorance of true conditions—among other sins. The Kansas State Board of Agriculture also reacted, issuing a declaration that the "one-hundredth meridian theory is a fit companion of the mythical American Desert." The desert had been conquered by the plow, and the lands west of the 100th meridian would as surely succumb.[8]

Perkins had made no reference to the rain-follows-the-plow theory but the use of that theory in rebuttal by the Kansas board was nonetheless appropriate. It was considered the most effective weapon against the desert theorists, old or new. Its prominence, however, also meant that it would be among the first of the promotional promises to come under attack. In Kansas T. C. Henry, himself a boomer of some stature, denied as early as 1878 that rain followed anything, but Henry was an irrigationist and hence his motives were immediately suspect.[9] If it continued to rain, the irrigation projects in which he had

6. Wilber, *The Great Valleys and Prairies of Nebraska and the Northwest*, p. 138. T. C. Henry of Kansas also criticized Hazen for retarding settlement ("The Settlement of Our Common Country," *Commonwealth* [Topeka], March 17, 1875).

7. Eli Perkins, "Let Emigrants Westward Look Out!," in *New York Sun*, reprinted in Brockett, *Our Western Empire*, p. 39.

8. Brockett, *Our Western Empire*, p. 39; KSBA, *Quarterly Report . . . for the Quarter Ending March 31, 1879* (Topeka, 1879), p. 37.

9. For Henry's comments and subsequent career, see *Henry's Advertiser*, Spring 1878; *Daily Commonwealth* (Topeka), February 2, 3, 7, 1882; *Field and Farm*, December 10, 1887; "Agriculture in Colorado," in *Annual Report . . . 1887–1888* of

an interest would become little more than fossilized remains of an earlier civilization.

But other commentators, less directly involved, quickly took up the issue of increased rainfall. Henry Gannett, an officer of the United States Geological Survey, was one of the first. Gannett realized that challenging the notions of Aughey and Wilber was like "questioning the Copernican system," but he issued that challenge nonetheless. Rain did not follow plows, he wrote, or trees, or railroad tracks, or any other artificial construction. It resulted solely from the interaction of certain physical forces which were beyond the control of man. Stewart Henry was even more certain in his rebuke, and more indignant. The notion that rain followed the plow was "a remarkable fallacy" which produced much suffering, for as Henry realized, "on the strength of it hundreds of families are induced each year to locate on the plains." They should have recognized that man cannot "so easily control Nature and her laws." Frederick Newell, a noted hydrologist and a leader in the reclamation movement, was equally disturbed by this promotional misrepresentation, or "popular delusion," as he called it. It "ensnared many emigrants" and gave them an inflated view of their own power.[10]

Newell was not alone among members of the scientific community in condemning the promotional excesses that resulted from the theory of increased rainfall. Howard Miller, a meteorologist, also denied that rain followed the plow, as did Cleveland Abbe and Willis Moore of the United States Weather Bureau, and J. S. Emory, a Kansas hydrologist.[11]

Colorado State Horticultural and Forestry Association (Denver, 1888), pp. 330, 336. For his irrigation schemes, see James Malin, "Grassland, 'Treeless', and 'Subhumid'," *Geographical Review* 37 (April 1947): 243–44; Joseph O. Van Hook, "Development of Irrigation in the Arkansas Valley," *Colorado Magazine* 10 (January 1933): 10; *Field and Farm*, April 27, 1889; Petition of F. C. Young to the State Land Board, 1889, original copy, John A. Cooper Papers, Colorado Archives.

10. Henry Gannett, "Is the Rainfall Increasing on the Plains?" *Science* 11 (March 2, 1888): 99–100; Stewart Henry, "Rainfall on the Plains," *Popular Science Monthly* 36 (February 1890): 535–38; F. H. Newell, "The Reclamation of the West," in *Annual Report of the Board of Regents of the Smithsonian Institution . . . for the Year Ending June 30, 1903* (Washington, D.C.: GPO, 1904), p. 834. See also F. H. Newell, "Hydrography of the Arid Regions," in U.S. Geological Survey, *Twelfth Annual Report . . . 1891–1892*, pt. 2 (Washington, D.C.: GPO, 1892), p. 234; "Irrigation on the Great Plains," U.S. Department of Agriculture, *Yearbook, 1896* (Washington, D.C.: GPO, 1897), p. 172; "The Public Lands and Their Water Supply," in U.S. Geological Survey, *Sixteenth Annual Report . . . 1894–1895*, pt. 2 (Washington, D.C.: GPO, 1895), p. 513.

11. U.S., Congress, Senate, *Preliminary Report on the Possibilities of the Reclamation*

All recognized that belief in theories of increased rainfall had a pernicious influence on the settlement patterns of the Plains and prevented
a realistic survey of the agricultural potential of the area.

Other critics, although undoubtedly aware of the theories of increased
rainfall, concentrated their attention on the more general abuses of the
boomers. They were occasionally quite trenchant in their comments.
Thomas Donaldson, for example, complained bitterly about the misrepresentations which the promoters used to entice immigrants.
"The arid regions," he wrote, "become in their advertisements areas of
broad, glowing, wheat bearing fields. . . . The boundless sage brush
plains become orange groves . . . and the lack of water a cause for
congratulation, because there will be no swamps to produce ague." 12
The consequences of such deception were tragic. Settlers were attracted
to the Plains, but they were almost totally unprepared for what they
found there. A correspondent for an eastern agricultural journal
wrote that "everything was depicted in the most attractive colors . . .
luring thousands to settle in the wilderness in which many of them are
now starving." *Field and Farm*, a western paper of similar interest,
agreed. "Land companies, railroad corporations and a subsidized
press," one of its editors wrote, "have so glaringly painted the prospects
of success . . . that men's minds have been bewitched and . . . they have
. . . given up the comforts of civilized life to live in dugout hovels,
isolation, beggary—nay, even starvation." 13

Few of these critics attempted to explain the basic reason for such
madness. They blamed the promoters, and with considerable justice,
but they neglected to account for the ready willingness of the prospective immigrant to believe. Rodney Welsh, in a remarkably perceptive
article, supplied that explanation. Americans, he wrote in 1890, were

---

of the Arid Regions of Kansas and Colorado by Utilizing the Underlying Waters
[by Howard Miller], 52d Cong., 1st sess., 1891–92 S. Exec. Doc. 41, pp. 301–6;
Cleveland Abbe, *Monthly Weather Review* 23 (September 1895): 337; Willis Moore,
Monthly Weather Review 27 (June 1899): 257, and vol. 33 (June 1905): 260–61; J. S.
Emory, in *Omaha Bee*, January 1, 1894.

12. U.S., Congress, House, *The Public Domain* . . . (by Thomas Donaldson),
47th Cong., 2d sess., pt. 4, 1882–83, H. Misc. Doc. 45, p. 535. Donaldson was also
something of a nativist. The promotional misrepresentations attracted many undesirables to American shores and this was another reason for his objections (ibid.,
pp. 536–37).

13. *Cultivator and Country Gentleman* 56 (April 23, 1891): 333; *Field and Farm*,
December 10, 1904; see also *Field and Farm*, January 10, 1891, and September 22,
1900.

too much taken with the myth of the happy yeoman, too quick to accept the poetry of Whittier and the writings of Jefferson and Franklin as part of the revealed truth. This was a relatively harmless mistake in the earlier years of America's westward movement, but once the Plains were reached it became a tragic one.[14]

In the late 1880s and into the '90s these charges had a certain disconcerting truth to them. Periodic drought and grasshopper invasions were a source of constant embarrassment to the promotional community and one agency began to reassess its role. The Kansas State Board of Agriculture admitted that it had not always been entirely candid in describing the agricultural potential of the state. Since 1877 the board had been the chief promotional agent in Kansas. Seldom during those years had it concerned itself with the welfare of its resident farmers. Its function had been to seduce, not educate. In 1887, however, the board began to reexamine its role. By that date eastern Kansas had shown itself to be one of the best general farming regions in the United States, and western Kansas had proved to be one of the worst. For both reasons promotion was considered less important to the state than previously.[15] It was also less praiseworthy, as a correspondent to the state board pointed out. Immigrants, he wrote, had come into the state partly "in response to [the] glowing accounts of this land of promise scattered everywhere." They were now facing starvation, a condition for which the board had to assume some responsibility.[16]

By 1893 it had. In that year Martin Mohler, secretary of the board, reported that the theory of increased rainfall was a "delusion and a snare."[17] Two years later, F. H. Snow, one of the leading disciples of the rain-follows-the-plow theory, suffered one of his periodic lapses of

14. Rodney Welsh, "Horace Greeley's Cure for Poverty," *Forum* 8 (January 1890): 586–93. For an expression of similar ideas, see the statement of R. J. Clark in U.S., Congress, Senate, *Report of the Special Commission of the United States Senate on the Irrigation and Reclamation of Arid Lands*, 51st Cong., 1st sess., 3, pt. 4, 1889–90, S. Rept. 928, p. 163.

15. KSBA, *Sixth Biennial Report . . . 1887–1888* (Topeka, 1889), p. 5.

16. W. E. Tweeddale, "Irrigation for Homesteaders in Western Kansas," in *Quarterly Report . . . for the Period Ending March 31, 1891* of KSBA (Topeka, 1891), pp. 79–80.

17. Martin Mohler at the World's Fair, quoted in *Kansas Farmer*, November 29, 1893; see also E. C. Murphy, "Is the Rainfall in Kansas Increasing?" *Transactions of the Kansas Academy of Science* 13 (1891–92): 16–19. But see J. T. Lovewell, "Climate of Kansas," in *World's Fair Report . . .* of KSBA (Topeka, 1893), pp. 31–32, for more rain-follows-the-plow statements.

faith. Rain, he was now saying, no longer followed anything. Rather its timing and amount were the result of a cyclical pattern which neither he nor anyone else was capable of controlling.[18] The board published these remarks in its biennial report, a significant departure from form in itself, but indicative of its changing emphasis.

By 1895 it had reverted almost completely to its original function of supplying agricultural information, and was no longer in the promotion business. Thomas Potter, the new president, explained.

> Probably more than any of its predecessors [the report of 1895] . . . is planned to be an agricultural volume instead of an immigration document. It is intended to be helpful in *promoting the prosperity and advancement of the population the state already has,* rather than to persuading the millions of less fortunate strangers that the mere fact of coming hither with unalterable ready-made views of Kansas people and Kansas agriculture means a life of ease, perpetual June weather, a steady diet of milk and honey, monotonous political harmony, and tireless pursuit of lucrative offices by everybody whomsoever.

This was a rather complete list of promises made by the promoters, and its inclusion in this context marks quite a change from the glory days of the seventies and eighties.[19]

The board took its new responsibilities seriously, publishing among other dissenting articles an account by Charles Lebdell in which the boomers' frontier was held up to scathing criticism. The promoters, according to Lebdell, had behaved so irresponsibly that many people disbelieved everything said about Kansas, or at least discounted it by an appreciable percentage. Promotional accounts of "farms that exist only in the imagination" served to repel rather than attract, and it was time for Kansas to promote on the basis of what she had rather than what she wished she had. Failing that, she should cease to promote at all.[20] Obviously, that type of comment was meant for home consumption only, further evidence of the board's new policy. As the drought of the early 1890s continued it confirmed in the minds of many the wisdom of diminishing the promotional output of the state, and Leb-

18. F. H. Snow, "Periodicity in Kansas Rainfall and the Possibility of Storage of Excess Rainfall," in *Ninth Biennial Report . . . 1893–1894* of KSBA (Topeka, 1895), pp. 338–40.

19. Thomas Potter, in *Tenth Biennial Report . . . 1895–1896* of KSBA (Topeka, 1897), pp. vii, viii.

20. Charles Lebdell, "Western Kansas: Her Needs and Possibilities," in *Twenty-sixth Annual Meeting, 1897 . . . Proceedings* of KSBA (Topeka, 1898), p. 222.

dell's article and others like it seem to have been received with an objectivity unlikely earlier.

But better times returned, and Kansas reverted to her well-practiced sensitivity to criticism. The dissenters were scarcely given a hearing. William Allen White, the Sage of Emporia, was one of those who felt that the time for thoughtful introspection had passed. He was eager to get back to the established values, among them a forward-looking promotionalism. His famous article "What's the Matter with Kansas?" makes the point as only White could.

> The newspaper columns and magazine pages once devoted to praise of the state, to boastful facts and startling figures concerning her resources [he complained] now are filled with cartoons, jibes and Pefferian speeches. . . . We have decided to send three or four harpies out lecturing, telling the people that Kansas is raising hell and letting corn go to weeds. . . . We don't need population, we don't need wealth. . . . We don't need cities on the fertile prairies, you bet we don't.[21]

White's editorial coincided, fortunately, with a general return of confidence in the agricultural potential of Kansas. The drought years had passed. Populist agitation had reached its nadir and once again Kansas could assume a combative posture before the world. The best example of this revived chauvinism came in the early summer of 1902. Though beyond the scope of this study it deserves mention. James Wilson, secretary of agriculture, had committed the unpardonable sin of including western Kansas in the "semi-arid zone." As fate would have it, the spring of 1902 brought devastating floods to much of the central part of the state, and the residents of that area took a perverse sort of comfort in this misfortune. Wilson was due to visit them and they did not intend to let him forget his indiscreet remarks. The *State Journal* of Topeka led the citizens in their ridicule. A headline of July, 1902, announced Wilson's arrival: "The Secretary of Agriculture pronounces Kansas semi-arid—VISITS THE SEMIARID REGION TO FIND IT UNDER WATER." Obviously, the story continued, the secretary would need some assistance to complete his tour. He was then "at Ottawa and tomorrow he [was to] penetrate still further into the heart of the 'semi-arid' belt. To be sure he may have to charter a boat or two before he gets there." Failing that, Wilson could always avail himself of the *Journal*'s offer: "Life Preservers for the Semi-Arid Region," one of its

21. *Emporia Weekly Gazette*, August 20, 1896. Reprinted many times.

advertisements stated, "70 Cents a Pint." Wilson could manage only the lame and somewhat bewildered comment that "you people here seem touchy about that term semi-arid." Actually, what else could be said about a people who took pride and solace from a flood?[22]

Although they generally saved their sharpest comments for those critics who lived outside the Plains, the promoters were scarcely more generous in their dealings with those who would dispute the boomers' frontier from within. Chief among these native critics were the same sturdy yeomen who had been led to the Plains by the blandishments of the promoters. The farmer had much to complain about, including grasshoppers, wind, isolation, drought, and poverty. Of these, drought was undoubtedly the most important, since upon it so many of the other conditions rested, and since it was so totally incompatible with the basic premise on which settlement was based. Plowing the soil, the immigrants discovered, did not produce rain; indeed, all too often it did not produce anything. For some this discovery came quickly. For other, more stubborn men it came only with total failure. But regardless of the time of its arrival it forced thousands of settlers out of the Plains. To the boomers this was bad business and bad publicity; every settler who left was a living testimonial to the weaknesses of their promotional arguments. A number of such testimonials were at large by the end of the century. Charles Harger compiled figures on the population movement out of the plains counties of Nebraska and Kansas between 1887 and 1898. They were not statistics to gladden a promoter's heart. Comanche County, Kansas, had a population of 5,004 in 1887; by 1898 this figure was reduced to 1,369. Greeley County in the same state went from 4,646 to 502 during the same period. Stanton County suffered a loss from 2,864 to 326, Morton, from 2,560 to 255, and Stevens, from 2,663 to 519. In Nebraska the losses were not quite so striking, although here Harger's figures do not begin until 1890 and hence do not include those people who entered the state during the boom of the late 1880s. Nonetheless, Blaine County fell from 1,146 to 300, and Perkins, from 4,370 to 1,975.[23]

These statistics, admittedly, are subject to misrepresentation. Some of those who moved may have remained in the state, some may have been afflicted with wanderlust, and some may have been guilty of using

22. *State Journal* (Topeka), July 15, 1902.
23. Charles Harger, "The Short Grass Country," *Harper's Weekly Magazine* 45 (January 26, 1901): 88–89. See also Fred Shannon, *The Farmers' Last Frontier: Agriculture, 1860–1897* (New York: Harper Torchbooks, 1968), p. 308.

drought and depression as an excuse rather than a reason for their migratory habits.[24] But it seems just as reasonable to assume that many were driven out by drought only after making a determined and genuine effort to succeed on the Plains. Their life was seldom an easy one even under the best conditions; and never did it approach the halcyon picture painted for them by the boomers.

The promoters, however, operated on the assumption that they were performing a rare public service in attracting people to the Plains. Hence any criticism of conditions found there, any appeals for aid when those conditions turned out to be less than ideal, were greeted with derision. They were considered the wailings of a few malcontents and ingrates. Still, appeals for aid were a nuisance that had to be curbed lest the outside world get the wrong impression. The recriminations began early.

In 1860 eastern Kansas suffered from a devastating drought, one of the worst in that region's history. The newspapers were full of details, until the *Daily Conservative* of Leavenworth reminded them of a higher duty to promotion. Doleful accounts of drought and crop failure were considered to be in bad taste; relief measures were unthinkable. Who, the *Conservative* reasoned, would want to immigrate to a region where drought relief was necessary?[25] In Nebraska a similar attitude was shown in 1874, when a lack of rain and an abundance of grasshoppers conspired to destroy most of the corn crop. There was considerable suffering, but Governor Robert Furnas was less concerned with that than with the tarnished image the state would have should news of the drought be released.[26] As he explained to a farmer in the county named after him, "Your destitution dare not be made public; *if it were known, it would blast your hopes for immigration.*"[27] Whether there should have been further immigration without a thorough review of the area's agricultural potential was not considered.

---

24. The latter is James Malin's view. See "Local Historical Studies and Population Studies," in *Cultural Approach to History*, ed. by Caroline Ware (New York: Columbia University Press, 1940), pp. 301–2, 305; *Winter Wheat in the Golden Belt of Kansas* (Lawrence: University of Kansas Press, 1943), p. 109; *The Grassland of North America: Prolegomena to Its History* (Lawrence, Kans.: Privately published, 1947), p. 281.

25. February 14, 1861.

26. Message of Governor Robert Furnas to the public, August 21, 1874, in *Messages and Proclamations*, 1: 435–36.

27. Robert Manley, "In the Wake of the Grasshoppers: Public Relief in Nebraska, 1874–1875," *Nebraska History* 44 (December 1963): 256–57.

Nevertheless, Nebraska was forced to appeal to the secretary of war for drought relief.[28] The adverse publicity which accompanied the action was a source of much irritation to certain elements of the state. A banker from Beatrice claimed to speak for the entire community when he wrote that "immediate steps [must be] taken by the State Officers to contradict the outrageous lies that have been and are now being told about the State." The outrageous lies he referred to were those being circulated by the army relief forces, and they were doing great harm to Nebraska's immigration prospects. One easterner of substantial means notified the bank that he was reconsidering an earlier decision to immigrate because of "the reports [he] had heard of the destitution in the State."[29] If certain Nebraskans had not forgotten where they were and asked for aid, such reports would never have received notice and the state would have secured another recruit. Whether he would have succeeded is problematical, but the Beatrice banker thought he certainly should have been given the chance.

The entire question of relief arose because of what the Union Pacific called "the begging propensities of some of the people ... bringing the State into bad repute."[30] The U.P. was not alone in this judgment. Somehow a number of chronic complainers had been admitted to the Plains, people who overlooked their own inadequacies and poisoned the entire image of this newest garden. The boomers had a number of terms to identify them. "Worthless fellows," "too lazy to work for a living," "grumblers," "lazy and poor business men," "shiftless," "liars"—all were used at various times to describe anyone who complained of drought or grasshoppers.[31] Other commentators went into

28. Gilbert Fite, "The United States Army and Relief to Pioneer Settlers, 1874–1875," *Journal of the West* 6 (January, 1967): 100. Kansas refused even to take this step. As Governor Anthony put it, "Kansas is not beggared. . . . No appeal need be made . . . to the Secretary of War" (I. D. Graham, "The Kansas State Board of Agriculture: Some Highlights of Its History," KSHS, *Collections* 17 [1926–28]:795).

29. Smith Bros., Bankers, to J. B. Wiston, personal secretary to Governor Garber, June 3, 1875, Garber Papers, NSHS. A. E. Touzalin, the Burlington promoter, was similarly unhappy (Touzalin to Garber, June 25, 1876, ibid.).

30. *Pioneer*, April 1878.

31. L. D. Burch, *Kansas As It Is*, pp. 100–101; *Courier* (Winfield, Kansas), December 21, 1882; F. D. Coburn, "Our Mutual Friend, Grumble," in *Report . . . for the Quarter Ending March 31, 1888* of KSBA (Topeka, 1888), pp. 41–44; Charles Sage, "Colorado's Attractions for Young Men," *Colorado Magazine* 1 (April 1893): 76–79; *Field and Farm*, July 4, 1891; *Nebraska State Journal* (Lincoln), April 22, 1897; John Martin, "The Progress of Kansas," *North American Review* 142 (April 1886): 348–55.

greater detail. "The human mind," wrote Samuel Aughey with surprising restraint, "has a tendency to exaggeration. Owing to this, during every locust invasion, the damage done has been over-estimated. . . . Human indolence and carelessness did much more damage."[32] Norman Colman, commissioner of agriculture, agreed. "It is the crop of the bad cultivator," he reported, "that is burned with drought, eaten by insects, or caught by the frost."[33] According to James Canfield, chancellor of the University of Nebraska, more than just poor judgment was involved. In western Nebraska 1893 and 1894 had been extremely lean crop years. Drought and hot winds had reduced the farmers of that region to near-starvation, and again they appealed for aid. Canfield was contemptuous. The appeals revealed a "want of spirit that leads some men to forget their manliness."[34] Canfield's was not an uncommon belief. Those whose conditions contradicted the garden image or those who complained about those conditions were accused of violating every trust placed in them.

The drought-stricken farmers of eastern Colorado were particularly sensitive to charges of betrayal. In 1891 a number of them appealed to Governor John Routt for aid. A petition from Yuma County was careful not to ask for money but for seed wheat, that the farmers might have something with which to start again. This, they assured the governor, was not a request for charity, indeed they "would scorn the thought of being called beggars."[35] A similar petition from Kit Carson County made an even more persuasive appeal. The free distribution of wheat they requested would be used "as an inducement to [the farmers] to stay on their homesteads, and develop the resources of our county, thereby *adding to the prosperity . . . of the whole state.*"[36] The reference to development and prosperity was no doubt intended to forestall any objections that promoters might have to advertising the drought. But, as a group of farmers in the Cheyenne Wells vicinity discovered, the boomers were not so easily mollified. These farmers also petitioned Routt for aid. They made the standard references: most were native

32. Aughey, *Sketches of the Physical Geography and Geology of Nebraska*, p. 143.

33. *Report of the Commissioner of Agriculture, 1887* (Washington: GPO, 1888), p. 143.

34. James Canfield, "Is the West Discontented? A Local Study of Facts," *Forum* 18 (December 1894): 449. See also James Furnas to J. Sterling Morton, August 29, 1894 (Letter Press Books, NSBA, NSHS).

35. Petition from the "Farmers of Yuma County" to Governor John Routt, February 8, 1891, Routt Papers, Colorado Archives.

36. Charles Nealley, John Goff, and Francis Goff to Routt, 1891, ibid.

Americans, all had been in the area at least four years, all were devoted to Colorado, its people and institutions. Unfortunately, in the last three years they had not "raised anything but some fodder," and it appeared as though they would "starve here if [they could not] get aid of some kind." It seemed a reasonable request, but the newspaper of the town disagreed. The *Cheyenne Wells Gazette*, cited earlier for examples of flamboyant promotionalism, had written that "the settlers do not need any ade [*sic*]." The farmers thought they knew why. "Why do they say it? because they think it will keep out settlers. They want us to go now for they have all our money. They want some more to come in that they may get . . . their money."[37] This was no doubt an overly simplistic and conspiratorial explanation, but as other evidence has shown, it was not entirely improbable.

Actually, the entire issue resulted from the original misconception regarding the nature of the Plains. Condemned as a desert, restored as a garden, the area had never been realistically described. Had it been either desert or garden its history would undoubtedly have been different and far less tragic. Americans thought they were accustomed to gardens; they had, so they told themselves, confronted nothing else in the advance westward. They knew what to expect. But had the Plains been a desert they would as surely have been recognized and understood as such. It is impossible to mistake a desert and certainly no one enters one without first preparing to meet the different challenges it presents. The Plains were neither desert nor garden, though at different times they resembled both. They were capable of great extremes, from bountiful productivity to what must have seemed near sterility. The boomer saw only the first extreme; the farmer all too often knew only the second. This was not a condition designed to inspire mutual confidence. To the promoters, dissent from the boomers' proclamations was an admission of either failure or ignorance, and they countered it with every resource they could command. To deny the fertility of the Plains was to deny the American experience, and whatever calumny was cast on the naysayers was thus well deserved. This was especially true if the critic was an outsider such as James Wilson, or especially, John Wesley Powell.

The promoters saved their choicest invectives for Powell and they administered them generously. The reasons are not difficult to see. Powell attempted to understand the Plains and this necessarily involved

37. L. M. Downing, George W. McKain, C. J. Spere, and H. W. Kellogg to John Routt, February 21, 1891, ibid.

a denial of the garden idea. He was, moreover, well trained and well placed. Between 1867 and 1877, he made thirty trips across the Plains, observing, collecting, and working out the basic outlines of what Wallace Stegner called his "blueprint for a dryland democracy."[38] As a member of the Public Land Commission of 1879 and later director of both the United States Geological Survey and the Irrigation Survey, he was in a position to exert considerable influence on the formation of western land policy. In the minds of the promoters his influence was pernicious and sinister, his crimes against the boomers' frontier heinous and committed without provocation.

Powell began his long career of dissent in 1877 upon the accession of Rutherford B. Hayes to the presidency. Hayes appointed Carl Schurz to the post of secretary of the interor with what Schurz interpreted as a mandate to cleanse the agency of past corruption.[39] The time seemed propitious for crusading reform of the land laws, and Powell, then the director of the Geographical and Geological Survey, proposed such changes in his seminal *Report on the Lands of the Arid Regions.* The alienation of the boomers dated from the publication of that report.

Powell began by assailing the present system of land laws, denying that 160 acres was sufficient land for successful agriculture in the arid and semiarid zones. He proposed instead a 2,560-acre homestead which would permit the cattlemen to own their land legally rather than control it through manipulation and abuse of the existing land laws. For the irrigator Powell would offer 80 acres, a workable agricultural unit which could be placed under ditch and cultivated efficiently. He next directed his attention to the contract system of land survey, which he considered "incoherent and worthless,"[40] and to the existing laws governing water rights which made irrigation of small units all but impossible.[41] These substantive reforms would have required significant changes in the conduct of the settlement of the West.

38. William Culp Darrah, *Powell of the Colorado* (Princeton: Princeton University Press, 1951), p. 221; Wallace Stegner, *Beyond the 100th Meridian: John Wesley Powell and the Second Opening of the West* (Boston: Houghton Mifflin Co, 1962), pp. 202–43.

39. Smith, *Virgin Land*, p. 229.

40. Powell to Carl Schurz, September 28, 1878, in U.S., Congress, House, *Report of the Public Land Commission*, 45th Cong., 3d sess., 1, 1879, H. Misc. Doc. 5, pp. 17, 18.

41. J. W. Powell, *Report on the Lands of the Arid Regions*, ed. by Wallace Stegner (Cambridge: Harvard University Press, 1966). The original edition is in U.S., Congress, House, 45th Cong., 2d sess., 1878, H. Exec. Doc. 73. Stegner's edition is complete and authoritatively done.

But Powell was not finished. In the course of his attacks he had occasion to dispute that favorite theory of the boomers, rain follows the plow.[42] It was a theme he was to return to many times, for as he learned to his discomfort, the promoters were undeterred by his original statement. Anyone, they reasoned, who termed the Plains semiarid could hardly be expected to understand the complexities of increased rainfall, so Powell was forced to repeat his earlier warning. "That there is any material change in the climate of this country, due to its settlement," he stated in 1890, "is denied by the experience of mankind everywhere."[43]

Powell, obviously, was fighting a losing battle. The boomers' frontier was too firmly based on the rain-follows-the-plow theory to be upset at that late date. The final irony, however, came in 1892 when the Union Pacific Railroad issued a promotional pamphlet describing its lands in eastern Colorado. Rain, the pamphlet insisted, was steadily increasing because of "the artificial changes wrought by man on the earth's surface." The source for this piece of news was John Wesley Powell's *Report on the Lands of the Arid Regions!*[44]

It was not the only time he was to be intentionally misunderstood. His entire *Report* was subjected to some of the most irrelevant criticism conceivable as western congressmen strove to sustain the boomers' frontier. They saw no reason to change the prevailing land system, particularly when those changes were proposed by a man of heretical ideas such as Powell. Actually Powell's projected plan for the semiarid regions was anything but radical. His ideas and those of his congressional opponents regarding the future of the Great Plains were remarkably similar. Powell had said that the Plains could "maintain but a scanty population," and this, of course, was contrary to the dearly held beliefs of the Gilpins and Augheys.[45] He had also called for a thorough

42. Powell, *Arid Regions*, pp. 105–6.

43. Statement of J. W. Powell to the House Committee on Irrigation, March 27, 1890, in U.S. Geological Survey, *11th Annual Report . . . 1889–1890*, pt. 2 (Washington, D.C., 1890), p. 259. See also J. W. Powell, *Physiographic Regions of the United States*, National Geographic Society Monographs, vol. 1, no. 3 (New York: American Book Co., 1895), pp. 70, 71–72; U.S., Congress, House, *Report to Special House Committee on Irrigation*, 51st Cong., 2d sess., 4, 1891, H. Rept. 2767, p. 138; and J. W. Powell, "Our Recent Floods," *North American Review* 155 (August 1892): 152–53.

44. U.P. Railroad *Colorado: A Complete and Comprehensive Description*, 5th ed. (St. Louis, 1892), pp. 101–2. The same comments were repeated in the 8th edition, 1899, p. 90.

45. Powell, *Arid Regions*, pp. 33–34.

revision of the land laws, that future prosperity might more readily be achieved; again the promoters demurred. The land laws had served them well; they "combined the wisdom of a century," and the promoters saw no need to change them.[46] But these were differences of opinion on means. The ends both sides sought were the same. Powell believed, as presumably did his critics, that the plains were to be the home of the yeoman farmer. These lands, he claimed, "were to be reserved for actual settlers, in small quantities, to provide homes for poor men, on the principal involved in the homestead laws."[47] There was nothing in this statement to justify Colorado Representative Thomas Patterson's comment that Powell's suggested 2,560-acre homestead would fill the Plains "with baronial estates, with an aristocratic and wealthy few, each owning land sufficient for a European principality."[48] That obviously was not Powell's intention. His sixteen-section homestead was designed to permit the successful settlement of the nonirrigable lands. These were not to be baronies, but homes for bona fide, Jeffersonian yeomen, the nation's "bulwark in its hour of supremest danger," as Patterson described them.[49]

Martin Maginnis, a territorial delegate from Montana, had a further criticism of Powell's suggested reforms. To Maginnis, any change in the land laws would place obstacles in the way of the successful operation of the safety valve, and 1879, he reminded his listeners, was a particularly inopportune year for blocking the valve. The United States had just begun to pull out of the depression, but there were still thousands who looked to the Plains as a place of refuge. Maginnis described some of them. They were "the people who are crowded in your cities, the mechanics and laborers who roam your streets, seeking in vain for the privilege of earning by the sweat of their brows that daily bread for which their wives and children pray at home." Patterson was in full agreement. He spoke of the "stress of population" which would one day demand the agricultural settlement of the Plains, and

46. Rep. Horace Page (Calif.), U.S., Congress, House, *Congressional Record*, 45th Cong., 3d sess., 1879, 8, pt. 2: 1197.

47. Powell, *Arid Regions*, p. 39.

48. U.S., Congress, House, *Congressional Record*, 45th Cong., 3d sess., 1879, 8, pt. 2, Appendix: 221.

49. Ibid. See also pp. 219–22, for more of Patterson's comments. The Public Land Commission of 1879 took most of its ideas from Powell's earlier recommendations. This same commitment to the perpetuation of the yeoman appears in its report, *Preliminary Report of the Public Land Commission, 1879–1880*, 46th Cong., 2d sess., 1880, 22, H. Exec. Doc. 46, pp. lxiii, lxvi.

make them "the most productive lands upon the continent." Would
Powell, "this revolutionist, this charlatan in science and intermeddler in
affairs of which he has no proper conception," be allowed to deprive the
oppressed of this world of a happy home on the Plains? He hoped not.[50]

Again Powell's motives had been misrepresented. He recognized the
importance of the safety valve; indeed, it was in part because of this
that he had proposed his reforms. "Thousands of men," he explained,
"who repair to [the West] and return disappointed from the fact that
they are practically debarred from the public lands; and thousands of
persons in the eastern states without employment, or discontented with
the rewards of labor, would speedily find homes in the great Rocky
Mountain Region."[51] Many of those who supported him made
similar comments. The *Nation*, in a long review article of Powell's
Arid Regions, wrote of the "thousands who, not obtaining the rewards
of labor, are becoming a burden and a danger in the East."[52] Abram
Hewitt, of New York, a man long known for his interest in the safety
valve, also endorsed Powell's reforms. In response to a comment from
Maginnis on the proposed change in the survey system, he affirmed again
that "it's because we want to keep the valve open that we propose this
change."[53] The National Academy of Science said the same thing
about Powell's proposed consolidation of the four surveys then mapping the West. The consolidation was "imperatively demanded,"
according to the academy, if the frontier was to remain viable. Most of
the remaining lands were not cultivable by conventional methods anyway, and a consolidated survey could best determine what agricultural
adjustments would have to be made. In the process it could reassure
the American people that during times of stress a farther West awaited
them to give them succor.[54] The safety valve was as much in the minds
of the reformers as in those of the most inveterate boomers.

50. U.S., Congress, House, *Congressional Record*, 45th Cong., 3d sess., 1879,
8, pt. 2: 1202–3; 217, 220, 221.

51. Powell, *Arid Regions*, p. 42.

52. *Nation* 26 (May 2, 1878): 288–89.

53. U.S., Congress, House, *Congressional Record*, 45th Cong., 3d sess., 1879,
8, pt. 2: 1205. William Goetzmann states that Hewitt, incorrectly identified as
Abraham, endorsed the change to 2,560 acre homesteads because of his own extensive ranch holdings and his well-known prejudice in favor of the business class
(*Exploration and Empire*, p. 584). Actually Hewitt's background offers ample evidence of his belief in the safety valve as an aid to labor.

54. Letter from the National Academy of Science, November 26, 1878, in *Report
of the Public Land Commission*, p. 5.

So, too, was the notion that the West had to be settled as quickly and expeditiously as possible. Powell's critics were given to considerable exaggeration when they claimed that his reforms would hold up settlement while a few overpaid scientists mapped out their geodetic lines. The critics were more than content with the present system of mapping conducted through the good offices of the district surveyor general. Powell thought this system worthless and prejudicial to the permanent settlement of the area. He hoped to replace it with a more scientific system of mapping. But, according to Maginnis, the settler was not interested in science; it was "of no earthly importance to him whether he is a hair's breadth out of the exact astronomic calculation." Besides, Maginnis continued, it had been the scientists who had originally designated the area a Great American Desert, sufficient proof of their blindness to the future of the region.[55]

Others of the Maginnis persuasion also came to the defense of the existing system of land surveying. Patterson, for example, described the surveyor general as "a sentinel upon a watch tower. . . . He sees the first indications of emigration" and surveys the land in advance. This was a valuable service which Patterson did not wish to see eliminated in a general reform of the land laws. Representative Mark H. Dunnell of Minnesota had another complaint. The immigrant, according to Dunnell, knew what he was getting with the old system, but the new one proposed by Powell was to be "scientific and theoretical, rather than practical" and immigrants were practical people. Besides, added Congressman John H. Baker of Indiana, the United States had no choice but to trust the development of its resources to the unaided ingenuity of the people. They had shown themselves capable in the past and it was an insult to think that they were unable to conquer the Great Plains without prior scientific investigation.[56]

Here, too, the critics misinterpreted Powell's intentions. He expressed on at least two occasions his confidence in the abilities of the American people, once warning the government simply to "furnish the people with institutions of justice and let them do the work for themselves."[57] On another occasion, in language almost Gilpinesque in its fervency,

55. U.S., Congress, House, *Congressional Record*, 45th Cong., 3d sess., 1879, 8, pt. 2: 1202.

56. Ibid., Appendix, p. 221; 8, pt. 2: 1203; see also the comments of Rep. Dudley Haskell of Kansas, p. 1210; p. 1563.

57. J. W. Powell, "Institutions for the Arid Lands," *Century Magazine* 40 (May 1890): 111. See also his comments to the House Committee on Irrigation, U.S. Geological Survey, *Eleventh Annual Report*, pt. 2, pp. 254–56.

Powell had written of the mission of these people. It was nothing less than the "ultimate spread of Anglo-Saxon civilization over the globe." He wished to see American science, institutions, and arts become the norm as all nations became integrated in a general federation of republican states.[58] Nor was he any less devoted to the idea of man's innate superiority and dominion over nature. Certainly there was no great ecological humility in his statement that man was "the master of his own destiny and not the creature of the environment." The American, in particular, was eminently capable of adapting the natural environment to his own wants and thus creating a new order to his own specifications. In Powell's view, this dynamism did not extend to increasing the rainfall, but it stopped only a little short of that.[59]

Such moderation, however, was enough to ensure the undying enmity of the boomers. The promoters placed no limits on the power of the plow. This once humble instrument was the catalyst for the climatic revolution then in progress and, as such, was in and of itself capable of effecting the settlement of the Plains. The plow needed no assistance; it was capable of working the necessary transformation alone. Soil and climatic conditions were of little consequence. The new law of progression on the Plains demanded that they obey the will of the omnipotent plow and the farmer who wielded it. It was this belief that prompted the opposition of the boomers to any attempts to change the methods of land disposition. The existing land laws, whatever their theoretical weaknesses, had the undoubted advantage of stimulating immigration. It made little difference to the promoters that the land which the government was so freely giving away was only partially understood. They were similarly untroubled by the frequent charges of corruption in the General Land Office or by claims that the system of surveys was lagging hopelessly behind settlement demands. They knew only that people were coming in, filing on the land, and instituting the changes which were thought to follow in their wake. By definition, then, any change in land disposition policies jeopardized the continued influx of new settlers and new plows. Any reform in the land laws, even if moti-

58. J. W. Powell, "Technology," *American Anthropologist* 1 (April 1899): 724–25.

59. Darrah, *Powell of the Colorado*, p. 357. In this belief Powell was much like his friend and contemporary, Lester Ward. Ward's dynamic sociology, according to Powell, was "America's greatest contribution to scientific philosophy" (*Science* 2 [August 24, 1883]: 226). Ward returned the compliment. See "Professor John Wesley Powell," *Popular Science Monthly* 20 (February 1882): 390–97.

vated by the same considerations which moved the promoters, was essentially self-defeating. An understanding of the nature of the Plains was not necessary; it was, in fact, pernicious if it involved even temporary delays in the disposal of the land. Besides, so long as rain followed the plow, attempts at a scientific survey of the Plains were little more than exercises in planned obsolescence.

Thus when President Hayes expressed dissatisfaction with existing land laws he was respectfully asked by one promoter to suffer his complaints in silence lest he upset the delicate balance of the boomers' frontier.[60] But Hayes had done more than complain. He had endorsed the 2,560-acre homestead proposed by John Wesley Powell, a blasphemy which led another promoter to accuse him of prejudice against those "whose interest it is to encourage industry, make beautiful homes, erect churches, and support schools."[61]

None of the land reformers, Hayes included, ever expressed any opposition to that sentiment. Indeed, they were as dedicated to the perpetuation of the yeoman ideal as the promoters. Unfortunately, the reformers were never able to convince their western critics of this dedication. Grover Cleveland, for example, was fully committed to the welfare of the agricultural class. He and his commissioner of the General Land Office, William Sparks, were indefatigable in their efforts to preserve the public domain and prevent its alienation to persons of questionable habits.[62] If Cleveland and Sparks were guilty of anything it was overexuberance in trying to legislate farmers into a region where agriculture was a hazardous occupation at best. In spite of this position, however, Cleveland's views were misrepresented and Sparks' were subjected to some of the harshest criticism to come from the boomers. Representative James Laird of Nebraska stated that Sparks, in his zeal to end the corruption in the Land Office, was "running a vendetta against the best interests of all the territory beyond the Missouri River." He was a public menace, a man who would drive

60. Rutherford B. Hayes, First Annual Message, December 3, 1877, in *Messages and Papers of the Presidents*, ed. by Richardson, 6: 4428; Fourth Annual Message, December 6, 1880, in ibid., p. 4309. For the criticism of this opinion see Moses Stocking, in *Nebraska Farmer*, June, 1878.

61. C. H. Walker, in *Nebraska Farmer*, April, 1878.

62. For Cleveland's proposals, see First Annual Message, December 6, 1885, in *Messages and Papers of the Presidents*, ed. by Richardson 7: 4944; Second Annual Message, December 6, 1887, ibid., p. 5106; Fourth Annual Message, December 3, 1888, ibid., p. 5379.

people from the land that he might "pose as a reformer, and drink the paid flattery of his gang of spotters, spies and poisoners."[63]

But Sparks's real difficulty arose when he attempted to suspend entry into new lands until the laws could be amended to conform to the semiarid conditions of the Plains. This would have delayed settlement, a heinous enough crime in itself; but in addition the boomers preferred not to have the existence of any semiaridity publicized. Many of them had spent a lifetime trying to dispel whatever lingering notions of aridity remained from the days of the Great American Desert, and all of them were agreed that what dryness remained was a temporary condition only, or at least would be if men like Sparks could be prevented from retarding immigration. The remarks of Representative Lewis E. Payson of Illinois are typical of this western attitude. Payson insisted that Sparks had been duped by the new desert theorists into believing that everything west of the 100th meridian was by definition arid. Representative Payson knew better. "The safety and security of the nation," he continued, "rested . . . in the distribution of those lands," and fortunately the nation could be assured that its safety and security could have found no more attractive place to rest. The changes "wrought by civilization, cultivation, tree planting, sowing of grass, and covering the earth with verdure" had made of the Plains a land capable of fulfilling this trust.[64] Vigilance had to be exercised, however, that misguided men not be permitted to shake such faith by irresponsible reforms.

A deadlock had thus been reached. The boomers' frontier had been built on the existing land laws. These laws spurred immigration, and immigration, in the minds of the promoters, was self-sustaining. Every new arrival, by changing the climatic conditions, was the agent of not only his own salvation but that of thousands of others. The greater the influx of new settlers, the sooner these changes could begin. It was a system which fed and sustained itself and the promoters were loud in their demands that it not be upset by scientific quacks and amateur reformers, regardless of how pure their motives.

63. U.S., Congress, Senate, *Congressional Record*, 49th Cong., 1st sess., 1886, 17, pt. 6: 5734. Senator Joseph Carey of Wyoming thought that all of Sparks's proposed changes should be labeled "bills to prevent the settlement of the Great West" (*Field and Farm*, July 31, 1886). A "well informed Denver lawyer" wrote that Sparks had given Colorado "the worst sort of a black eye" (ibid., June 21, 1886).

64. U.S., Congress, House, *Congressional Record*, 49th Cong., 1st sess., 1886, 17, pt. 5: 5378.

In 1888, when John Wesley Powell resumed his earlier demands for land law reform, he discovered again just how loud the promoters could be. In that year, upon the urging of Nevada Senator William Stewart, Powell was appointed to head a United States Irrigation Survey of the semiarid regions. In order to facilitate his labors, President Cleveland and the Congress suspended entry into all of the lands to be investigated. Since Powell had anticipated ten years as the time necessary to complete his survey, this suspension began to take on a sense of near permanency.[65] A decade was all but an infinity to the boomers. To have the land locked up for that length of time was to lose thousands of potential immigrants; as one Wyoming critic put it, suspension "would act on the Territory like a wet blanket on a buffalo-chip fire."[66]

Powell's justification for the imposed delay was not entirely satisfactory to the West, a region where shortsightedness had become traditional. As he explained it, "I think it would be almost a criminal act to go on as we are doing now, and allow thousands and hundreds of thousands of people to establish homes where they can not maintain themselves."[67] In Powell's mind the government, perhaps unwittingly, had been giving away shoddy merchandise. After almost two hundred years the United States had exhausted its garden, but it had not exhausted its storehouse of garden images. Powell's irrigation survey would create new images more in keeping with actual conditions, yet, he hoped, not totally unacceptable to traditionalists. The yeoman would still be there, together with his plow, his mule, and his numerous progeny. He might be irrigating 80 acres rather than sowing corn broadcast over the traditional 160. He might even be running a few head of cattle, but, hopefully, without leaving himself completely vulnerable to the brutalizing influences of that industry.[68] Once Powell had had an opportunity to classify the lands as irrigable or nonirrigable, the Americans could begin again their subjugation of the last part of the continent. The delay would barely be felt, and the advantages to be gained from an understanding of the land would more than justify it.

65. Wallace Stegner, "Editor's Introduction," in *Arid Regions*, by Powell, p. xxi; U.S., Congress, Senate, *Sundry Civil Appropriations Bill*, 51st Cong., 1st sess., 1890, 8, S. Rept. 1453, p. 57.

66. U.S., Congress, Senate, *Report of the Special Commission on the Irrigation and Reclamation of Arid Lands*, 51st Cong., 1st sess., 1889–90, S. Rept. 928, 3, pt. 4, p. 513.

67. *Sundry Civil Appropriations Bill*, p. 60.

68. J. W. Powell, "The Irrigable Lands of the Arid Region," *Century Magazine* 39 (March 1890): 766–76.

Nor would American values have to undergo any change. Irrigation required more cooperative effort perhaps than Americans were accustomed to but there was no cause for alarm here. As to the charges that government-sponsored irrigation was discriminatory and paternalistic, Powell had insisted that "the money shall be furnished by the people; and [had said] to the Government: Hands Off!"[69]

Despite this obeisance to Jeffersonian liberalism, Powell's proposed survey was discontinued in 1890. The people of the West discovered that he truly intended to study their region. Perhaps they feared the consequences of such a study; perhaps they simply refused to surrender the time necessary to complete it. Whatever the cause, it was a study they felt they could not afford. William Stewart, one of the first to advocate an irrigation survey, reflected western attitudes when he explained the kind of scientific investigation he favored. Powell, he wrote, "took the place of Hayden, who was a real geologist, who died of grief by being crowded out."[70] Senator S. G. Moody of South Dakota was even more explicit in his criticism of Powell's irrigation survey. "It is detrimental to our country," he told the Senate. "Ay, . . . it is not merely detrimental, it is paralyzing. . . . The land offices are closed. . . . Not one acre of public land can be taken by the poor."[71] Twelve years later Senator Joseph L. Rawlins of Utah confirmed Moody's dire remarks. The irrigation survey, Rawlins said, "instead of promoting the settlement of the West, . . . [had] obstructed its settlement."[72]

In spite of considerable evidence to the contrary, Powell was never able to convince his congressional critics that he was anything but a subverter of the American dream. He had no more success with two

69. J. W. Powell, "Institutions for the Arid Lands," pp. 111–16; Powell's statement to the House Committee on Irrigation, U.S. Geological Survey, *Eleventh Annual Report . . . 1889–1890*, pt. 2, pp. 254–56.

70. U.S., Congress, Senate, *Congressional Record*, 51st Cong., 1st sess., 1890, 21, pt. 7: 6305. See Stewart's earlier remarks in the *Industrialist* (Manhattan, Kansas), August 24, 1889; and William Stewart, "Reclaiming the Western Deserts," *Forum* 7 (April 1889): 201–8.

71. Senate, *Congressional Record*, 51st Cong., 1st sess., June 20, 1890, 21, pt. 7: 6308.

72. Ibid., 57th Cong., 1st sess., March 1, 1902, 35, pt. 3: 2284. Elwood Mead, later a leading irrigationist, agreed. So did the land commissioner of the Union Pacific Railroad. See *Report of Governor Francis P. Warren of Wyoming to the Secretary of the Interior, 1889*, (Cheyenne, 1890), 631; testimony of Allen Woodcock of the U.P. Railroad, in *Report of the Special Commission on the Irrigation and Reclamation of Arid Lands*, p. 566; and *Daily Nebraska State Journal* (Lincoln), April 9, 1890.

of his most determined opponents outside of Congress. Samuel Aughey and Charles Dana Wilber were understandably unhappy with Powell's activities. He had denied their theory that rain followed the plow; he had suggested a thoroughgoing reform of the surveying system; and he had insisted that the cattlemen had at least an equal claim to the lands of the Great Plains. He was, then, heartily disliked by both. Aughey much preferred the scientific methods of some of Powell's critics, notably Edward Cope.[73] Cope, first of all, had championed the cause of Ferdinand V. Hayden in the struggle over consolidation of the surveys,[74] but in addition to this valuable service, he was himself a boomer of some ability. W. E. Webb, whose gazette *Buffalo Land* has been referred to earlier, cited Cope as saying that the Great Plains were equal to those of Lombardy "in point of fertility, and ... would undoubtedly become before 1890 the great wheat-producing region of the world."[75] This was the kind of scientist Aughey could understand. As for Powell, Aughey could not imagine the reasons that prompted his voluntary effort to "defame some of the most fertile lands in the world." The only explanation Aughey could offer was that Powell was totally ignorant of the actual conditions or deliberately misstated the case in order to curry favor with the new desert theorists who so determinedly pursued the consolidation of the surveys.[76]

Wilber was even less charitable. The Public Land Commission of 1879, of which Powell was a member and the leading spokesman, was composed of "wiseacres, kid-gloved experts, and closet philosophers." Fortunately, the farmer "with his plow tears them asunder, leaving us to remember the experts only as charlatans or quacks."[77] Anyone who had read Wilber knew what the farmer was doing with his plow.

Certainly Robert Furnas of Nebraska knew, and in 1880 he asked Wilber and Aughey to draft a reply to the recommendations of the Public Land Commission, specifically those dealing with the 2,560-acre homestead.[78] The two boomers complied, insisting in their rebuttal that the commision had visited the Plains with the preconceived notion that the land laws needed changing, and no amount of evidence to the

73. Aughey, *Sketches of the Physical Geography and Geology of Nebraska*, p. 192.
74. Wallace Stegner, *Beyond the 100th Meridian* (Boston: Houghton Mifflin Co., 1962), pp. 284–86.
75. W. E. Webb, *Buffalo Land* (Philadelphia: Hubbard Bros., 1872), p. 194.
76. *Daily Nebraska State Journal* (Lincoln), August 8, 1879.
77. Wilber, *The Great Valleys and Prairies of Nebraska and the Northwest*, p. 143.
78. Ibid., p. 168. The request and the reply were published in NSBA, *Transactions ... September, 1876,* to *September, 1879....* (Lincoln, 1880), pp. 107–13.

contrary could convince them otherwise.[79] The consequences of their "nefarious" scheme would be fatal to the immigration interests of Nebraska. It would, in addition, be a "fearful robbery" of the birthright of the people, and all who were coconspirators in this "crime against society" should be held up for "public execration." They were, after all, trying to reintroduce the Great American Desert into American geography.[80]

Wilber thought he knew why, and in offering his explanation he gave voice to another important element in the boomers' frontier. The Public Land Commission, he wrote, was working "vi et armis, with the wealthy combination of cattle kings," or "nomadic herdsmen" as he called them on another occasion. Wilber knew well the mutual hostility between ranchers and farmers, and hence had no difficulty detecting the mainspring of the movement for land reform. The cattlemen, of course, had much to gain by the implementation of the land commission's report. It was readily understandable that they would prefer a gift of 2,560 acres to having to piece together their ranches from a variety of different land laws. What is not so easily understood is Wilber's objection to this seemingly legitimate desire. It was true that the cattlemen were the obstructionist element in the spread of the boomers' frontier. It was also true that Wilber was an agrarian, dedicated to the settlement of Nebraska with one family per 160 acres. But more was involved. Wilber was in full accord with the notion that the cattlemen were only partially civilized, only half-evolved, to borrow a standard reference of the late nineteenth century. In Wilber's mind the preservation of vast tracts of land for the exclusive use of a few cattle barons was "semi-barbaric," and beyond the pale of civilized society.[81]

Ideas of this sort had a long history. As early as 1831, John Mason Peck in his guidebook for emigrants wrote of "three classes, like the waves of the ocean, . . . rolling one after the other." The first of these classes were the "pioneers" who depended upon pasturage for their subsistence.[82] There as nothing inherently wrong with this dependence;

79. Wilber, *The Great Valleys and Prairies of Nebraska and the Northwest*, pp. 106–7.

80. Ibid., p. 172; see also pp. 146, 164–65.

81. Ibid., pp. 71, 143, 144, 264.

82. "Guide for Emigrants, 1831," in *The West: Contemporary Records of America's Expansion Across the Continent, 1607–1890*, ed. by Bayrd Still (New York: Capricorn Books, 1961), p. 86.

indeed, it was perfectly natural under the circumstances. The problem arose only when those devoted to pastoral pursuits failed to recognize that they had been superseded by a more highly evolved social group, the farmers. When the agriculturalist began to press his claims to the land the nomadic herdsman was expected to graciously step aside, just as the Indian and the trapper had stepped aside for him. It was all part of cosmic plan which man was impotent to change even if he wished.[83]

No disgrace was involved in such abdication. As Humboldt had written, the pastoral age of human development was a "beneficent intermediate state which . . . promotes agriculture."[84] It supplied the necessary period of adjustment which allowed the once fierce hunters to become accustomed to a more sedentary existence. From there it was but a short evolutionary step to the cultivation of plant food and the completion of the evolutionary cycle. Andrew Johnson, devoted champion of agrarian interests, agreed, though without the cool detachment of Humboldt. In 1858 Johnson quoted the Swiss publicist Emerich Vattel on the social retardation of the herdsman. In Johnson's mind the cattleman was scarcely less objectionable than the large slaveholder, and Vattel offered him confirmation of this opinion. "There are those," Vattel was quoted as writing, "who avoid agriculture, that would only live by hunting and flocks. This might doubtless be allowed in the first stages of the world," but given the advances of civilization those who still retained this idle life were an anachronism and a curse upon the land.[85]

As the nineteenth century progressed this became an even more popular notion. R. S. Elliott, for example, insisted that his experiments for the Kansas Pacific would permit the yeoman to exercise his natural superiority over the cattleman. John Tice, author of a popular gazette, hoped Elliott was right since it was obvious to all that the cattle industry was retarding "the growth, settlement and improvement of Kansas and the surrounding states." Another gazetteer, Linus Brockett, concurred. Cattle ranching was a particularly objectionable life since it tended toward a "condition of semi-civilization. . . . This isolated life inevitably leads to results directly opposed to the whole genius

83. For example of this thinking, see Paul Honigsheim, "Max Weber as Historian of Agriculture and Rural Life," *Agricultural History* 23 (July 1949): 182.

84. Humboldt, *Views of Nature*, p. 12.

85. U.S., Congress, Senate, *Congressional Globe*, 35th Cong., 1st sess., 1858, pt. 3: 2265.

of our institutions." Even John Wesley Powell, thought by Wilber to be a coconspirator with the cattlemen, considered their life to be "semi-nomadic." His proposed land reforms, hopefully, would correct this and regain for them a modicum of civilization. Others were not so optimistic. A Senate committee, meeting to determine the best method of disposing of federal lands in the Plains region, concluded that "it would be better that these lands should remain forever a desert than be monopolized by great private landed estates."[86]

However, these were not the only alternatives. The irresistible forces of evolution would ensure that there would be neither desert nor landed estates. William E. Smythe, one of the prime movers in the irrigation movement, explained. "Cattle raising is a pursuit which does not develop the higher possibilities of the country, either in a material or a social way."[87] This was a standard lament, but Smythe did not consider the situation critical. There was an immutable law which supplied the needed corrective. "Civilization," Smythe wrote in 1892, "is driving barbarism before it. . . . The conflict is between the civilization of irrigated America and the barbarism of cattle ranching." There was no doubt in his mind as to the ultimate victor, for "whoever defies the spirit of progress, the march of civilization, will be destroyed."[88]

The best that could be said about the stockmen was that they were a necessary, though impermanent, step in a long system of social evolution. The man who best expressed this belief was Frederick Jackson Turner. In his commencement address to the University of Washington in 1914, he said of the Great Plains that "successive industrial waves are passing. The old free range gave place to the ranch, the ranch to the homestead, and now in places in the arid lands the home-

---

86. Elliott to James Wilson, March 9, 1870, Elliott LPB; Tice, *Over the Plains; on the Mountains*, p. 43; Brockett, *Our Western Empire*, p. 79; Powell, *Arid Regions*, pp. 41–42. See also, in this same context, V. B. Paine, "Our Public Land Policy," *Harper's New Monthly Magazine* 71 (October 1885): 741–46; T. C. Henry's comments in the *Dickinson* (Kans.) *County Chronicle*, March 3, 1882; U.S., Congress, Senate, Committee on Public Lands, *Report*, 50th Cong., 1st sess., 1889–90, S. Rept. 778, p. 7.

87. William E. Smythe, *The Conquest of Arid America* (New York: Macmillan, 1905), p. 222.

88. *Irrigation Age* 3 (May 1, 1892): 30. For similar comments, see Binger Herman, *Annual Report of the Department of the Interior, 1902* (Washington: GPO, 1902), pp. 167–75; William Street, "The Victory of the Plow," Kansas State Historical Society, *Transactions* 9 (1905–1906): 33–34; Frank Blackmar, "The Mastery of the Desert," *North American Review* 182 (April 1906): 676–88.

stead is replaced by the ten or twenty acre fruit farm."[89] From this point of view, there could be no opprobrium attached to the intermediate stages of development, including the range and ranch cattle industries. That generous attitude persisted, however, only so long as the cattlemen recognized their social inferiority and willingly surrendered to the forces of civilization. If they behaved arrogantly or overstayed their welcome they were subjected to scathing criticism. Unfortunately for harmony on the Plains, they violated both of these canons of decorum.

But arrogance was just one of the cattlemen's sins. They also had the effrontery to disagree with the aims of the boomers—ample evidence, to the promoters, of their primitivism, and more than ample reason for their removal. As might be expected, the cattlemen were convinced that their own industry was the only one suited to conditions on the Plains. Within limits they were right. Grass was the one commodity which the Plains could offer in abundance and upon it they built their empires. It was a sensible arrangement until the cattlemen began to abuse this essential resource by overgrazing. At that point the Plains proved their ability to retaliate. The dry summer and harsh winter of 1886–87 left the range industry on the verge of collapse, which made it appreciably easier for the homesteaders to exercise their alleged natural right of succession.

Until that time, however, the cattlemen were convinced of the futility of the boomers' frontier. They mocked the promoters' slogans and scorned their naiveté. The Almighty, declared one of them, intended the Plains to be cattle country; even the boomers could not reverse that verdict.[90] Their efforts were not only futile but presumptuous, particularly in connection with the rain-follows-the-plow theory. Rainfall, the cattlemen insisted, was not likely to increase at the bidding of the promoter. Certainly there had been no noticeable change owing to the stockmen's importunities.

89. Frederick Jackson Turner, "The West and American Ideals," in *Frontier and Section: Selected Essays of Frederick Jackson Turner* (Englewood Cliffs, N.J.: Prentice Hall, 1961), p. 104.

90. H. E. Teschemacher, 1884, in *Interviews with Wyoming Cattlemen*, by H. H. Bancroft, Microfilm, Western Range Cattle Industry Study, CSHS; see also the address by Silas Bent of the Las Animas County (Colorado) Cattle Growers' Association, "The Arid Region, the Permanent Range," delivered at the meeting of the Colorado Cattle Growers' Association, December 28, 1886, in *Field and Farm*, January 2, 1887; and the remarks of William Sturgis of the Wyoming Cattle Growers' Association in the *Democratic Leader* (Cheyenne), December 30, 1884.

Still, the fiction persisted that rain would follow the farmer, and the cattlemen were forced to watch as the range was overrun by yeomen attracted by this promise.[91] It was not an encouraging sight. As one stockman allegedly said, "I want nothing to do with anything which will have a tendency to bring more people into Wyoming. There are too many people here now—too many people—too few cattle."[92] Besides, the cattlemen reasoned, cattle could survive on the Plains—people could not. Silas Bent of the Colorado Stock Growers' Association described the condition very simply. "These lands," he wrote, "as they stand and will forever stand, are not fit for agriculture." The government should recognize this fact and set aside the semiarid regions for the cattle industry alone. The farmers might protest. Bent assumed they would but, as he explained, there was really no injustice involved. For those who might ask when agricultural interest had ever been accorded such generous treatment, Bent had a ready answer: "Ever since Mr. Jefferson began to attract immigration to this country by proclaiming to the world [America's great store of free land]." Silas Bent was a wise man, wiser than most of his generation.[93]

But there were only a very few who agreed with him. Some, like Theodore Roosevelt in his prepolitical years, were attracted by the romance even then connected with the cattle industry.[94] Others, like Senator J. J. Ingalls of Kansas, had never progressed beyond William Gilpin's original and reasonably accurate definition of the Plains as the pasturage of the world.[95] Most of those who clung to the notion that the Plains were cattle country, however, did so from a determination of the actual conditions in the area, or from a personal interest in the cattle

91. For examples of cattlemen denying that rain followed the plow, see testimony from Elbert County, Colorado, in *Preliminary Report of the Public Land Commission, 1879–1880*, p. 296; a letter in the *Nation* 41 (August 27, 1885): 172–74; Stephen Dorsey, "Land Stealing in New Mexico: A Rejoinder," *North American Review* 145 (October 1887): 396–405; *Cheyenne Wells Gazette*, July 16, 1887.

92. *Irrigation Age* 3 (May 1, 1892): 30.

93. Joseph Nimmo, *Range and Ranch Cattle Traffic*, in U.S., Congress, House, 48th Cong., 2d sess., 1884–85, H. Exec. Doc. 267, p. 99.

94. "Ranch Life in the Far West," *Century Magazine* 37 (February 1888): 500, 502; see also Joseph Nimmo, "The American Cowboy," *Harper's New Monthly Magazine* 73 (November 1886): 880–84.

95. See U.S., Congress, Senate, *Congressional Record*, 44th Cong., 2d sess., 1877, 5, pt. 3: 1967; J. J. Ingalls, "Westward the Course of Empire Takes Its Way," *Lippincott's Monthly Magazine* 49 (June 1892): 716–20; J. J. Ingalls, "Blue Grass," in *A Collection of the Writings of John James Ingalls* (Kansas City, Mo: Hudson-Kimberley Publishing Co., 1902), p. 102.

industry.[96] But whatever their reasons, the champions of the cowman over the farmer were in a distinct and unpopular minority. The boomers' frontier could not support itself on cows. It demanded yeomen, not only for itself but as its gift to the nation.

For this reason it countered every argument of the stockman, and eagerly sought to replace him and his culture with an agrarian pattern of life. Occasionally the conflict became deeply embittered, particularly (and unexpectedly) in Wyoming. The general tone of the conflict was sounded on January 8, 1887, when the *Laramie Sentinel* congratulated Cain, "the tiller of the soil," for killing Abel, "the stock grower," and thereby establishing a precedent which might still be useful in Wyoming. After all, the paper continued, in "no county on the globe and at no period of the world's history has any nation or people who devoted themselves exclusively to stock raising ever risen much above semi-barbarism."

Such a comment would have been unusual in Wyoming ten years earlier. At that time the cattlemen were the dominant interest in the territory and they were not markedly sympathetic to the boomers' frontier. By the late eighties, however, Wyoming had awakened to the promises of that frontier and convinced itself that the chief obstacle to its prosperity was the presence of large cattle companies. Governor Thomas Moonlight led the territory in its fight to prove its agricultural potential. Moonlight insisted that there was a "future for this territory as soon as men begin to satisfy themselves that Cattle! Cattle! Cattle!!! are not the only things." [97] Parts of Wyoming, most notably Johnson County in the northeast quarter of the state, took Moonlight at his word and began to seek more attractive neighbors. On May 28, 1891,

96. *Message of Governor Thayer to the Fourth Legislative Assembly of Wyoming Territory, 1875* (Cheyenne, 1875), p. 18; Nathanial Shaler, "Improvement of Native Pasture Lands," *Science* 1 (March 23, 1883): 186–87. Shaler was answered by Samuel Aughey in *Science* 1 (April 27, 1883), p. 335. See also Frank Wilkeson, "Cattle Raising on the Plains," *Harper's New Monthly Magazine* 72 (April 1886): 778–95; and especially, H. M. Taylor, "Condition of the Cattle Interests West of the Mississippi River," in U.S., Department of Agriculture, Bureau of Animal Industry, *Fourth and Fifth Annual Reports . . . 1887–1888* (Washington, D.C.: GPO, 1889), p. 332.

97. W. Turrentine Jackson, "The Administration of Thomas Moonlight, 1887–1889," *Annals of Wyoming* 18 (July 1946): 147; see the same author's "Territorial Papers of Wyoming in the National Archives," *Annals of Wyoming* 16 (January 1944): 45–53; for similar comments, see *Laramie Boomerang*, December 17, 1891; *Lusk Herald*, August 12, 1887; *Wyoming Industrial Journal* (Cheyenne), September, 1900, pp. 98–99; statement of Joseph Carey, in *Report of the Special Commission on the Irrigation and Reclamation of Arid Lands*, 3, p. 461.

the *Buffalo Bulletin*, the leading paper of the county, listed the many advantages of that section, concluding with the prediction that "with these inducements, the homesteader, the miner, and the sheepowner will surely come and at no distant day." To a cattleman a more onerous threesome would be impossible to imagine.

The large stockmen of Wyoming did not surrender their range without a struggle. In April, 1892, they launched their "invasion" of Johnson County, ostensibly in an attempt to rid that area of "rustlers," but actually to throw one final challenge to the promoters who would boom the cattlemen off the range. Their defeat in this ill-conceived engagement was thought by many to mark the end of the stockmen's influence over the state.[98] However, as late as 1914 a Wyoming agricultural promoter was still bemoaning the fact that the cattlemen were blocking the state's "advance toward civilization."[99] This was intolerable to a boomer but it was one of the prices he had to pay for ignoring the natural conditions of the Plains.

In the other states of the central Great Plains, the cattlemen's war against the homesteader did not take so violent a turn, primarily because the stockmen were never so firmly entrenched. Still, the same arguments were made: the cattlemen were too nomadic to fit comfortably into the American tradition, too out of touch with basic American values. Governor John Routt of Colorado was certainly of this mind. "Don't you know," the governor was reported to have said in 1887, "that when man wants the range, [the] cow must go? The Colorado cattle range is growing smaller because man, with Nancy and the baby, puts a home there, and when man wants it, man is entitled to it and the bull and cow must find other places to graze."[100] Four years later Routt was besieged with petitions from the farmers of eastern Colorado asking for drought relief. Nancy and the baby, it seemed, did not have enough to eat. But the reason for this condition, according to the *Rocky Mountain News*, was not a lack of attention to the climate of the Plains but rather the monopolizing tendencies of the "cattle syndicates." It was part of "the old fight between the toiling many and the monied few." Old legends die hard on the plains of eastern Colorado.[101]

98. See, for example, Message of Governor John Osborne, 1893, in *Wyoming, Messages of the Governors, 1890–1933*, p. 18.

99. A. E. Bowman, Address delivered at the Ninth International Dry Farming Congress, *Proceedings . . . October 12–15, 1914* (Wichita, 1914), p. 39.

100. *Cheyenne Wells Gazette*, July 30, 1887.

101. *Rocky Mountain News*, June 1, 1892. See also the Merino Commercial Club,

The drive to eliminate the cattle industry from the region was so determined that it even sought to erase the word "ranch" from the western vocabulary. At least two spokesmen for Colorado promotional interests joined the *Logan Sentinel* in the campaign to "banish forever . . . the word 'ranch' as now generally used." The *Sentinel* believed that "this word has done more to repel the home-loving farming people of the east and to deter them from settling among us, than any other thing." The editorial went on to explain: The term "ranch" was a "relic of frontier days, and is suggestive only of the adobe hut and the corral. Turn it over to the Mexicans and the cowboys, and adopt once more the good old English word 'farm' that we left in the states with our old names and our religion." Thus in one sentence did an eastern Colorado newspaperman manage to combine every objection to the cattle kingdom. The cowboys were not "home-loving," nor by implication were they very religious. In addition, many of them were Mexican, a race held to be notoriously ill-adapted to agricultural pursuits. If that were not enough, "ranch" was a remnant of frontier days and, though later generations were to find considerable romance in that era, the farmers of eastern Colorado obviously preferred a more modern and civilized existence.[102]

It was sincerely hoped that the cattlemen would not prove obstinate when asked to vacate the Plains. Many of the boomers, in fact, expressed appreciation for the stockmen's contribution to social progress, and few actively sought an open conflict with them. The promoters asked only that the cowmen recognize that their period of ascendency was over. Should such a response not be forthcoming, however, the boomers were prepared to use their principal promotional weapon and drive the stock interests from the Plains. That weapon was, of course, the rain-follows-the-plow theory, and it was of more than incidental importance to the cattlemen. A number of observers had noticed the significance of aridity in the maturation and curing of the grasses of the Plains. In an arid or semiarid region the native grasses were cured by

---

The Land of Opportunity, Merino in the South Platte Valley, Colorado (Merino, 1899), in which the same rich vs. poor interpretation was given to the cattleman vs. farmer conflict.

102. *Logan Sentinel* in *Field and Farm*, October 1, 1887. The *Sentinel* probably took this statement from Nelson Millett, "Horticultural Humbugs," Colorado State Horticultural Society, *Third Annual Report . . . 1886* (Denver, 1886), p. 107. A year later the Union Pacific Railroad used the exact words in *Colorado: A Complete and Comprehensive Description. . . .* (Council Bluffs, 1887), p. 13.

the dry weather and then preserved by the early frost. According to H. M. Taylor of the Department of Agriculture, this fact precluded any possibility of peaceful coexistence between cattlemen and farmers. As he put it, "Whenever the natural rainfall is sufficient and frequent enough to produce a grain crop the grasses remain green and full of sap until the frost kills them." Conversely, any region where the grasses were cured on the ground before the frost was obviously too dry for general farming. Frank Wilkeson, a former Kansas cattleman, put the matter more succinctly. "If the West is to remain a grazing country, it is essential that it remain arid." [103]

This was exciting news to the rain-follows-the-plow advocates. The elimination of aridity was the object of their plowing and they looked on with undisguised delight at what they thought was a permanent change in the nature of the grass cover on the Plains. R. S. Elliott anticipated "great changes in the *grasses* of the Plains," reporting that "the 'buffalo grass' has almost entirely disappeared." [104] Elliott not only predicted a change, he also correctly identified the species which the boomers were most eager to eliminate. Buffalo grass was a favorite of the stockmen. It cured quickly, had high nutritional value, and possessed remarkable recuperative powers. Obviously it could not be allowed to remain. Samuel Aughey was pleased, then, to report that it was "disappearing because of the increase in rainfall." [105] The Kansas State Board of Agriculture was similarly encouraged by the westward march of what it called "tame grasses." Timothy, clover, orchard grass, and bluegrass were slowly replacing the old cover of buffalo and grama grass. [106] The change was observed by an old German in Nebraska who was quoted by a Burlington official as saying, "Goes der Bufflo, Comes dis blue yoint." The official went on to add that "the blue joint has rapidly killed out and taken the place of the buffalo . . . and this has extended westward until now there is but little buffalo grass in Nebraska." [107]

103. H. M. Taylor, "Importance of the Range Industry," U.S., Department of Agriculture, Bureau of Animal Industry, *Second Annual Report . . . 1885* (Washington, D.C.: GPO, 1886), p. 294; Wilkeson, "Cattle Raising on the Plains," p. 789.

104. Elliott to [illegible], August 7, 1870, Elliott LPB.

105. *Sketches of the Physical Geography and Geology of Nebraska*, p. 115.

106. KSBA, *Fourth Biennial Report . . . 1883–1884* (Topeka, 1885), pp. 5–6.

107. T. E. Calvert to "Mr. Manderson," May 22, 1898, Val Kuska Collection, NSHS. This seven-page letter from one of the Burlington's high officials gives an interesting account of the history of the line in Nebraska. Calvert emphasizes the original desert character of the area and the remarkable changes caused by the plow.

All this was discouraging enough to the cowmen but, theoretically, the plow brought with it more than just tame grasses and the rain which produced them. It also brought heavy winter and spring snows. Again the farmers were delighted with the prospect. Snows made the soil more friable and guaranteed a good start for spring-planted crops. But snow was the bane of the cattlemen, as the winter of 1886–87 showed. The plow and its consequences were thus doubly injurious to the cattlemen, a fact which the boomers were quick to note. John Tice, the gazetteer and publicist of R. S. Elliott's experiments, warned the ranchers of Nebraska that they would soon have to begin winter feeding of their stock. They would be unable to find enough native grass as soon as the plow had done its work.[108] This meant that the farmer could enter the Plains without first having to deal with the recalcitrant cowmen, and that meant not only the development of the West and the perpetuation of the Jeffersonian ideal, but also the continuation of an evolutionary process begun centuries earlier and now approaching completion on the central Great Plains.

One man, H. R. Hilton of Kansas, caught what he perceived to be the true significance of these changes and managed to bring all of these various theories into one cohesive argument. It was an extraordinary effort and his article must be considered one of the most remarkable documents to come out of the boomers' frontier. Hilton was a thorough-going evolutionist with an unflagging belief in the inevitability of progress. In 1888 he set forth a law of progression on the Plains. He established five categories, all of which were evolving in complementary fashion toward a system of perfect social harmony. The first of these categories was what Hilton called "population progression." In order, the population of the Plains had progressed from Indian to cowboy to squatter to pioneer farmer to scientific farmer. Hilton offered little here that was new, except to note that the fourth group in the progression, the pioneer farmer, introduced the plow. This was to have profound effect on the other four categories. Hilton next turned to the climate of the Plains and told how it had progressed from arid to semi-arid to moist. That change directly affected the third category, grass cover, and Hilton traced its progression from buffalo to bunch to bluestem to tame grasses. Likewise the animal population, in response to the social, climatic, and vegetational changes, had progressed from

108. Tice, *Over the Plains; On the Mountains,* p. 159. The *Lamar* (Colo.) *Leader* made the same point in a story reprinted in the *Cheyenne Wells Gazette,* January 21, 1888. So did the *Lusk* (Wyoming) *Herald,* May 20, 1887.

the buffalo, antelope, and coyote to Texas longhorns to half-breed stock to high-grade beeves to pure-bred cattle. Even the last of these, though the perfected form, was not expected to remain a permanent fixture on the Plains. The cattleman, although a more responsible figure by then, was soon to give way to the agriculturist. The new scientific farmer, moreover, was to have a much wider variety of grains in the selection of his crops: Hilton's last category was forage crops and a similar progression obtained here as well. Sorghum was the first commercially feasible crop, but as the rain increased it was to be replaced in order by millet, wheat, rye, barley, oats, and finally the king of midwestern grains, corn.

Here, then, was an evolutionary cycle to boggle the imagination of the most inveterate promoter. It included reference to social, meteorological, botanical, zoological, and agricultural progression and it concluded on a grand and expansive note: scientific farmers working in an area of bountiful rain, grazing their pure-bred cattle on tame grasses, and growing corn. All of this would develop in a once arid region where Indians hunted bunch-grass-fed buffalo, and a few squatter farmers grew sorghum. That was progress![109] But a guarded optimism would not have sustained the boomers' frontier. The promoters were convinced that they had to proclaim the millennium or surrender the Plains either to the cattlemen or, worse still, to those scientific "quacks" who would poke and probe at the land in an effort to discover its weaknesses.

The one unpardonable sin of the dissenters and the reformers, then, was that they would block this new law of progression on the Plains. Any reform in the disposition, survey, or classification of land meant a delay in the workings of the progression. There was land and there were people. It mattered little to the promoters that in this case the two were not necessarily on the best of terms. As soon as the people had had a chance to mold the land into a preconceived form, any incompatibility would be overcome, and it was the promoters' job to hasten this forced reconciliation. So long as there was land available they were determined to promote its settlement. Unfortunately, as the promoters were becoming increasingly aware, the exhaustion of arable land was rapidly approaching. In 1893 Frederick Jackson Turner formally announced its disappearance, but even before then a disturbingly large number of observers had warned that America's supply of usable

109. H. R. Hilton, "The Influence of Climate and Climatic Changes upon the Cattle Industry of the Plains," in *Report . . . for the Quarter Ending March 31, 1888, . . .* of KSBA (Topeka, 1888), p. 145.

lands in the public domain was dwindling.[110] Americans had begun to predict the end of the frontier as early as the 1870s, and by the 1890s such gloomy pronouncements were quite common. The boomers could defend their kind of frontier against those who dissented from its basic principles but they could hardly resist the alleged exhaustion of the object of their salesmanship: the land. They were becoming salesmen without a product.

It would be a mistake, however, to assume that promotion ceased upon the announcement that Americans had run out of arable land. Boomers were active well into the 1900s, some of them unreconstructed rain-follows-the-plow men. But generally the mid-1890s witnessed a new kind of promotion, one which emphasized irrigation and dry farming. This in turn involved new land laws, new promotional methods, new farming techniques, and new areas of concentration. The safety valve theory was still a very real part of the promotional effort but the other features of the Garden were strangely absent. Irrigation and dry farming, whatever other promises they held, involved an admission that semiaridity and garden images did not form an effective promotional combination. The attempt to transfer the Garden to the grassland ended with the realization that Eden could not be recaptured by fervent prayers and incantations, and that proper land utilization in the central Great Plains required more than the boomers' combination of naiveté, wishful thinking, and fraud.

The change had a sobering effect on Americans, east and west. They began to investigate more closely the actual conditions of their remaining public domain, and the boom began to diminish to respectable levels. Science and sanity came to replace hazy images of the Garden regained. It was a welcome change, for during its glory days in the 1870s and '80s the boom reached a crescendo that carried it from Kansas and Nebraska to New York, London, Berlin, and points east.

The boomers had played a vital role in the final phase of the frontier era. In spite of overwhelming physical evidence to the contrary, they had managed to keep alive the notion that the Plains were a viable part of the frontier settlement process, that the semiarid grasslands which they had so long promoted were worthy of a nation's confidence. It was a massive exercise in persuasion, but it nurtured the idea that America was not without a region in which it might find relief and redress in time of difficulty. This was the traditional function of the

110. Turner, "The Significance of the Frontier in American History," in *Frontier and Section*, p. 62.

frontier and the boomers worked to convince a credulous public of the ability of the Plains to meet these demanding standards. Success required, admittedly, some skill in meteorological sleight of hand, but the boomers' image of the frontier propped up the public faith in America's mission. It was grand and exciting and almost totally irresponsible, but it served a central purpose. It sustained, and was in turn sustained by, the image of America as a garden. And this was a fortunate arrangement, for on the central Great Plains, neither could have survived without the other.

Selected Bibliography

PRIMARY MATERIAL—UNPUBLISHED

Manuscripts

Colorado Historical Society and Colorado Archives, Denver.
  Bancroft, H. H. *Interviews with Wyoming Cattlemen.* Western Range
    Cattle Industry Study. Microfilm.
  Colorado Executive Records.
  Colorado Territorial Board of Immigration. Letter Press Books.
  John A. Cooper Papers.
  Benjamin Eaton Papers.
  James B. Grant Papers.
  John Routt Papers.
University of Colorado, Western History Collections, Boulder.
  Elbert, S. H. "Public Men and Measures." Bancroft MSS.
  "Governor Gilpin, a Pioneer of 1842." Bancroft MSS.
Kansas State Historical Society, Topeka.
  George Anthony Papers.
  "An Appeal from the Kansas Bureau of Immigration to the People of
    Kansas, March 7, 1868." Letter from George A. Crawford, Commis-
    sioner, to the "People of Kansas." Samuel Crawford Papers.
  Thomas Carney Papers.
  Samuel Crawford Papers and Scrapbooks.
  S. W. Glick Papers.
  Governors' Letter Press Books.
  James Harvey Papers.
Missouri Historical Society, St. Louis.
  The Early Papers of Lt. William Gilpin Narrating Experiences with the
    Dragoons Protecting the Western Frontier.
  Richard Smith Elliott. Letter Press Book.
Nebraska State Historical Society, Lincoln.
  George T. Anthony Papers.
  James Boyd Papers.

Burlington Railroad, Val Kuska Collection.
William Dawes Papers.
Silas Garber Papers.
George Holdrege Papers.
Albinus Nance Papers.
Nebraska State Board of Agriculture. Letter Press Books.
Wyoming State Historical Society, Cheyenne.
Francis P. Warren Papers.

PRIMARY MATERIAL—PUBLISHED

Collections of Documents and Papers

Abbott, Edith, ed. *Historical Aspects of the Immigration Problem*. Chicago: University of Chicago Press, 1923.

Clay, Henry. *The Works of Henry Clay*. Edited by Calvin Colton. 9 vols. New York: G. P. Putnam's Sons, 1901–1904.

Commons, John R., et al., eds. *A Documentary History of American Industrial Society*. 13 vols. Cleveland: Arthur Clark Co., 1910.

Debo, Angie, ed. "An English View of the Wild West." *Panhandle Plains Historical Review* 6 (1933): 24–44.

Franklin, Benjamin. "Observations Concerning the Increase of Mankind." In *The Papers of Benjamin Franklin*. Edited by Leonard Labaree. 12 vols. New Haven: Yale University Press, 1961. 4: 225–35.

Jefferson, Thomas. *The Writings of Thomas Jefferson*. Edited by Paul Leicester Ford. 10 vols. New York: G. P. Putnam's Sons, 1892–99.

———. *The Writings of James Madison*. Edited by Gaillard Hunt. 9 vols. New York: G. P. Putnam's Sons, 1900–10.

Messages and Proclamations of Nebraska Governors. 3 vols. Lincoln: Nebraska State Historical Society, 1942.

Messages of Kansas Governors. 4 vols. Topeka: The State Printer, 1937.

Porter, Kirk, and Johnson, Donald, eds. *National Party Platforms, 1840–1956*. Urbana, Ill.: University of Illinois Press, 1956.

Richardson, James D., ed. *A Compilation of the Messages and Papers of the Presidents*. 11 vols. Washington, D.C.: Bureau of National Literature and Art, 1910.

Wyoming, Messages of the Governors, 1890–1933. Cheyenne, 1934.

Public Documents: Federal

Annals of Congress, 1789–1824.

Annual Report of the United States Geological and Geographic Survey of the Territories, 1871. Washington, D.C.: Government Printing Office, 1871.

Baker, F. P. *Preliminary Report on the Forestry of the Mississippi Valley and Tree Planting on the Plains.* U.S. Department of Agriculture. Washington, D.C.: Government Printing Office, 1883.

Congressional Globe, 1838–74.

Congressional Record, 1875–93.

Elliott, Richard Smith. "Experiments in Cultivating the Plains along the Line of the Kansas Pacific Railway." In F. V. Hayden. *Preliminary Report of the United States Geological Survey of Montana and Adjacent Territories.* Washington, D.C.: Government Printing Office, 1872.

Executive Documents. U.S. House and Senate, 1840–95.

Gilpin, William. "The Agricultural Capabilities of the Great Plains." In U.S. Patent Office. *Report on Agriculture, 1857.* Washington, D.C.: Government Printing Office, 1858.

Hayden, F. V. *Preliminary Report of the United States Geological Survey of Wyoming and Portions of Contiguous Territories. . . .* Washington, D.C.: Government Printing Office, 1872.

Johnson, Willard. *The High Plains and Their Utilization.* U.S. Geological Survey. *Twenty-first Annual Report.* Washington, D.C.: Government Printing Office, 1899–1900. Pt. 4.

Miscellaneous Documents. U.S. House and Senate, 1840–95.

Papers Relating to the Foreign Relations of the United States, 1862–1886. Washington, D.C.: Government Printing Office, 1863–87.

Register of Debates in Congress, 1825–37.

Reports. U.S. House and Senate, 1840–95.

Senate Committee on Education and Labor. *Report upon Relations Between Labor and Capital.* 48th Cong., 2d sess. Vol. 1. Washington, D.C.: Government Printing Office, 1883.

Thomas, Cyrus. "Agriculture in Colorado." In F. V. Hayden. *Preliminary Field Report of the United States Geological Survey of Colorado and New Mexico. . . .* Washington, D.C.: Government Printing Office, 1869.

———. "Physical Geography and Agricultural Resources of Minnesota, Dakota, and Nebraska." In F. V. Hayden. *Sixth Annual Report of the United States Geological Survey of the Territories Embracing Portions of Montana, Idaho, Wyoming, and Utah.* Washington, D.C.: Government Printing Office, 1873.

U.S. Geological Survey. *Eleventh Annual Report . . . 1889–1890.* Washington, D.C.: Government Printing Office, 1890.

———. *Third Annual Report of the . . . Survey of the Territories . . . 1872.* Washington, D.C.: Government Printing Office, 1872.

Watts, Frederick. *Report of the Commissioner of Agriculture for the Year 1869.* Washington, D.C.: Government Printing Office, 1870.

———. *Report of the Commissioner of Agriculture for the Year 1870.* Washington, D.C.: Government Printing Office, 1871.

Wilson, Joseph. *Report of the Commissioner of the General Land Office for the Year 1868*. Washington, D.C.: Government Printing Office, 1868.

Young, Edward. *Special Report of Immigration, Accompanying Information for Immigrants*. Department of the Interior. Washington, D.C.: Government Printing Office, 1872.

Public Documents: State and Territory

Colorado

Colorado State Board of Agriculture. *Agricultural Statistics of the State of Colorado, 1892. . . .* Denver, 1893.

Colorado State Bureau of Immigration and Statistics. *Natural Resources and Industrial Development and Condition of Colorado*. Denver, 1889.

Colorado State Horticultural and Forestry Association. *Annual Reports, 1887–1888*. Denver, 1888.

Colorado Territorial Board of Immigration. *Official Information of the Resources of Colorado, 1872*. Denver, 1872.

——. *Report . . . for the Two Years Ending December 31, 1873*. Denver: Wm. Byers Public Printer, 1874.

——. *Report . . . 1874*. Denver, 1874.

Faurot, C. S. *A Report on the Resources and Industrial Development of Colorado, 1893 . . . Colorado Exhibit, World's Columbian Exposition*. Denver, 1893.

House Journal of the Legislative Assembly, Territory of Colorado. Denver: Thomas Gibson, Colorado Herald Office, 1861.

Millett, Nelson. "Horticultural Humbugs." Colorado State Historical Society. *Third Annual Report . . . 1886*. Denver, 1886.

Kansas

Kansas Bureau of Immigration. *Kansas As She Is: Free Homesteads in the Garden of the World*. 2d ed. Lawrence, 1870.

——. *Report . . . 1868*. Topeka, 1869.

——. *The State of Kansas: A Home for Immigrants . . . Offered to Persons Desiring Homes in a New Country*. Topeka, 1867.

Kansas State Board of Agriculture. *Annual Report, 1872–1893*. Topeka, 1873–94.

——. *Biennial Reports, 1880–1896*. Topeka, 1881–97.

——. *Kansas: Its Resources and Capabilities, Its Position, Dimensions, and Topography*. Topeka, 1883.

——. *Monthly Report, April, 1891*. Topeka, 1891.

——. *Proceedings of the Annual Meetings, 1889–1897*. Topeka, 1890–98.

——. *Quarterly Reports, 1879–1891*. Topeka, 1880–92.

Lovewell, J. T. "Climate of Kansas." In Kansas State Board of Agriculture. *World's Fair Report.* . . . Topeka, 1893.

Nebraska

Alexander, George S. *Nebraska: Its Resources, Prospects, and Advantages of Immigration . . . Together with Suggestions to Immigrants.* Bureau of Immigration. Lincoln, 1870.

Brown, George. *The State of Nebraska as a Home for Emigrants.* Bureau of Immigration. Lincoln, 1875.

Nebraska Bureau of Immigration. *Eine Wortheile und Huelfsquellen; oder; Wohin soll Man auswandern und warum*? Lincoln, 1871.

————. *Nebraska: Containing a Brief Account of the Soil, Productions, Agricultural and Mineral Resources.* . . . Lincoln, 1866.

Nebraska: Her Resources, Advantages, and Development. Prepared and compiled by Joseph Garneau, commissioner general, Nebraska Columbian Exhibit. Omaha, 1893.

Nebraska State Board of Agriculture. *Annual Reports, 1871–1892.* Des Moines, Iowa, and Lincoln, 1871–93.

————. *Transactions . . . from September, 1876 to September, 1879.* . . . Lincoln, 1880.

Nebraska State Board of Immigration. *Nebraska: A Sketch of Its History, Resources, and Advantages It Offers to Settlers.* Nebraska City, 1870.

Nebraska State Horticultural Society. *Annual Reports, 1878–1883.* Lincoln, 1879–85.

Noteware, J. H. *The State of Nebraska.* Nebraska State Board of Immigration. Lincoln, 1873.

Report of the Superintendent of Immigration for Nebraska, 1874. Lincoln: State Printers, 1875.

Wyoming

Message of Governor Campbell to the Third Legislative Assembly of Wyoming Territory . . . 1873. Laramie, 1873.

Message of Governor Francis E. Warren to the Eleventh General Assembly, 1890. Cheyenne, 1890.

Message of Governor J. W. Hoyt to the Sixth Legislative Assembly of Wyoming Territory . . . 1879. Cheyenne, 1879.

Message of Governor Thomas Moonlight to the Tenth Legislative Assembly of Wyoming Territory . . . 1888. Cheyenne, 1888.

Report of Governor Francis P. Warren of Wyoming to the Secretary of the Interior, 1889. Cheyenne, 1890.

"Report of Governor Thomas Moonlight of Wyoming to the Secretary of the Interior, Sept. 27, 1887." Typescript copy in the Wyoming State Historical Society.

Newspapers

Colorado

Cheyenne Wells Gazette, 1886, 1888.
Denver Tribune-Republican, 1882.
Field and Farm (Denver), 1886, 1887, 1889, 1900, 1904.
Greeley Tribune, 1871.
Rocky Mountain News (Denver), 1862, 1870.

Kansas

American Desert (Millbrook), 1887.
Daily Commonwealth (Topeka), 1873, 1881, 1882, 1883.
Daily Journal (Leavenworth), 1866.
Dickinson County Chronicle (Abilene), 1882.
Garden City Herald, 1883.
Henry's Advertiser (Leavenworth), 1878.
Kansas City Times, 1883.
Kansas Farmer (Topeka), 1877, 1888, 1893.
Kinsley Mercury, 1887.
Kirwin Chief, 1876.
Topeka Capital, 1882, 1888, 1891.
Western Cyclone (Nicodemus), 1886.
Wichita Weekly Beacon, 1876.

Nebraska

Daily Nebraska State Journal (Lincoln). Also published as *Daily State Journal* and *Nebraska State Journal*. 1874, 1879, 1890, 1892.
Lincoln Journal, 1876.
Nebraska Farmer (Lincoln), 1877, 1890.
Nebraska Herald (Plattsmouth), 1869, 1870.
Nebraska Statesman (Nebraska City), 1866, 1871.
Omaha Bee, 1894.
Omaha Herald, 1870, 1873, 1876.
Omaha Republican, 1873, 1876.

Wyoming

Buffalo Bulletin, 1891.
Cheyenne Leader, 1867.
Laramie Sentinel, 1887.
Lusk Herald, 1886, 1887.
Wyoming Industrial Journal (Cheyenne), 1900.

Railroad and Other Newspapers

Irrigation Age (Chicago), 1892, 1897.
Kansas Pacific Homestead (Kansas Pacific), 1877, 1878.

Pioneer (Union Pacific), 1874, 1875.
Star of Empire (Santa Fe), 1869.
Western Trail (Rock Island), 1886, 1887.

Articles, Pamphlets and Speeches

Adams, Charles Francis, Jr. "The Rainfall on the Plains." *Nation* 45 (November 24, 1887): 417.

Address of Mr. Orange Judd at the Nebraska State Fair, Lincoln, September 16, 1885. Lincoln, 1886.

Address of the Honorable G. M. Lambertson at the Nebraska State Fair, Omaha, September 12, 1883. Omaha: Herald Printing Co., 1883.

Aughey, Samuel. *The Geology of Nebraska: A Lecture Delivered in the Representative Hall at Lincoln . . . January 20, 1873. . . .* Lincoln, 1873.

Benton, Thomas Hart. *Central National Highway from the Mississipppi River to the Pacific.* Louisville: The Lost Card Press, 1960. Microcard.

———. *Discourse of Mr. Benton of Missouri Before the Boston Mercantile Library Association . . . Delivered in Tremont Temple at Boston, December 20, 1854.* Washington, D.C.: J. T. & L. Towers, 1854.

Dillon, Sidney. "The West and the Railroads." *North American Review* 152 (April 1891): 443–52.

Dorsey, Stephen. "Land Stealing in New Mexico: A Rejoinder," *North American Review* 145 (October 1887): 396–405.

Ernst, C. J. "The Railroads as a Creator of Wealth in the Development of a Community or District." *Nebraska History and Record of Pioneer Days* 7 (January–March, 1924): 16–22.

Fink, Louis. *Kansas: Its Resources, Capabilities, etc., With Very Valuable Information for Catholic Immigrants.* Pamphlet in Kansas State Historical Society.

Furnas, Robert. *Nebraska: Her Resources, Advantages, Advancements, and Promises; World's Industrial and Cotton Centennial Exposition* New Orleans: E. A. Brandon & Co., 1885.

Gannett, Henry. "Is the Rainfall Increasing on the Plains?" *Science* 11 (March 2, 1888): 96–104.

Harger, Charles. "The Short Grass Country." *Harper's Weekly Magazine* 45 (January 26, 1901): 88–89.

Hay, John. "The Central State, Its Physical Features and Resources." *Harper's New Monthly Magazine* 77 (June 1888): 39–50.

Hazen, W. B. "The Great Middle Region of the United States and Its Limited Space of Arable Lands." *North American Review* 120 (January 1875): 18–37.

Henry, Stewart. "Rainfall on the Plains." *Popular Science Monthly* 36 (February 1890): 535–38.

Historical and Descriptive Review of Kansas. Vol. 1, *The Northern Section.* Topeka: Jon. Lethem, 1890.

"Homesteads, the Republicans and Settlers Against Democracy and Monopoly, The Record, 1868." *Kansas Speeches* 4, Kansas State Historical Society.

Inman, Henry. "On Climatic Changes in the Prairie Region of the United States." *Kansas City Review of Science and Industry* 2 (July 1878): 228–41.

Julian, George. "Our Land Policy." *Atlantic Monthly* 43 (March 1879): 325–37.

———. "Railway Influence in the Land Office." *North American Review* 136 (March 1883): 237–56.

Martin, John. "The Progress of Kansas." *North American Review* 142 (April 1886): 348–55.

Monthly Weather Review 23 (September 1895): 337; 27 (June 1899): 257; 33 (June 1905): 260–61.

Murphy, E. C. "Is the Rainfall in Kansas Increasing?" *Transactions of the Kansas Academy of Science* 13 (1891–92): 16–19.

Powell, John Wesley. "Institutions for the Arid Lands." *Century Magazine* 40 (May 1890): 111–16.

———. "The Irrigable Lands of the Arid Region." *Century Magazine* 39 (March 1890): 766–76.

———. "The Non Irrigable Lands of the Arid Region." *Century Magazine* 39 (April 1890): 915–22.

———. "Our Recent Floods." *North American Review* 155 (August 1892): 149–55.

———. "Technology." *American Anthropologist* 1 (April 1899): 695–745.

Smalley, E. V. "The Future of the Great Arid West." *Forum* 19 (June 1895): 466–75.

———. "Our Sub Arid Belt." *Forum* 20 (June 1896): 486–93.

Smythe, William E. "The Irrigation Idea and Its Coming Congress." *Review of Reviews* 8 (October 1893): 394–406.

Spalding, John. "Is Our Social Life Threatened?" *Forum* 5 (March 1888): 16–26.

Speeches Delivered at the Southern Hotel, St. Louis, June 14, 1867. St. Louis: S. Levison, 1867.

Stewart, William. "Reclaiming the Western Deserts." *Forum* 7 (April 1889): 201–8.

Turner, Frederick Jackson. "The Significance of the Frontier in American History." American Historical Association *Annual Report for 1893.* Washington, D.C.: Government Printing Office, 1894.

Ward, Lester. "Professor John Wesley Powell." *Popular Science Monthly* 20 (February 1882): 390–97.

Warren, Gouverneur K. "Explorations of the Country Between the Missouri and the Platte Rivers." *North American Review* 87 (July 1858): 66–94.

Welsh, Rodney. "Horace Greeley's Cure for Poverty." *Forum* 8 (January 1890): 586–93.

Wilkeson, Frank. "Cattle Raising on the Plains." *Harper's New Monthly Magazine* 72 (April 1886): 778–95.

Railroad and Land Company Literature

Burlington Railroad. *Land In Nebraska, 600,000 Aker, des besten Landes . . . in Nebraska.* Lincoln: Burlington Railroad, 1880.

———. *Southwestern Nebraska and Northwestern Kansas.* Omaha: Journal Co., 1887.

Colorado Homestead Company. *Prosperity in Colorado, and Health to Enjoy It. . . .* Denver: Colorado Homestead Co., n.d.

Greeley Board of Trade. *Farming in Colorado . . . With a Short Review of the Climate and Resources of Weld County.* Greeley: Greeley Board of Trade, 1887.

Husted Investment Company. *Some Facts About Kansas.* Compiled by Foster D. Coburn. Kansas City: Husted Investment Co., 1890.

Kansas Land and Emigration Co. *Emigration to Kansas, the Glory of the West.* London: Privately printed, 1871.

Kansas Pacific Railroad. *Emigrants' Guide to the Kansas Pacific Railway Lands: Best and Cheapest Farming and Grazing Lands in America, 6,000,000 Acres. . . .* Lawrence, 1871.

Kern, Maxmillian. *Forest Tree Culture on the Kansas Prairies.* Kansas City, Mo.: Kansas Pacific Railroad Co., 1879.

Northern Kansas Immigration Association. *Corn is King: The Advantages Northern Kansas Offers to Home Seekers and Land Buyers.* Kansas City, Mo.: Ramsey, Mollett & Hudson, 1888.

Northern Pacific Railroad. *Die Nord Pacific Eisenbahn, Der Staat Dakota, Mittheilungen fuer Landbauer und Alle, die ein eignes Heim suchen.* New York: Love & Alden, 1883.

———. *Guide to the Arkansas Valley Lands of the Atchison, Topeka, and Santa Fe Railroad Company in Southwestern Kansas.* Topeka: Santa Fe Railroad, 1879.

———. *How and Where to Get a Living.* Topeka: Santa Fe Railroad, 1876.

———. *Kansas in 1875: Strong and Impartial Testimony to the Wonderful Productiveness of the Cottonwood and Arkansas Valleys; What Over 200 Editors Think of Their Present and Future.* Topeka, 1875.

———. *Le Kansas . . . sa situation, ses ressources, et ses produits: Le chemin de fer d'Atchison, Topeka, et Santa Fe.* Topeka: Santa Fe Railroad, n.d.

Santa Fe Railroad. *A New Sectional Map of Seven Counties in the Arkansas Valley of Kansas.* Topeka: Santa Fe Railroad, 1883.

Schmidt, Carl B. *Official Facts about Kansas.* Topeka: Santa Fe Railroad, 1884.

Syndicate Land and Irrigation Company. *Valuable Data.* Denver: Syndicate Land & Irrigation Co., n.d.

Union Pacific Railroad. *Colorado: A Complete and Comprehensive Description.* . . . Council Bluffs, Iowa: Union Pacific Railroad, 1887.

———. *Colorado: A Complete and Comprehensive Description.* 5th ed. St. Louis: Union Pacific Railroad, 1892.

———. *The Emigrant Guide and Handbook of the Central Branch, Union Pacific R.R., &c.: Homes for the Homeless and Superior Locations for Capitalists and Other Business Men.* Omaha: Advertising Co., 1878.

———. *Five Million Acres: The Union Pacific Guide: Homes and Farms in Kansas and Colorado at Low Prices and Eleven Years' Credit.* Kansas City, Mo.: Union Pacific Railroad, 1882.

———. *Guide to the Lands of the Union Pacific R'y Co. in Nebraska.* Omaha: U.P. Land Department, 1882.

———. *Guide to the Union Pacific Railroad Lands, 12,000,000 Acres.* . . . Omaha: Union Pacific Railroad, 1871.

———. *Kansas: The Golden Belt Lands.* Omaha: Union Pacific Railroad, 1882.

———. *Kansas: The Golden Belt Lands Along the Line of the Kansas Division of the U.P. R'W.* Kansas City, Mo.: Union Pacific Railroad, 1876.

———. *Nebraska: A Complete and Comprehensive Description of the Agricultural Resources, the Stock Raising, Commercial, and Manufacturing Interests.* 3d ed. Omaha: Union Pacific Railroad, 1897.

———. *Omaha to the Mountains on the Union Pacific Railroad.* Chicago: Union Pacific Railroad, 1868.

———. *Progress of the Union Pacific Railroad West from Omaha . . . across the Continent.* New York: Union Pacific Railroad, 1868.

———. *The Resources and Attractions of Nebraska.* . . . Omaha: Union Pacific Railroad, 1893.

Books

Adams, F. G. *The Homestead Guide, Describing the Great Homestead Region in Kansas.* Waterville, Kansas: By the Author, 1873.

Andreas, A. T. *History of Nebraska.* Chicago: A. T. Andreas, 1882.

Aughey, Samuel. *Sketches of the Physical Geography and Geology of Nebraska.* Omaha: Daily Republican Book & Job Office, 1880.

Beadle, J. H. *The Undeveloped West; or, Five Years in the Territories.* Philadelphia: National Publishing Co., 1873.

Bodine, L. T. *Kansas, Illustrated: an Accurate and Reliable Description of This Marvellous State.* . . . Kansas City, Mo.: Ramsey, Mollett & Hudson, 1879.

Bowles, Samuel. *Across the Continent.* New York: Hurd & Houghton, 1869.
———. *Our New West.* Hartford: Hartford Publishing Co., 1869.
Boynton, Charles, and Mason, T. B. *A Journey Through Kansas with Sketches of Nebraska.* Cincinnati: Moore, Wilstach, Keyes & Co., 1855.
Brockett, Linus. *Our Western Empire.* Philadelphia: Bradley Garretson & Co., 1881.
Burch, L. D. *Kansas As It Is: A Complete Review of the Resources, Advantages, and Drawbacks of the Great Central State.* Chicago: C. S. Burch, 1878.
Butler, James. *Nebraska: Its Characteristics and Prospects.* Omaha: Privately printed, 1873.
Copp, Henry Norris, ed. *The American Settlers' Guide.* Washington, D. C.: By the Editor, 1880.
Davis, F. M. *Nebraska: Its Advantages and Resources.* Lincoln, 1880.
Elliott, Richard S. *Industrial Resources of Western Kansas and Eastern Colorado.* St. Louis: Levison & Blythe, 1871.
———. *Notes Taken in Sixty Years.* St. Louis: R. P. Studley & Co., 1883.
Frémont, John Charles. *Memoirs of My Life.* Chicago: Belford, Clarke & Co., 1886.
George, Henry. *Our Land and Land Policy.* New York: Doubleday & McClure, 1901.
———. *Progress and Poverty: An Inquiry into the Causes of Industrial Depressions and of Increase of Want with Increase of Wealth; The Remedy.* 50th Anniversary Ed. New York: Robert Schalkenback Foundation, 1942.
Gilpin William. *The Central Gold Regions: The Grain, Pastoral, and Gold Regions of North America.* Philadelphia & St. Louis: Sower, Barnes & Co., 1860.
———. *The Cosmopolitan Railway, Compacting and Fusing Together All the World's Continents.* San Francisco: History Co., 1890.
———. *Guide to the Kansas Gold Mines at Pike's Peak, Including an Address on the New Mines.* Cincinnati: E. Mendenhall, 1859.
———. *Mission of the North American People: Geographical, Social, and Political.* 2d ed. Philadelphia: J. B. Lippincott & Co., 1874.
———. *Notes on Colorado and Its Inscription in the Physical Geography of the North American Continent.* London: Witherby & Co., 1870.
Goddard, Frederick. *Where to Immigrate and Why.* Philadelphia: People's Publishing Co., 1869.
Greene, Max. *The Kanzas Region: Forest, Prairie, Desert, Mountain, Vale, and River.* New York: Fowler & Wells, 1856.
Griswold, Wayne. *Kansas: Her Resources and Development.* Cincinnati: Robert Clarke & Co., 1871.
Hale, E. E. *Kanzas and Nebraska . . . An Account of the Emigrant Aid Co.'s Directions to Emigrants,* Boston: Phillips, Sampson & Co., 1854.

Hall, Edward H. *The Great West: Emigrants', Settlers', and Travellers' Guide and Handbook.* New York: Tribune Office, 1864.

Hayden, F. V. *The Great West: Its Attractions and Resources.* Philadelphia: Franklin Publishing Co., 1880.

Hazen, William Babcock. *Our Barren Lands: the Interior of the United States West of the One-Hundredth Meridian and East of the Sierra Nevadas.* Cincinnati: R. Clarke & Co., 1875.

Hutchinson, C. C. *Resources of Kansas.* Topeka, 1868.

Ingalls, J. J. *A Collection of the Writings of John James Ingalls.* Kansas City, Mo.: Hudson-Kimberley Publishing Co., 1902.

James, Edwin. *Account of an Expedition from Pittsburgh to the Rocky Mountains, 1819–1820.* Vol. 15 of *Early Western Travels.* Edited by Reuben G. Thwaites. 39 vols. Cleveland: Arthur H. Clark Co., 1904–1907.

Julian, George. *Speeches on Political Questions.* New York: Hurd & Houghton, 1872.

Keeler, B. C. *Where to Go to Become Rich. . . .* Chicago: Belford, Clarke, & Co., 1880.

Malthus, T. R. *An Essay on Population.* 2 vols. London: J. M. Dent & Sons, 1958.

Marcou, Stephen. *Homes for the Homeless: A Description of Marion County, Kansas, and the Cottonwood Valley! The Garden of the State!* Marion Centre, Kans.: Marion County Record Book & Job Office, 1874.

Marsh, George Perkins. *Man and Nature; or, Physical Geography as Modified by Human Action.* New York: Charles Scribner, 1864.

Marx, Karl. *Capital.* Translated by Eden and Cedar Paul. 2 vols. London: J. M. Dent & Co., 1930.

An Old Settler [C. W. Dana]. *The Garden of the World; or, the Great West.* Boston: Wentworth & Co., 1856.

Powell, John Wesley. *Physiographic Regions of the United States.* National Geographic Society Monographs, vol. 1, no. 3. New York: American Book Co., 1895.

————. *Report on the Lands of the Arid Region.* Edited by Wallace Stegner. Cambridge: Harvard University Press, 1966. Originally published as *House Exec. Doc. 73,* 45th Cong., 2d sess., 1878 (Sn 1805).

Redpath, James, and Hinton, Richard. *Handbook to Kansas Territory and the Rocky Mountain Gold Regions.* New York: J. H. Colton, 1859.

Richardson, Albert D. *Beyond the Mississippi: From the Great River to the Great Ocean, Life and Adventure on the Prairies, Mountains and Pacific Coast.* Hartford: American Publishing Co., 1867.

Smith, Adam. *An Inquiry into the Nature and Causes of the Wealth of Nations.* New York: Modern Library, 1957.

Smythe, William E. *The Conquest of Arid America.* New York: Macmillan Co., 1905.

Spalding, John L. *The Religious Mission of the Irish People and Catholic Colonization.* New York: Catholic Publications Society, 1880.

Strong, Josiah. *Our Country.* Edited by Jurgen Herbst. Cambridge: Harvard University Press, 1963.

Sumner, William Graham. *Earth Hunger and Other Essays.* Edited by Albert Galloway Keller. New Haven: Yale University Press, 1913.

———. *War and Other Essays.* Edited by Albert Galloway Keller. New Haven: Yale University Press, 1911.

Tewksbury, A. C. *The Kansas Picture Book.* Topeka: A. S. Johnson, 1883.

Thayer, William. *Marvels of the New West.* Norwich, Conn.: Henry Publishing Co., 1890.

Tice, John. *Over the Plains; on the Mountains.* St. Louis: Industrial Age Printing Co., 1872.

Tocqueville, Alexis de. *Democracy in America.* Edited by Richard Heffner. New York: New American Library, 1956.

Turner, Frederick Jackson. "Social Forces in American History." In *Frontier and Section: Selected Essays of Frederick Jackson Turner.* Englewood Cliffs, N. J.: Prentice Hall, 1961.

Von Humboldt, Alexander. *Cosmos: A Sketch of the Physical Description of the Universe.* Translated by E. C. Otte. 5 vols. London: G. Bell, 1891–93.

———. *Views of Nature; or, Contemplations on the Sublime Phenomena of Creation.* Translated by E. C. Otte and H. G. Bohn. London: George Bell & Sons, 1896.

Webb, William E. *Buffalo Land.* Philadelphia: Hubbard Brothers, 1872.

Weston, W., ed. *Weston's Guide to the Kansas Pacific Railway.* Kansas City, Mo.: Missouri Bulletin Steam Printing & Engraving Co., 1871.

Wheeler, A. C. *The Iron Trail.* New York: F. B. Patterson, 1876.

Wilber, Charles. *The Great Valleys and Prairies of Nebraska and the Northwest.* Omaha: Daily Republican Printing Co., 1881.

Willard, J. F., ed. *Experiments in Colorado Colonization.* Boulder: University of Colorado Press, 1932.

Witter, Daniel. *The Settlers' Guide to the Entry of Public Lands in Colorado.* Denver: News Printing Co., 1882.

Secondary Material

Articles

Appel, Livia, and Blegen, Theodore C. "Official Encouragement of Immigration to Minnesota During the Territorial Period." *Minnesota History Bulletin* 5 (August 1923): 167–203.

Athearn, Robert G. "The Great Plains in Historical Perspective." *Montana* 7 (Winter 1958): 13–30.

Blackmar, Frank. "The History of the Desert." Kansas State Historical Society, *Transactions* 9 (1905–1906): 100–117.

———. "The Mastery of the Desert." *North American Review* 182 (April 1906): 676–88.

Bowden, Martyn. "The Perception of the Western Interior of the United States, 1800–1870: A Problem in Historical Geosophy." *Proceedings of the Association of American Geographers* 1 (January 1969): 16–21.

Carruth, William. "The New England Emigrant Aid Company as an Investment Society." Kansas Historical Society, *Collections* 6 (1903): 90–96.

Curti, Merle, and Birr, Kendall. "The Immigrant and the American Image in Europe, 1860–1914." *Mississippi Valley Historical Review* 37 (September 1950): 203–30.

De Voto, Bernard. "Geopolitics With Dew On It." *Harpers* 188 (March 1944): 313–23.

Ellis, David M. "The Forfeiture of Railroad Land Grants, 1867–1894." *Mississippi Valley Historical Review* 33 (June 1946): 27–60.

Fite, Gilbert. "The United States Army and Relief to Pioneer Settlers, 1874–1875." *Journal of the West* 6 (January 1967): 99–108.

Gates, Paul W. "The Homestead Law in an Incongruous Land System." *American Historical Review* 41 (July 1936): 652–81.

Hedges, James Blaine. "Promotion of Immigration to the Pacific Northwest by the Railroads." *Mississippi Valley Historical Review* 15 (September 1928): 183–203.

Hickman, Russell. "Speculative Activities of The Emigrant Aid Company." *Kansas Historical Quarterly* 5 (August 1935): 235–67.

House, Albert V., Jr. "Proposals of Government Aid to Agricultural Settlement during the Depression of 1873–1879." *Agricultural History* 12 (January 1938): 46–67.

Jackson, W. Turrentine. "The Administration of Thomas Moonlight, 1887–1889." *Annals of Wyoming* 18 (July 1946): 139–62.

———. "Territorial Papers of Wyoming in the National Archives." *Annals of Wyoming* 16 (January 1944), 45–53.

Johnson, Samuel. "The Emigrant Aid Company in the Kansas Conflict." *Kansas Historical Quarterly* 7 (February 1937): 21–33.

Lewis, G. Malcolm. "William Gilpin and the Concept of the Great Plains Region." *Annals of the Association of American Geographers* 56 (March 1966): 33–50.

Malin, James. "Grassland, 'Treeless', and 'Subhumid'." *Geographical Review* 37 (April 1947): 241–50.

Manley, Robert. "In the Wake of the Grasshoppers: Public Relief in Nebraska, 1874–1875." *Nebraska History* 44 (December 1963): 255–76.

———. "Samuel Aughey: Nebraska's Scientific Promoter." *Journal of the West* 6 (January 1967): 108–18.

Morris, Ralph. "The Notion of A Great American Desert East of the Rockies." *Mississippi Valley Historical Review* 13 (September 1926): 190–200.

Sageser, A. Bower. "Attempted Economic Adjustments in Holt County During the 1890's." *Nebraska History* 40 (June 1959): 105–18.

Shelford, V. E. "Deciduous Forest Man and the Grassland Fauna." *Science* 100 (August 18, 1944): 135–62.

Smith, Henry Nash. "Rain follows the Plow: The Notion of Increased Rainfall for the Great Plains, 1844–1880." *Huntington Library Quarterly* 10 (February 1947): 169–93.

———. "Walt Whitman and Manifest Destiny." *Huntington Library Quarterly* 10 (August 1947): 373–89.

Welter, Rush. "The Frontier West as Image of American Society: Conservative Attitudes Before the Civil War." *Mississippi Valley Historical Review* 46 (March 1960): 593–614.

Books

Bogue, Allan. *Money at Interest: The Farm Mortgage on the Middle Border.* Ithaca, N.Y.: Cornell University Press, 1955.

Darrah, William Culp. *Powell of the Colorado.* Princeton: Princeton University Press, 1951.

Decker, Leslie. *Railroads, Lands, and Politics: The Taxation of the Railroad Land Grants, 1864–1897.* Providence: Brown University Press, 1964.

Dick, Everett. *The Sod House Frontier.* New York: D. Appleton Century Co., 1937.

Fogel, Robert. *The Union Pacific Railroad: A Case in Premature Enterprise.* Johns Hopkins University Studies in Historical and Political Science, vol. 78, no. 2. Baltimore: Johns Hopkins Press, 1960.

Gates, Paul W. *Fifty Million Acres: Conflicts Over Kansas Land Policy, 1854–1890.* Ithaca, N.Y.: Cornell University Press, 1954.

———. "The Homestead Act: Free Land Policy in Operation, 1862–1935." In *Land Use Policy and Problems in the United States,* edited by Howard Ottoson. Lincoln: University of Nebraska Press, 1963.

———. *The Illinois Central Railroad and Its Colonization Work.* Cambridge: Harvard University Press, 1934.

Goetzmann, William. *Exploration and Empire.* New York: Alfred Knopf, 1966.

Hargreaves, Mary Wilma. *Dry Farming on the Northern Great Plains.* Cambridge: Harvard University Press, 1956.

Henthorne, Mary Evangela. *The Career of the Right Reverend John L. Spalding as President of the Irish-Catholic Colonization Association of the United States.* Urbana: University of Illinois Press, 1932.

Higham, John. *Strangers in the Land: Patterns of American Nativism, 1860–1925.* New Brunswick, N.J.: Rutgers University Press, 1955.

Johnson, Samuel. *The Battle Cry of Freedom: The New England Emigrant Aid Company in the Kansas Crusade*. Lawrence: University of Kansas Press, 1954.

LaFeber, Walter. *The New Empire: An Interpretation of American Expansion, 1860–1898*. Ithaca, N.Y.: Cornell University Press, 1963.

Lewis, R. W. B. *The American Adam*. Chicago: University of Chicago Press, 1955.

Mack, Edward C. *Peter Cooper, Citizen of New York*. New York: Duell, Sloan, & Pearce, 1949.

Malin, James. *The Grassland of North America: Prolegomena to Its History*. Lawrence, Kan.: Privately published, 1947.

———. "Local Historical Studies and Population Studies." In *Cultural Approach to History*, edited by Caroline Ware. New York: Columbia University Press, 1940.

———. *Winter Wheat in the Golden Belt of Kansas*. Lawrence: University of Kansas Press, 1943.

Marx, Leo. *The Machine in the Garden*. New York: Oxford University Press, 1964.

Nash, Roderick. *Wilderness and the American Mind*. New Haven: Yale University Press, 1967.

Nevins, Allan. *Abram S. Hewitt with Some Account of Peter Cooper*. New York: Harper & Brothers, 1935.

Osgood, Ernest. *The Day of the Cattleman*. Chicago: University of Chicago Press, 1963.

Overton, Richard. *Burlington West: A Colonization History of the Burlington Railroad*. Cambridge: Harvard University Press, 1941.

Robbins, Roy. *Our Landed Heritage: The Public Domain, 1776–1936*. Lincoln: University of Nebraska Press, 1962.

Sanford, Charles. *The Quest for Paradise: Europe and the American Moral Imagination*. Urbana: University of Illinois Press, 1961.

Shannon, Fred. *The Farmers' Last Frontier: Agriculture, 1860–1897*. New York: Harper Torchbooks, 1968.

Shannon, James. *Catholic Colonization on the Western Frontier*. New Haven: Yale University Press, 1957.

Smith, Charles H. *The Coming of the Russian Mennonites*. Berne, Ind.: Mennonite Book Concern, 1927.

Smith, Henry Nash. *Virgin Land: The American West as Symbol and Myth*. New York: Vintage Books, 1962.

Stegner, Wallace. *Beyond the 100th Meridian: John Wesley Powell and the Second Opening of the West*. Boston: Houghton Mifflin Co., 1962.

Webb, Walter Prescott. *The Great Frontier*. Austin: University Press, 1964.

———. *The Great Plains*. New York: Grosset & Dunlap, 1931.

Index